Dust Bowl, USA

Depression America and

the Ecological Imagination,

1929–1941

BOWL,
USA

Brad D. Lookingbill

Ohio University Press

Athens

Ohio University Press, Athens, Ohio 45701
© 2001 by Brad D. Lookingbill
Printed in the United States of America

Ohio University Press books are printed on acid-free paper ⊗ ™

09 08 07 06 05 04 03 02 01   5 4 3 2 1

Library of Congress Cataloging-in-Publication Data

Lookingbill, Brad D., 1969–
      Dust Bowl, USA: Depression America and the ecological
imagination, 1929–1941 / Brad D. Lookingbill.
          p. cm.
      Includes bibliographical references (p.) and index.
      ISBN 0-8214-1375-9 (cloth: alk. paper)—ISBN 0-8214-1376-7
(pbk.: alk. paper)
          1. Dust storms—Great Plains—History—20th century. 2. Dust
storms—Environmental aspects—Great Plains—History— 20th
century. 3. Dust storms—Great Plains—Historiography. 4. Great
Plains—History—20th century. 5. Great Plains—Environmental
conditions. 6. Great Plains—Historiography. 7. Frontier and pioneer
life—Great Plains. 8. Human ecology—Great Plains. 9.
Depressions—1929—Great Plains. I. Title: Dust Bowl, U.S.A. II.
Title.
      F595 .L66 2001
      978'.032—dc21   00-054535

Contents

Illustrations

Preface

My grandfather Augustus Henry Webb came to the Oklahoma panhandle in 1907 and farmed a plot of land for more than a half-century. As a boy, I heard his stories about surviving the dirty thirties but losing a son to dust pneumonia. A desire to understand his troubles fired my interest in the environment in general and the dust bowl in particular. His dedication through falls and recoveries until his death in 1998 inspired me to honor his labor with mine. I have labored to produce a post-western history that is about the mythologies of the frontier. It is my conviction that we recognize in the past the dreams of our own buried lives. Thus, this work is dedicated to the memory of Augustus.

My work has been advanced by the kindness of others. Special appreciation goes to Richard Lowitt of the University of Oklahoma for his suggestions concerning sources and his reading of an early draft. Lisa Dorill of Gettysburg College shared prints and paintings with me and helped me to sharpen my perspective. John Wunder, Allan Bogue, Robert Dorman, Michael Steiner, Elizabeth Raymond, Alvin Turner, and Thomas Walther offered constructive criticisms of my research at various stages. The expertise of Todd Kosmerick and Michael Lovegrove guided me through the Carl Albert Center at the University of Oklahoma. At the Ohio University Press, David Sanders, Nancy Basmajian, and Trudie Calvert provided vital editorial expertise. From the University of Toledo, Ronald Lora, Diane Britton, William Longton, Charles Glaab, Guoqiang Zheng, Marcela Calisto, and David Nemeth made supportive recommendations. Most of all, I am grateful to the late Gerald Thompson, my mentor and adviser. His complimentary closings summed up his craft well. Best.

Several institutions have earned my gratitude for their generosity. The Visiting Scholars program at the Carl Albert Center of the University of Oklahoma underwrote a portion of the research through a grant. Also, the faculty development committee of Columbia College and the Graduate Student Association of the University of Toledo provided funding for trips. An Outstanding Dissertation award from the Oklahoma Historical Society in 1995 acknowledged my work in progress. The Western History Association's annual conference allowed me to present and to clarify my thoughts in 1996, as did other scholarly venues afterward. Timely gifts have aided my visits to archives and museums: the Carl Albert Center and the Western History Collection at the University of Oklahoma; the Special Collections of Oklahoma State University; the Oklahoma Historical Society in Oklahoma City, Oklahoma; the No-Man's Land Museum in Goodwell, Oklahoma; the John L. McCarty Collection at the Amarillo Public Library; the Southwest Collection at Texas Tech University; the Panhandle-Plains Museum of Canyon, Texas; the Kansas State Historical Society at Topeka, Kansas; and the Nebraska State Historical Society at Lincoln, Nebraska. During my traveling, someone was kind enough always to leave the light on for me.

Words are not enough to express my debts to others, but they will have to suffice. I am indebted to Roger Bromert, Associate Professor of History at Southwestern Oklahoma State University, for pushing me to begin the book. When I became lost, Julie Ward directed me toward the fascinating field of cultural geography. Deidra Moses designed a useful map, while Joshua Hauser and Jana Whitehurse organized the index. Sheila Brynjulfson, Graham Higgs, John McHale, Melissa Young, Tonia Compton, Bob Boon, Larry West, Michael Polley, David Roebuck, Anthony Alioto, and Terry Smith suffered with me through my revisions. Without the many comments, questions, and suggestions of colleagues, the book would never have been published. They kept me on track through their indefatigable empathy. My journey down a long and winding road would have arrived nowhere without a little help from my friends and family.

Dust Bowl, USA

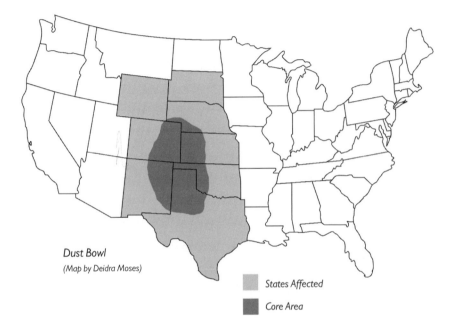

Dust Bowl
(Map by Deidra Moses)

States Affected

Core Area

Introduction

This book is about the dust bowl and its historical dimensions. The word "dust" came through Old English by way of the German "dunst," which meant vapor, smoke, or cloud. The word "bowl," of course, evolved from "bolla," a round vessel rather wide though not deep. During the 1930s, the hybrid phrase defined a site in the United States subject to disaster. With negative connotations, it also signified emptiness, vegetative absence, or an exhausting experience.[1] Because language is continuously reworked and re-shaped to represent a dynamic human relationship with external worlds, it renders a powerful expression of human suffering from a place seemingly long ago and far away. In other words, the North American dust bowl and the stories about it demonstrate that the human understanding of nature is itself historical.

The understanding of the dust bowl originated with an irregular but dreadful environment, a dystopia. The term "dystopia" literally means "a bad place," a locus of agony. While literary utopias depict a perfect society, dystopias recognize a collapse of human design. As an overtly didactic genre of writing, they extrapolate terrifying near futures from troubling contemporary trends. Even as the emotional tensions of a tragic plot slip away from romantic dreams, a sense of anxiety resonates with an audience. The nightmarish scenes reveal social ills and unseemly chaos, albeit magnified and horrific. Besides offering a morbid form of entertainment, they typically present cautionary tales about the ends awaiting a culture in decline. Grounded in the darker side of modernity, a story located there has been predominantly though not entirely an invention of the twentieth century.[2]

Dystopia inspires not just stories about nature but stories about stories about nature.[3] In the process, they add another layer to a people's sense of myth. Whether offered as parables, legends, lore, fables, ballads, allegories, poetry, or fictions, the assumptions of mythos are seldom far from the surface of cultural narratives about landscapes. A landscape appears to be still and solid, but narrating its cycles may quickly present disturbing patterns. Some narrators of disturbances in modern times and places pine for a return to an Edenic paradise while considering the signs of an apocalyptic moment. Through narration, the terms appropriate pieces of artifactual language and memory. Because knowledge arises phenomenologically out of the sensory engagement with circumstances through languaging, the distinction between an objective reality and an observing subject is untenable in discourse.[4]

What begins with discourse, in effect, takes a linguistic turn onto a greater plane where metanarratives swirl. The environment and its infinite permutations extend into this kind of terrain, then. Journeying into a discursive field demands a tolerance for the uncertainties of referential relationships. Relationships to the landforms are made with the flawed and limited tools that language provides. Languaging coheres with partial observations, experiences, and perceptions, which socially constructs both commonplace and meaningful terms. Across paths of communication and forms of representation, the trails of fragmentary evidence appear in and through codes, ideologies, and metaphors. Furthermore, they follow the opaque and transparent configurations of history constituted by the imposition of plots upon plots. The deconstruction of history entails interpreting, decoding, and deciphering the latent content of stories. A historian thus makes an archaeological expedition into the ecological imagination, ending with stories about stories quite different from where each actually began.

The first noted historian to excavate stories about the dust bowl was James C. Malin. Throughout his career, he remained rooted in the Great Plains and ultimately became the foremost American scholar on the history of the grasslands. The publication of *The Grasslands of North America* (1947), for example, constructed a multidisciplinary model for environmental histories. The prolegomena, as Malin denoted his romance with the land, bundled together evidence from climatology, geology, geography, soil sciences, and historical sources. He intended to write history "from the bottom up," while considering the adaptations of "folk movements" through the grasslands. Privileging the perspectives of the European settlers, his "forest man" evolved and became the hybrid "grass man" with a resistant nature. Only a few areas of the grasslands remained stable, claimed Malin, while the environment of the region appeared in an inconstant state of flux and impermanence. This intemperate landform, so given to oscillations of "boom and bust," nonetheless appeared superior to forest expanses elsewhere. His native vegetation deserved a new terminology, or at least recognition and respect.[5]

Moreover, the irascible historian from the University of Kansas criticized the "evangelical conservationists" for distorting the ecology of the region. Blowing dirt, Malin contended with great passion, was a recurring phenomenon and fitted into the whole "economy of nature." The agitation of politicians, the sensationalism of social activists, and the lack of historical perspective, however, exaggerated the dust bowl. He raged: "No more brazen falsehood was ever perpetrated upon a gullible public than the allegation that the dust storms of the 1930s were caused by the 'plow that broke the Plains.'" In defense of his homeland, Malin dismissed the mythopoetic nature of the stories about a blistering sun, the marching dunes, and an eroded homestead. Federal agencies and naive outsiders, in particular, unjustly maligned the landscape and built up a deceptive set of negative images about its iterations. While the hot tempests blew and internal colonization continued, Malin challenged those authorities who were reporting that a desert was forming in the heartland of the country.[6]

The historian Donald Worster's survey *Dust Bowl: The Southern Plains in the 1930s* (1979) presented the most alarming story about the dirty thirties. Though trained at Yale University in American studies—and later to become a professor of history at the University of Kansas—Worster returned home to study the Great Plains during the 1970s in an effort to come to grips with the past. Offering a didactic history, he described an ecological crisis that began with the refusal by greedy Americans to accept essential limits. At the outset, Worster envisioned a wretched soil, "our cultural boneyard, where the evidences of bad judgment and misplaced schemes lie strewn about like bleached skulls." The materialistic values and agricultural system of "an almost pathological state," asserted the polemical historian, perpetuated misconceptions concerning the dialogue between people and the environment. His story was about the environmental insensitivity of Americans; it was a tragedy caused primarily by human agency and not by nature.[7]

Desertification represented a sign of failure and would continue to plague a capitalistic culture. The Great Plains, Worster concluded with passion, "cannot be pushed and pushed to feed the world's growing appetite for wheat without collapsing at last into a sterile desert." To be sure, he was sensitive to the terrible blight after 1968 in the African Sahel, the border country south of the Sahara desert. In fact, a picture from that locus appeared in his book with the caption "Sahelian dust bowl" below it. While overstating the probabilities for self-destruction, though, his thesis subsumed shifting scenes and cultural assumptions under materialistic processes causing failure. The extreme years of the 1930s anticipated more days of judgment for a society committed to capitalism, or so Worster opined. Although he insisted that historians confront contemporary problems, he analyzed the past in ideological terms. Ostensibly, his story accentuated the essentialist values of the modern environmental movement. He descended from a generation of revisionist historians, who took up the burdens of a new western history.[8]

Enframed by Malin and Worster, a host of historians have written the narrative of events by filling in the interpretive space between them. In particular, the monographs of R. Douglass Hurt, Pamela Riney-Kehrberg, and Paula Nelson exemplify outstanding case studies. Their studies include engaging anecdotes about human perseverance and adaptation, even while emphasizing the lapses of commercial agriculture. They have staked their claims on qualitative assessments of magazines, newspapers, letters, bulletins, reports, pamphlets, verse, novels, monographs, songs, and diaries. They generally agree that federal, state, and local policies and a strong sense of community enabled people in the dust bowl to persist.[9] However, historians have yet to answer the question: How did Depression America conceive the dust bowl?

Because no historian has analyzed its ethnography, the story of the dust bowl needs retelling. Using deconstructive methods to analyze the nature of dystopia, the chapters that follow consider the variations on distinct yet related themes of cultural narratives. The themes thread the discourses on both the power and the presence of the frontier as metanarrative, the grandest mythopoetic song of American history. The howling black blizzards of the Great Depression composed a crucial movement for the march of civilization, albeit a darker one. While lapsing into a momentary crisis, motifs derivative of social drama accounted for a terrible stage somewhere at the bottom. Descending lines of composition moved downward to the end, but the cycle turned with an eventual recovery and positivist assumptions. After the recovery from the pitiful ordeal, the story constituted another episode in the saga of the nation.

That is why the story was and is so compelling. In a world out of balance, it has been recounted in multiple versions with differing layers of meaning and resonant with tragic and romantic lines. For Depression America, the condition of modernity was associated with stories about an environmental phenomenon. The association did not simply begin with the hard times of one era but was an outgrowth of assumptions that were generations in the making. The assumptions were historically reinforced from 1929 to 1941 by the mediation of texts, which created an allusive, illusive, and elusive landscape for the entanglements of the ecological imagination. Having spun a web of relationships, cultural narratives on the whole strengthened the interconnections between humans and the environment. For those who dwell there still, the connections have become vital for living with the dust bowl.

Chapter 1

CONQUEST On August 4, 1930, Byron Clark, an Omaha, Nebraska, attorney for the Chicago, Burlington, and Quincy Railroad, spoke to a local homecoming festival. The *Custer County Chief* of Nebraska printed his address, which began with his solemn musing that a pioneer "goes before, as into the wilderness, preparing the way for others to follow."[1] As Clark praised the forerunners of civilization, he recalled a time when the land before the people was a "Great American Desert":

> But you pioneers by your own initiative came through the gates to this western wilderness. You prepared the way for the people; you have and are casting up the highways. You have gathered out the stones, but above all you have lifted up a standard for the people. . . . Pioneers of the flesh, in the evolution of this community since the advent of this pioneer railroad in 1886, you have progressed from the sun baked sand duned land to the friable fertile soils, from prairie grass and cactus to vegetable and cereal crops, from the desert to the oasis.[2]

Although he could only imagine the trauma that men and women would soon experience, his story celebrated an epic of conquest.

An epic exists across a great plane of interconnected myths. Myths constitute real or fictional stories, whose recurring themes embody the identity of people by expressing the complex emotions of their psyche. The deepest and the broadest dimensions, wrote the anthropologist of religion Mircea Eliade, inform consciousness of nature and history.[3] Traceable in modern as well as traditional archetypal patterns, the formal devices of language punctuate the cultural awareness of a landscape with a sense of time and place. Through originary tales, the lofty, luminous, eerie, scary, and wondrous features set the stage for ongoing evolution. The more disorienting the environment, though, the more magical the human agency becomes at the outset. Out of the chaos, the transcendent spirit of a culture dwells within the majestic mountains, vast oceans, dark forests, or great deserts distinguishing a homeland. With spatial relationships fixed through the angles of vision, myths attempt to grasp an environment and give it life.[4]

Through narrative, myths come to terms with the mysteries of nature. That is not to deny *a priori* nature but to underscore the artifactual nature of stories. With eras of referential layering, the artifacts accumulate and embed in linguistic strata. The layers of meaning cover the ecological imagination, wherein deep knowledge takes root just below the gloss of the surface. Narrative, in effect, recognizes terms as real as the referents in the environment. While organizing reality through beginnings, middles, and ends, a metanarrative continuously recycles localized stories as a grand and unified one. It creates a world wherein signifiers have no holistic relation to the signified but only relative or relational coherence. Mythopoetic tales enable people to ground themselves as well as to imagine the matrix of the cosmos.[5]

The extension of Western civilization and its dream of living space after 1492 generated a metanarrative reaching mythopoetic proportions. As conquerors of Native America proclaimed the manifest destiny of their crusades, popular millennialism allegorically inspired revisions of the landscape. Crusading patriarchs claimed dominion over an invented wilderness before them, charged by providence for a mission to subdue the earth. Furthermore, the mission was accelerated by the projection of the Enlightenment, which called the cadence of an imperial march. While moving away from a state of nature toward an emancipation of humanity, the premises of development harmonized national liberation, modern science, and institutional power. Through codes, ideologies, and metaphors, cultural narratives created colonial realms, placing the terra incognita under new authority. The new authorities then projected the anxieties of conquerors across the continent. As the border lands became enclosed, transplanted storytellers recorded the process of westward expansion while often ignoring the stories of indigenous people. This process, or at least the grand stories about the movement, enabled strangers of disparate backgrounds and perspectives to possess the occupied territories.[6]

While dispossessing others, people from around the world encountered enigmatic turf at the center of Native America—the Great Plains. The uncommon physiography contained contours and waves of living polycultures, with eccentric variations of swales, coulees, potholes, moraines, gullies, rimrocks, buttes, and dips. Extreme temperature shifts and visible irregularity appeared in this landlocked country. Over the millennia, vast fans of sands and stones displaced from the Rocky Mountains by wind, water, and gravity formed a sloping landscape eastward toward the Missouri River. Along the one hundredth meridian, rainfall ranged from seven to twenty inches annually. While resting in a rain shadow, the short-grass prairies experienced drying winds.[7] The indigenous people, who lived through the droughts, localized horticulture in the river valleys of the region and devised sophisticated bison-hunting cultures. The Comanche, for instance, claimed to have emerged from the clouds of dust. Cycles of above-average precipitation alternated with those of below-average precipitation, although the weather could be extreme. When a wet cycle broke with a sudden force, unsettling conditions ensued.[8]

The unsettling conditions obtained notoriety when nonindigenous explorers, scientists, and colonists reached the trans-Missouri region. After the Louisiana Purchase of 1803, United States army officers such as Meriwether Lewis described the lack of timber and scarcity of water in parts of the country he called "the Deserts of America." Lieutenant Zebulon Pike in 1806 compared the bewildering space to the "sandy deserts of Africa," a conclusion based on his journey into Spanish provinces. After Major Stephen Long's expedition in 1819 labeled the rolling tract of land stretching to the Rocky Mountains as the "Great Desert," that caption remained on maps of the United States as late as 1870. Delimiting the area as inappropriate for cultivation and uninhabitable by a people dependent on agriculture, the reports invented the "Great American Desert" of legend and lore. Without a doubt, the ostensible emptiness of the midcontinental belt became one of its most puzzling features. The early Anglo-American visitors conceived of a nation born in the primordial forests but not in a vision of distance and scarcity.[9]

Across the wide Missouri River, Thomas Jefferson's chosen people, the virtuous yeomen, still craved more land. It was no coincidence, then, that unjust federal Indian removal policies made the undesirable interior the destiny for dispossessed Native Americans of the eastern United States. Concerned about the degradation of civil society, writer Washington Irving of New York cautioned that any European population moving into the West might become nomadic brigands, violent mercenaries, or worse. Artists such as George Catlin and Karl Bodmer entered the perceived nothingness and captured in portraits a mysterious exoticism of deserted ruins enclosing pagan peoples. Some of these troubling depictions appeared in journals, periodicals, and books. In 1844, the merchant and entrepreneur Josiah Gregg opined in *Commerce of the Prairies* that "some favorable mutation should be wrought in nature's operations to revive the plains and upland prairies," which seemed fit only for "their migratory lord, the Prairie Indian."[10] To a tourist facing the shape of things to come, crossing this rugged terrain was a dangerous undertaking.

Consider the stories offered by the historian Francis Parkman, who published an exhilarating chronicle, *The Oregon Trail*, in 1849. Although several of the New England elite considered the desert a barrier to westward expansion, he recognized the landscape as a challenge to masculinity. In the narrative, he beheld a barren, trackless waste, extending for hundreds of miles to the Arkansas River on the one side and the Missouri River on the other. Undaunted, he envisioned a challenging path for a savvy traveler:

Should any one of my readers be impelled to visit the prairies . . . I can assure him that he need not think to enter at once upon the paradise of his imagination. A dreary preliminary, a protracted crossing of the threshold, awaits him before he finds himself fairly upon the verge of the "great American desert" those barren wastes, the haunts of the buffalo and the Indian, where the very shadow of civilization lies a hundred leagues behind him. . . . As he advances, indeed, he will see mouldering in the grass by his path the vast antlers of the elk, and farther on the whitened skulls of the buffalo, once swarming over this now deserted region.[11]

An unattractive climate alarmed visitors across the trails overland, or so the travel literature of Parkman suggested. Imagining an uninviting locus fraught with peril, the romantic impulse prepared for the headlong drive westward through hellish winds.

The epithet for the "Great American Desert" did not interrupt that drive for long, though, as argonauts, trappers, bullwhackers, and migrants moved through Indian country. The savage nature of the middle passages —the sterility of the soil, absence of fuel, scarcity of water, scantiness of vegetation, and isolation of the experience—punctuated travelers' vignettes.[12] One journalist reported that the conditions recalled a scene at "the death of Christ." Horace Greeley, a prominent newspaper editor and propagandist for the West, lamented grim contours on his overland journey. *Freedom's Champion* in Atchison, Kansas, appraised the howling tempests as similar to those "in the desert of Sahara." One memorable account came from the British adventurer and writer Sir Richard Burton, who proclaimed in 1860 that the "desert is mostly uninhabited, unendurable even to the wildest Indian." The *Southern Quarterly Review, De Bow's Review, North American Review,* and *Lippincott's Magazine* were among the national periodicals introducing the fierce and harsh region to readers in graphic features. Emigrant guides echoed the troubling sentiments about the continental interior, warning readers about the dreariness of the prairies as they moved westward toward greener pastures. For a nation engaged in a great Civil War, the fate of "free soil" was crucial to the Union.[13]

The fate of free soil, no less than the land itself, precipitated the reconstruction of the Union. The explorer, military veteran, Colorado territorial governor, and land speculator William Gilpin published *Mission of the North American People* in 1874, musing that the expanses were no longer "deserts." The author prophesied with great promotional effect redemption for the environment, where a "Garden of the World" would feed an expanding population. His geographical conception emphasized population moving westward and transforming what he once called "an immense disc of howling wilderness."[14] The scientist and director of the U.S. Geologic Survey John Wesley Powell saw things differently. In his *Report on the Lands of the Arid Region of the United States* in 1878, he concluded that "no part of it can be redeemed for agriculture, except by irrigation." Worried about the potholes on a path to glory, he asserted that recovery of fertility from the wastes necessitated a "new phase of Aryan civilization" to adapt pastoralism.[15] Beyond the hundredth meridian, then, an agrarian republic would defer to a cattle kingdom extending from the Bad Lands of the Dakotas to the Llano Escatado in Texas.

While ranchers laid trails and enclosed ranges, speculative zealotry spread like prairie fire and transplanted new fields from old dreams. Irrespective of topographic features, the rectangular grid of townships and ranges, sections and quarter-sections, divisions and subdivisions, was imposed on the landscape. Meanwhile, the notion spread that even rainfall "followed the plow." That is why climatological experts such as Professor Samuel Aughey of the University of Nebraska divined that the breaking and cultivation of the sod altered climate by stimulating local showers and heavy dews.[16] Charles Dana Wilbur, a town builder and amateur scientist, argued that eternal law guaranteed the plowed dominion of a settler society. He scribed:

To those who possess the divine faculty of hope—the optimists of our times—it will always be a source of pleasure to understand that the Creator never imposed a perpetual desert upon the earth, but, on the contrary, has so endowed it that man, by the plow, can transform it, in any country, into farm areas. . . . It is indeed a grand consent, or, rather, concert of forces—the human energy or toil, the vital seed, and the polished raindrop that never fails to fall in answer to the imploring power or prayer of labor.[17]

Even while studying the climate with calm statistics, the voices for progress declared that intensive cultivation regenerated the unfortunate landforms.

That regeneration paralleled a last stand for an indigenous population resisting violent dispossession. The subsistence environment for Indian people collapsed as the U.S. Army, railroad companies, federal government agents, professional hunters, and deadly diseases virtually exterminated the bison. Kiowa, Comanche, and Cheyenne nations living near the Red River participated in an uprising during 1874, trying to save the remnants of the great beasts from buffalo skinners. U.S. Colonel Nelson A. Miles, who commanded a company of men during the buffalo war, described a dreadful ordeal with "intense heat" in a territory "parched, blistered, and burnt up in universal drought." He observed deposits of mineral gypsum blanketing vast areas at the base of the Staked Plains, exposed to erosion from high winds. The streams were nearly all dry during late summer, and what water he did find in stagnant pools was polluted with gypsum, alkali, and salt. Although the tribes devised different strategies for survival, the collapse of the bison ecology confined them to an ever-shrinking world of government reservations.[18]

For the first people of the Great Plains, the cosmos was crumbling. Plenty Coups, for instance, remained a Crow chief on a reservation, but his cultural reservoir evaporated with the end of the traditional hunts. In a dream, he envisioned the Four Winds blowing a great storm that destroyed a small forest, which tribal elders interpreted as a prophecy about impending doom. He ended his story about a lost world abruptly: "After this nothing happened."[19] Sitting Bull, a visionary warrior and shaman for the Sioux, in 1876 communicated with Wakantanka, the great living spirit, at the top of a butte overlooking his homeland. Months before the battle of Little Big Horn, he dreamed of a great dust storm propelled by high winds advancing from the east. Behind the tempest, he could see soldiers, their weapons and horse trimmings ablaze from the sun. When the approaching fury crashed into a cloud, the dust storm dissipated and left the vapor intact under an open sky. While living on the banks of the Grand River in the 1880s, he again foretold of the disappearance of rain, the withering of vegetation, and the evaporation of the waterways. If the Lakota accepted subsistence farming and stock raising on the "Great Sioux" reservation, then heavy droughts would come and "cause considerable suffering for man and beast."[20] In other words, the presence of a new regime generated an ecological nightmare for the tribes.

Under the new regime, the short-grass prairies offered a geography of hope for aliens, who found inspiration even in the darkest shadows. The

Salina Herald of Kansas maintained that the dramatic blows of dust were the "historic pillar of cloud that guided the Children of Israel." Even the names of new communities—Garden City and Zionville in southwestern Kansas, Nazareth in the Texas panhandle—announced the anthems of a great pilgrimage. One Oklahoma colonist explained his family's yearning for a chance to begin life anew in a sodhouse: "We were going to God's Country. We were going to a new land and get rich. Then we could have a real home of our own." The public domain constituted a "land flowing with milk and honey" that would "blossom like the rose," exulted the pioneer. By the 1880s, more than fifteen thousand African Americans migrated to Kansas in search of "free soil," earning the name "Exodusters" for their trek. Homesteaders and sodbusters from across the United States and Europe carried their dreams into the area, but thousands of them eventually drifted elsewhere in disappointment. When severe drought arrived, covered wagons in the 1880s carried the bittersweet phrase: "In God We Trusted, In Kansas We Busted." Others referred to the Oklahoma panhandle as "God's Land, But No Man's Land."[21] The sirens of failure thus told of paradise gained but soon lost.

Newcomers told their stories through folk songs, expressing ambivalence and uncertainty about the dips in the country. Hymnbooks were filled with lyrics such as "Canaan's Land" and "On Jordan's Stormy Banks I Stand," and many people knew these lines by heart. "Starving to Death on a Government Claim," however, appeared in Kansas folklore with the bitter refrain: "Hurrah for Lane County, the land of the free, the home of the grasshopper, bed-bug, and flea." While the cautionary tale admonished the hungry to "stick to your homestead and battle the fleas," the old bachelor farmer confirmed his manhood by returning to the East for a wife. Consider the ballad "Beulah Land, Sweet Beulah Land," which gave new life to an ancient motif in local parodies. In South Dakota the words commiserated: "We've reached the land of desert sweet, where nothing grows for man to eat; the wind it blows with feverish heat, across the plains so hard to beat. O Dakota land, sweet Dakota land, as on thy fiery soil I stand." In a different version titled "The Kansas Fool," the lyric testified of grasshoppers, debt, and bankers, that is, unforeseen parasites.[22] Although such themes echoed a forlorn hope, they also suggested self-creation in that only an exceptional people persevered in an unpromising land.

An essay titled "The Great American Desert" illustrated such claims in 1888. Writing for the popular *Harper's Magazine,* Frank H. Spearman appraised the rimrocks and the buttes with the positivist assumptions of Darwinian naturalism. Despite woebegone days, "the pioneers of a true civilization," he continued, "will build anew; and if the second attempt fails, success crowns a third effort." Therefore, the law of survival of the fittest reigned on the Great Plains in full effect. Indeed, a yeoman "will emerge from his barren one hundred and sixty acres of desert land with melons, potatoes, pumpkins, and squashes of simply prodigious size, capturing the premiums at the local fairs, to the intense chagrin of the farmers who have been laughing all summer at his lunacy in locating on sand." Whatever the barriers, the landscape sustained those cunning people who learned to overcome adversity. According to Spearman's irrational exuberance, "there is no known limit to the richness and depth of this desert soil."[23] While highlighting the aridity of the wilderness, the struggle to survive made the fit stronger and the land richer.

Though living in a potential disaster area, pioneers faced the dangers with great expectations and measured success. While Hard Spring wheat dominated the Dakotas, Turkey Red was introduced into Kansas by the Mennonites. Improved milling accompanied the rising waves of grain. Bonanza farms in the Dakota land boom drove agriculture into the wastes, even as homestead laws were amended to incorporate more acreage. While commercial agriculture forced a greater use of mechanization and accumulation of debt, an unexpected dry season returned to the Great Plains after 1887. Meanwhile, protests by farmers initiated a political attack on processors, railroads, elevators, and outsiders. Blistering populists demanded access to "nature's bounty" and to relief from distant plutocracy, falling prices, rising costs, and unexpected drought.[24] The farm novelist Hamlin Garland depicted a sweltering scene, where the "free land" of the West was nothing more than a "shanty on a barren plain, hot and lone as a desert." The intense political and social upheavals rendered frightful imagery of a lonesome prairie, parched fields, sterile poverty, hapless paupers, and unfulfilled dreams.[25] The darkening of the sun by dust, failures of crops in dry land, the foreclosures on debtors by creditors, and plagues of grasshoppers denoted an apocalypse.

By the end of the nineteenth century, westward expansion had seemingly reached its end. With the passing of a continuous line of settlement, a young historian, Frederick Jackson Turner, wrote an essay in 1893 titled "The Significance of the Frontier in American History." The frontier, which he denoted as "the existence of an area of free land," represented the key to unlocking the mysteries of American history. Turner's narrative accelerated through the "obstacles" along the path of that civilization, that is, vast forests, mountainous ramparts, the desolate, grass-clad prairies, barren oceans of rolling plains, and arid deserts. As a social evolutionary trope, his thesis cast a transformative experience wherein the trajectory of the population movement blended the parts of the nation into a whole. It staged progress, he mused, from "the buffalo" and "the Indian" to the "paternal enterprises of reclamation of the desert." Moreover, the trader, rancher, miner, and farmer developed nascent characteristics of civilization when and where America as a "free land" existed. With a mythic closure of an open continent, Turner thus defined the word "frontier" and presented it as a generalized or universal place.[26]

The place, in other words, existed nowhere in particular but on a mythic plane. While curving to demonstrate movement in time and space, the plane was surveyed as a baseline connecting ordinal points. A baseline of development achieved coherence through emplotments, which delineated the rise and fall of civilizations. In particular, the plots for romance and tragedy constituted meaning through different trajectories. Sloping upward, plots of romance departed from an incomplete stage but ended with a positive resolution. That line appeared ascensionist, moving from bad to good places. Sloping downward, plots of tragedy created tension that culminated with a scene of disaster, or at a negative conclusion. That line appeared declensionist, moving from good to bad places.[27] A linear movement in a narrative cast the plot in one direction and, in momentary lapses, reversed the plot toward the other. While the reversal of slopes recovered one domain, the presence of one denoted the absence of the other. With each oscillation, passages of a metanarrative moved back and forth between referential polarities. Through the cycles of an eternal return, romantic and tragic emplotments informed a scalable lineage of conquest. In its totality, conquest entailed both the romance of the garden and the tragedy of the desert.[28]

With the dawn of the twentieth century, the stories about the conquest underscored the ascension of a progressive era. While deploying science and modern institutions, the United States began reengineering nonarable lands. Fearing a future deficit of food with a rapidly exploding population, the federal government acted to support irrigation through the Carey Act of 1890 and the Newlands Act of 1902. Frederick H. Newell, a U.S. Geological Survey engineer and director of the Reclamation Administration, typified a new generation of empire builders. Since underdeveloped realms became "dry and brown, given over to the prairie wolf" during drought, he insisted that natural resource management stimulated "excessive fertility" and a "salubrious climate." Nebraska journalist William E. Smythe's book *The Conquest of Arid America* (1900) selected places where the lowest orders of society asserted mastery when aided by irrigation enterprises. They became partners with the state for creation, he foretold, empowered to accomplish in arid places what had been accomplished in the Nile valley of Egypt and in the Tigris-Euphrates valley of Mesopotamia. These cooperative efforts would uplift the best civilization yet known in "the desert and in a virgin area," where the hydraulic society created opportunities to begin life anew. On the cusp of modernity, the visions were of a western empire that would rise above geophysical constraints.[29]

Even if the luminaries of the great transformations planned to benefit from imperial projects, the vision resonated with the people who imagined what the environment might become. The *Earth,* a magazine published by the Santa Fe and Topeka Railroad, quoted experiment station and government reports about the bountiful future. One article noted that an inexhaustible shallow water belt, which originated from distant mountains or glacier water, resided below dry land.[30] Through the power of technological force, "the land of the underground rain" emerged as one of the most extensively irrigated areas in the United States.[31] In celebration, the *Earth* proclaimed:

It is evident that the Panhandle, as it has been and as it is now regarded in the popular mind, will soon be a thing of the past. The great cattle ranches, the wandering masses of cattle, the rounding cowboy, the vast circumference of unpeopled desert. . . . All these, it can be foreseen, will give way perhaps almost entirely in time, as they are now fast giving away to the spreading farming element. To have begun to conquer, by new methods, what has long been considered a repulsive desert, is in itself a monumental tribute to man's patience, ingenuity, and enterprise.[32]

Summoning forth the deepest impulses of the culture, the boosters of the region materialized their dreams in a progressive formula.

Material dreams, in fact, elevated the expertise, bureaucracy, and devices for modernization. Without much rainfall, a few communities on the Great Plains developed deep wells and built windmills but rarely obtained enough capital resources to thrive. By 1902, wheat farmer and propagandist Hardy Campbell of Nebraska advocated dry land farming. Using the principles of scientific management, he outlined ways in which his techniques could maximize the efficient use of water resources. Husbandmen were encouraged to develop proper cultivating motions—deep plowing, soil harrowing, and dust mulching—to prevent evaporation of scarce water. The Department of Agriculture's annual reports, moreover, included titles such as "The Weather Bureau and the Homemaker" (1901) and "The Water Economy of Dry Land Crops" (1912). Guides laid out the enticing "treachery" of the "region of periodic famine," where the hand of government sustained agriculture in an uncertain landscape.[33] With a state of nature under modern forms of cultivation, the advancing line illustrated that the frontier remained open for development.

An idyllic golden era of expansion and specialization appeared on the horizon, then. One promotional pamphlet in 1912 noted that "following the first flush of conquest over the desert we are prone to think our measure of success is full." More human sacrifice promised fulfillment of the American dream, which helped those with "slender means" and "broken health" to continue producing the staples of the wheat kingdom. The pamphlet assured that immigrants with both traits were the beneficiaries of reclamation. The occasional drought, sparse vegetation, and frequent dust storms marked only temporary setbacks. Of course, federal government calls to patriotism during World War I accelerated the development of arable land. To plant more hardy grains was to make the world safe for democracy. Also, favorable prices and an overseas mission drove farmers during this great plow-up to destroy native grasses. The profits gave rise to the "suitcase" farmer, or remote townspeople working the soils only to plant and to harvest a crop. While an extensive wheat monoculture appropriated even the marginal areas, it mustered a rising generation of self-made men in agribusiness.[34]

An impressive gain in economic productivity followed, opening opportunities for social mobility and community building. Waves of migrants arriving from humid realms of the United States and Europe continued to break the sod. The peak for internal colonization occurred from 1910 to 1920, when toilers in the region transformed more than one million formerly unplowed acres into farms. In Oklahoma, 1,179,178 residents in 1930 had been born elsewhere, nearly half of the entire state's population. In Kansas, likewise, the population in 1900 included 708,336 persons who had been born elsewhere. In 1930, the same figure remained remarkably high at 664,352, while the number of persons born in the state but living elsewhere had reached 728,311. Clearly, the turnover of population suggested a tenuous sense of place for people without deep roots.[35] With a deep desire to escape their pasts, however, the strangers who had come to a strange land looked to the horizon with anticipation. Whatever environment awaited the outsider, the transplanted migrants clung to stories about the frontier and desired to build a better future for their families.

In the midst of the great migrations, profound changes in the land were observed. Charles Moreau Harger, a popular Kansas journalist, for example, called his home "the promised land." While colonists continued an exodus into the deserts like "the fighting men who followed Moses to freedom," he maintained that dry farming conquered soils once thought perpetually barren and that technology harnessed rivers for irrigation. When population movements reached the "gray plains where mesquite and sagebrush alone relieve the monotony," the agencies of government accomplished the task of "redeeming it wherever the rivers can be turned upon the surface." Through cooperation and unity, he opined, they triumphed even in the marginal areas, which meant "a more substantial civilization, a peace of mind and a strength of purpose denied to the earlier army of homeseekers." Harger praised America's "new vision" developing from the occupation of the continent, providing an outlook rich in the "inspiration of bright skies and cheery sunshine." The multitudes emerged strong, sinewed with the struggle of hard labor, or so he applauded. In time, they arrived face-to-face with a marvelous vista of possibilities in social and economic terms.[36] In retrospection, the travail of suffering and sacrifice had passed, and the fullness of time appeared.

Of course, the vision of the travail derived from the period of colonization. When referring to colonization, that generation glorified the waves of population migration while obliquely recognizing the volatile environment of the place. Boosters, local historians, and pioneer associations recovered memories of bad places and hard times, while the multiple forms of mediation described feats of strength and tests of manhood. The embellishment of mythic experience rendered a tale for environmental as well as social development of unparalleled magnitude. The perceived agents for the transformative process appeared to be arboreal plantings, agricultural techniques, irrigation development, local entrepreneurship, federal government programs, and good fortune. Moreover, geographies and histories around the turn of the twentieth century inscribed the "Great American Desert" into school and college textbooks. They depicted the landscape before conquest in terms of absence, thereby establishing a point of origin mapping the presence of development afterward. In a re-enactment of the Judeo-Christian tradition, a chosen people possessed the earth and stewarded it with the potent effects of labor.[37]

Looking backward on originary stories punctuated the age of conquest with intense social drama, which this generation of writers cast primarily in terms of romance. Frank W. Blackmar and Randall Parrish, historians who evinced the uplifting sentiments, explained that the Great Plains were once a "real desert" where only the wild things grew. Accordingly, the people and policies of the United States redeemed the arid waste and made something out of very little. According to Charles Richard Van Hise, a University of Wisconsin geologist, since "the early days the great plains were known as the Great American Desert." He compared the region to "Palestine and Egypt," where alternate periods of "lean and fat years" appeared periodically; the lean years occurred during periods of deficient rainfall, but the fat years followed with an abundance of rainfall. A magical mutation was achieved with the regularity of civilization, then, which managed the ostensible rhythms of nature through the rational use of resources. A similar claim was endorsed by Ralph C. Morris, who in 1926 concluded: "Slowly in some years and more rapidly in others, the work of converting this region, handicapped to a considerable extent by nature, into a land of comfortable homes and prosperous citizens continues yet today and suggests in several aspects the pioneer stage."[38] Committed to the ascensionist plot, intellectuals narrated the holy work of saints.

Likewise, narratives in popular culture referred to a kind of holy land, although often with some ambivalence. By the 1920s, the imagery of wide, open spaces reached a mass audience through novels, magazines, and film. Willa Cather and Badger Clark, for instance, fashioned romantic tales about village people in a primitive locus. Modernist literature, however, could be less than positive about rural life. Sinclair Lewis in the satirical *Elmer Gantry* in 1927 created a quaint yet defective character with his description of the small town setting circumscribed by shifting eddies. While the brutish rabble were "plodding yokels" of an American peasantry, they displayed "sudden guffawing" and "milled like cattle, in dust up to their shoelaces, and dust veiled them, in the still heat, under the dusty branches of the cottonwoods." Ole Rolvaag's *Giants in the Earth* in 1927 reinforced the perceptions of loneliness, hardship, and drudgery with a chronicle about Scandinavian families colonizing the Dakota territory. The title of the last chapter hit home: "The Great Plains Drinks the Blood of Christian Men and Is Satisfied."[39] They wrested a livelihood from nature, to be sure, but the environment seemed to diminish folks without refinement.

With the rise of an urban life, the decline of a rural one accelerated. In Kansas, Oklahoma, and Texas over 60 percent of the population still lived in rural localities by 1930; and though not all residents farmed or ranched, communities depended on these activities for economic vitality. A global economic breakdown reduced the market price of the staple, wheat, from $1.16 per bushel in 1926 to $0.68 in 1930. As more and more acreage was turned to hardy grains, the price of the cash crop and thus land spiraled downward toward a crash. Foreign markets for grain collapsed, and the federal government abandoned the World War I price supports. Soon, all aspects of social life were descending on an unprecedented scale and scope, which further pushed producers to overextend marginal areas and to refinance their properties. As previous generations had learned through dips, paying off debts became a nightmare if a harvest failed or if livestock starved. In years of financial panic, which arrived almost as cyclically as the droughts, rural life languished.[40]

The heat rose to generate extreme temperatures, which, in conjunction with a country in decline, punctuated a miserable record of experiences. Drought struck across several states in 1931, when the entire nation averaged 13 percent below normal precipitation levels. With soil baked and sod broken, ominous black blizzards blanketed the hardest hit portions of western Kansas, southwestern Nebraska, southeastern Colorado, northeastern New Mexico, and the Oklahoma and Texas panhandle. Across eroding fields, there were twenty-two dust storms in 1934 and as many as seventy-two in 1937, although the number declined thereafter. Outbreaks of measles, strep throat, respiratory illnesses, and bronchial diseases called "dust pneumonia" exacerbated the physical distress. Furthermore, volatile patterns in population demographics paralleled the climatic extremes. The hard times of the 1930s ultimately winnowed as many as three and a half million people from their farms. Refugees, mostly unemployed sharecroppers and tenant farmers, drifted with the blight. Despite the conspicuous poverty, though, three out of four people in the region persisted.[41] Nevertheless, the intersecting forces of wind, drought, and erosion constituted a watershed in the world the neophytes had made.

In the context of the interwar years, a new world seemed out of balance. According to the historian David Wrobel, a troubled society assumed a sense of anxiety about a closing frontier. Ostensibly, the early twentieth century produced ebbs and flows of optimism about the possibilities for expansion. That is because the perception of the existence of free land, however myopic, was basic to American mythos. Therefore, intellectually charged debates often revolved around the idea of the frontier, if not the nature of the story itself. Conservative voices searched for new vistas in developing corporations and asserting individualism, particularly during the era of declining fortunes. In contrast, liberal advocates for development contended that disappearing opportunities necessitated increased state-centered capacities for relief, reform, and recovery. The discourses, in effect, formalized underlying cultural tensions about the fate of civilization.[42]

Of all the spectacles created by the frontier, none have been more compelling than those suggesting an unrelenting conflict with nature. The raging winds, searing heat, and wandering fugitives were featured in newspaper and magazine articles, broadsides, works of music and art, federal and state government publications, monographs, histories, and fictions. Such artifacts articulated the omens of a catastrophe. The omens insinuated the terrors of a shocking and confusing era, but the gap between expectations and realizations extended a series of perceptions that began with the conquest of the Great Plains. The perceptions about the environment appeared in the teleological plot lines for internal colonization, which gave form and meaning to the displacement of civilization materializing in modern life. Simply put, the evidence of displacement did not disappear in a vacuum but was settled in stories about a new world. The new world, or at least its social construction through an epic of conquest, contained the deep, commonly felt fears about a post-frontier society.

From one plot to another, an epic made conquering a desert central to regional and national self-consciousness. That self-consciousness was about making the most out of perceived emptiness in the landscape. It was about moving forward through the pain of disappointments. It was also about taking chances in fleeting moments and realizing dreams deferred. Most of all, it was about overcoming a bewildering cosmos. Between success and failure, an anxious grasp of the situation laid the foundation for accommodating to the changes in the land. Embedded in the culture, conquest devised language to communicate problems, to formulate possibilities for growth, and to comprehend what seemed incomprehensible. With no way out of the predicament, a people and a nation experienced one of the most terrible disasters in American history. Indeed, empty homesteads, overcast skies, and dislocated families signaled that there was trouble ahead.

Chapter 2

FALL   *Dust Bowl* (1933) depicts with oil on canvas the deserted wastes of a farm somewhere in the Great Plains. A raging storm floats along the background of a surreal setting. Near the center of the portrait, a blazing sunset breaks through the haze of the atmosphere, if only to shine on the excremental remains of crooked fenceposts and broken barbed wire. An eerie light reveals tracks and ripples across the sands, meandering off to nowhere in particular. A tiny farmhouse and windmill materialize on the distant horizon. In the foreground, an abandoned, eroded landscape unfolds, even as a lost civilization vanishes into the evening. The shadowing on the canvas evokes the desolate field of a biblical Armageddon or a quiet battleground along the western front of the Great War. The artist, Alexandre Hogue, pictures an apocalyptic moment for a region of doom, where a plot of land reveals a fallen civilization.[1]

According to this depiction of the fall, days of judgment disgraced the people living in what Hogue called the dust bowl. The term "dust bowl" had existed in Great Plains lore before this 1933 artifact, but its use in the vernacular thereafter denoted a country degraded by erosion, drought, and depression.[2] This vernacular, if articulating what the literary scholar Sacvan Bercovitch called an American jeremiad, expressed more than threnody in hard times. As testaments about signs and wonders in nature, jeremiads have echoed in a timeless fashion through the words of cultural authorities, remaining malleable to extraordinary ecological phenomena.[3] Through ritualized expressions of the jeremiad,

prophetic voices have cried out in bewilderment about the fate of civilization when observing disasters. They inform a nation about human suffering and raise awareness about it. They also bring attention to significant ills
that a society might otherwise attempt to ignore. They guide people when
all hope seems lost. Formalizing emotive fears into a cultural narrative,
moreover, transforms a landscape into a microcosm for great tribulation.
In expressing the emotional sense of an impending crisis, jeremiads become
creative as well as cathartic.[4]

Before the environmental problems became severe, the discourses local
to the Great Plains warned of a crisis as early as 1930. "The country is in a
bad way," lamented the editor of the *Baptist Messenger* of Oklahoma, since
"nearly every state east of the Rocky Mountains is in the grip of a disastrous
drouth." While admitting that the temperatures in the region had reached
higher than normal levels, the editor proceeded to suggest that "we need
only to read again the messages of God's prophets of old to know wherein
we have sinned against God, and have brought these conditions on us."
Ostensibly, tribulation and plague denoted Manichean sensibilities, that is,
an Old Testament vision of the end. Even though the "land was smitten by
a drouth and the fields yielded no food," declaimed his story, a cultural decline appeared far more alarming than rising temperatures.[5] He stirred
emotions with one rant: "God has taken care of his people in worse drouths
than this. Joseph passed through a seven years' drouth. Elijah prayed and it
rained not three and one-half years. He prayed again and the heaven gave
rain. In apostolic days the world suffered from a drouth. Drouths and low
prices and disturbed political and economic conditions are not nearly so
disastrous to a land as spiritual famine. Our greatest concern is that
point."[6] This admonition gave meaning to the irregularity of dips, explaining the mysterious ways of nature through eschatology.

Consider an editorial in a Kansas newspaper titled "Depression Tragedies," which appeared in 1932. The editor for the Methodist broadside
lamented a drought that extended from the Canadian border to the Texas
panhandle and from the Rocky Mountain slopes to the central states. The
pious editor surmised: "Man seems to have made a terrible failure, and sin
and riotous spending, and living in pleasure, and forgetting God, has
brought on God's judgments on our nation, by great areas of drought, and

withholding rain, to add to the miseries of a great nation, full of pride, sin, adultery, and forgetting God." Of course, the jeremiad in some sense expressed a human relationship to an encompassing world, or at least to an overwhelming force assumed active in tumults and silences. Through eschatology, then, it explained that "God's pay day comes" with certainty, delivering "withering heat and blighting drought, and a depression full of terrible tragedies, and the dreadful realities of fiery judgments!"[7] A tale of woe forecast the climatic, and even climactic, conditions in ritual terms of suffering.

Forecasting misery in the heartland and pleading for relief, local newspapers fixated on the unexpected severity of the weather. For example, the *Sublette Monitor* of Kansas during 1933 began to appeal for external aid to relieve an "acute situation" and to recondition "sand-swept farm lands." Livestock suffered, soil blew, and people starved in a region "whipped by winds and blasted by sand," one article testified. It added, though, that "three years ago this part of Kansas was among the most prosperous, considering its population, in the world." In those fulsome days, picturing the "desolation of wheat fields" now marking the region "would have been laughable." In fact, omnipotent forces were to blame for the crisis. The editor reasoned that "the drouth and high winds sapped the soil of life," a calamity beyond the control of the people. Although this account complained about the degree of suffering, the editor, nevertheless, followed with conventional promotional language, contending that "sooner or later the prairies will wave their green guidon again," and "Nature will cease her chastisement."[8] He was confident of a better "next year"; the blight composed a temporary punishment, but redemption would undoubtedly follow in the wake.

Not everyone extolled faith in such a scenario, especially as cultural authorities confronted the onset of dark dusters. Impressed by the blowing sand, the Reverend M. E. Markwell of Boise City, Oklahoma, in his newspaper column warned the community: "We are getting deeper and deeper in the dust." While slouching into depression, "material things are slipping away—get a hold of something eternal." Likewise, the Nazarene Church in Meade, Kansas, reported that the seating capacity was filled for every service "because people are awakening to the warnings of God's word, that financial conditions and crop shortages are dependent upon someone greater than man." The *Dodge City Daily Globe* in 1935 published a petition by ministers for citizens to reconsecrate their lives and prepare themselves for "God's own way and judgment to deliver us from this dust peril lest . . . a worse calamity come upon us."[9] The alarming appeal further stated:

Whereas, the drought and dust stricken area of the United States is in emi-nent [*sic*] danger of becoming a great desert and unfit for human habita-tion, life, health and happiness of our people are in danger because of the present perilous conditions. And whereas, it is beyond all control of indi-viduals, local committee and government agencies . . . [we] believe it inad-equate without the help of Almighty God, we appeal to all people to prepare themselves by their personal lives and pray that God may come to our rescue speedily.[10]

Although the language tended to be more of an expression of community solidarity than theological decree, it defined an understanding of the land-scape in terms of a fallen civilization.

With days of judgment arriving, the *Catholic Advance* of Kansas articu-lated the rhetoric of the downfall. In an editorial titled "Dust Storms in West Kansas," the newspaper alerted readers that "every day was Ash Wednesday. It was not hard to believe that we are dust and that to dust we shall return." Elsewhere, the editor explained that the "wind out where the West begins is no mere gentle breeze but a blowing current." Near Garden City, Kansas, the wind cut deep trenches in the landscape and covered roads and fences with dirt. Readers were told to "pity the farmers who saw their fields blown away, powerless to stop the havoc," offering charity for folks who suffered under the "plague" of storms. The editor admonished farmers to revive traditional farming techniques, complaining that the "modern combine pulverizes the soil" and was ill suited to the "dust belt." While considering the possibility that a "weather change might make the United States an arid land," the *Advance* noted that the "great Gobi desert in China was once a fertile country," at least until destructive practices dev-astated it.[11] As walls of dust came crashing against communities, cultural authorities sought to explain the fall.

The editor of the *Catholic Advance* counseled his readers about the fall. He warned that grasshoppers might wipe out the countryside before the next harvest. In fact, the sight of the expulsive dusters suggested a biblical precedent:

The plagues that overran Egypt in the days of the stubborn Pharohs [*sic*] are classics in the Scriptures. God punished Egypt with the plagues because the Egyptians had made slaves of an entire race of people and because Pharoh would not accept Moses as God's prophet. We have Pharoh's today, too many of them, and nations which promote a bad species of slavery. For instance, all the so-called civilized nations of earth are slaves to money, slaves to power, slaves to pleasure.[12]

Such analogues likened the desiccated locus to a biblical setting, thus composing narratives about a godforsaken place.

Meanwhile, nationally circulating news also described a godforsaken place. Reports in *Newsweek* described a field in Kansas that "now looks like the Great American Desert." In one storm, the wind blew five hundred million tons of topsoil from the nation's breadbasket, but a greater specter of soil erosion "threatens to turn half of the United States into a desert." The desert of the text and accompanying photos reminded the author of "an Old Testament plague," with plots of land wrecked from an apocalypse now.[13] For the *New York Times,* Russell Porter remarked in 1934 that the blight echoed the "Old Testament story of Joseph and the 'Seven Years of Dearth' in Egypt." With thousands of acres of pasture "burned to a crisp by the hot Southwest winds and lack of moisture," neither feed nor water could be obtained for livestock on ranges. Cryptically, the report dreaded what was to come, just "as in Pharaoh's dream interpreted by Joseph, the 'Seven Ill-Favoured and Lean-Fleshed Kine' have been accompanied into this once rich and fertile land by the Seven Thin Ears.'"[14] Even if the Depression and the drought represented two distinct phenomena, the stories in circulation rarely separated the two.

Alarmed by this calamity, the *New York Times Magazine* contemplated a fatal environment. During a visit to the region in 1934, Harlan Miller wrote: "A pallor has blanched the face of the parched earth. Tiny low dunes roll across the acres as the wind blows the surface dust." These dreadful vignettes reminded him of "the alien pictures of the sterile desert," or at least the ones he had observed in his geography book. After the economy had crashed, a wheat farmer faced a "coy and capricious Mother Nature who will reward him handsomely if he guesses her mood and forestalls her whim." Note the use of the feminine metaphors when describing the fall, projecting anthropomorphic assumptions of gender on nature. A year later, Miller recalled the "sterile grays and browns of the near deserts," when such blows appeared "comparable with the heavy sandstorms of the Sahara and Arabian Deserts."[15] The dust plague, according to Miller, tore away soil and left behind a denuded shame.

The jeremiad underscored the most frightening of ends for a civilization premised on wresting a living from the soil. After observing the terrible situation in 1934, A. W. Malone in *New Outlook* cautioned of a "Desert Ahead!" "Is there danger of the desert conquering our Middle West?" he asked rhetorically. "Will the now fertile regions, lying between the Alleghenies and the Rockies, some day become a forbidding desert, similar to the sands that once knew the footprints of the Queen of Sheba?" He argued in the affirmative that, indeed, the extreme drought signaled a national catastrophe with permanent diminution. In fact, he predicted that the intercontinental rail system "would soon be mere streaks of rust through a howling desert, which would separate by some 1500 miles the two habitable coastal regions." A bad place in the middle of North America had formed, Malone surmised, and a hellish fury continued to rage.[16]

Furthermore, Malone believed such destruction portended ill not only for commercial development but also for population distribution. Refugees scorned by the "lands which the desert was conquering" would have to be absorbed by the two coastal regions. The cities, which already suffered from overcrowding and unemployment, could not handle the dislocation. Those with doubts about his fears "need only be reminded of the great tracts of desert which once were 'lands of milk and honey,'" he opined. Plainly, the "great tragedy of metamorphosis from glowing wealth to sandy oblivion in Egypt and Arabia" had begun to spread across a different stage.[17] According to Malone's jeremiad, future generations would once again label the continental interior as the Great American Desert.

As disaster spread down the hardest-hit belt, the *Saturday Evening Post* covered the story with concern. Morris Markey in "Nature the Farmer" warned readers that the great spring wheat basin of America had turned into "an empty wilderness." He traveled through one dust storm, he reported, and saw firsthand "the desert nature of the land" simmering in the sun. As residents donned dust masks to filter the filthy air, hopes sank in a country "empty of vegetation" but covered under "the sand of a desert." Likewise, Putnam Dana McMillan deplored the "marginal land and marginal thinking." Alluding to the risky practices of farmers, bankers, and speculators, he regretted the circumstances that made a once bountiful wheat kingdom "now a desert."[18] Visiting journalists inspected the wreckage, although they seldom returned to view the repairs.

Meanwhile, Meridel Le Sueur narrated in the *American Mercury* a car drive "through the sizzling countryside." The journalist, who had decried unemployment lines in an eastern metropolis, discovered "something terrifying" about this visible catastrophe. While the pall of dust "went into your nostrils" so one could not breathe, "the smell of hunger" that pervaded "made you count your own ribs with terror." In vivid prose, she imagined that the "whole country cracks and rumbles and cries out in its terrible leanness, stripped with exploitation and terror—and as sign and symbol, bones—bones showing naked and spiritless, showing decay and crisis and a terrific warning, bare and lean in Mid-America." Ultimately, she became so disenchanted with the consequences of "bourgeois individualism" that she joined the Communist Party.[19] The graphic details of terror appeared to confirm journalistic commentaries about the plight of the underclass.

Moved by the dark dusters in 1934, an editorial in the *Commonweal* titled "The Call of the Land" got to the bottom of things. After comparing one storm to those experienced in the "Sahara Desert," the editor warned that the "denudation of vast areas and also the drying up of water courses" resulted from "the reckless and unchecked destruction of forests and woodlands in the past." The storm therefore echoed the call from "Mother Earth" to her children imprisoned, or self-exiled, in the cities. When nature called, the sounds could be heard as a "voice of anger" raging against neglect and abuse, claimed the editor. The editorial continued: "Signs and omens and wonders are usually the accompaniment, at least in popular imagination, of all periods of human crisis, and at the risk of being regarded as fanciful, we wonder if the great dust storm may not be considered as such a portent."[20] The modern age of the metropolis distanced Americans from nature, but the sweep of dust clouds seemed to awaken them to the call of the wild.

Without a doubt, the spring of 1935 produced circumstances that awakened the country. The *Boise City News* of Oklahoma opened one article about the grit blanketing the community with the Scripture from Ezekiel 22:12–13, in which the Lord declared: "Behold, therefore, I have smitten my hand at thy dishonest gain which thou hast made, and at thy blood which has been in the midst of thee." An editor for the *Amarillo Globe* reported telephone calls from readers about the "Curses of Disobedience" in the book of Deuteronomy, which warned of heat and sandstorms. In Kansas, the *Topeka Daily State Journal* announced in a headline: "The Garden of Eden Destroyed When Man Turned the Sod on the Prairies of Kansas." After an ominous black blizzard on 14 April 1935, the *Meade Globe News* of Kansas envisioned it as "the Wrath of God." The *Herald-Democrat* of Beaver, Oklahoma, reported the fear that "like Tyre and Sidon we were to be buried here." Other witnesses of blight thought "the end of the world" was at hand and panicked. For communities in the path of the daunting rollers, anxieties were ingrained in the assumptions of folk eschatology. Perhaps the sense of divine punishment was heightened by the fact that the most vicious of tempests struck a week before Easter on Palm Sunday, a Christian commemoration of ritual sacrifice.[21]

The spectacle of the tempests moved the nation to look into the situation. Charles Fitzhugh Talman, writing for *Nature Magazine* in 1935, compared the clouds of dirt and sand to "those of the 'habubs' for which the Egyptian Sudan is famous." He explained that when the topsoil blew, scattered showers became colored with reddish sand, which often created "showers of blood" arousing superstitious terror.[22] "If it rains. . . . These three little words rule life in the dust bowl of the U.S.," mourned Associated Press reporter Robert Geiger for the *Washington Evening Star* in 1935. During awesome sandstorms, Geiger not only offered the country the sobriquet of "dust bowl" but also labeled it "a vast desert, with miniature shifting dunes of sand." The journalistic penchant for analogies and sensation picked up, even as Geiger chose to use the term "dust belt" in a subsequent dispatch.[23] Whatever the terminology, the turbulent nature of the region became a dramatic feature of its fall.

In her stories about the fall, the writer Avis Carlson toured "that mighty strip of drought-baked prairie running from Canada to the Gulf and reaching to the Rockies." In the *New Republic* and *Harper's,* she warned a national audience that withering fields "are bare as the desert floor," and "the darkness is like the end of the world." She blamed the rapid rate of settlement for the collapse of her homeland, as the settler "pushed out to the fatal hundredth meridian," although the settler did not act alone. In a sense, it was as if "the government bet a man 160 acres that he couldn't live on them five years." Note the orientation of the frontier in her prose. The introduction of tractors, she observed next, allowed advancing tillers to conduct extensive plowing "under the hottest sun and in the midst of the most choking dust," a dangerous shift that "amounts to a major assault on nature." Perhaps the fields returned to "the desert from which they came," and so she cautioned that "the American people should begin to understand that they have in the plains a national problem."[24] The problem, if unsolved, threatened not only the livelihoods of residents but also the ideals on which the nation was premised.

The problem was frequently observed but seldom analyzed, though. Alfred Klausler, writing in the *Nation,* observed "fences torn, buildings unpainted, dust-drifts along the fence lines, fields of stunted Russian thistle, deserted farmyards—as far as the eye can see desolation and waste." In this fight to save the soils, M. E. Poyer mourned that "in other parts of the world men have made deserts by substantially the same processes we have been following."[25] W. I. Drummond in *Review of Reviews* surveyed "a desolated Sahara," and the terror of 1936 left "the present barren expanse of a new American desert land." An editorial in the *New Republic* that year explained that "the old delusion that this is a nation specially favored by God, which need take no thought for the morrow, is being burned to powder under the fierce blast of a scorching sun."[26] The social drama, in effect, raised the perturbations to the level of a fiery trial for civilization.

As the media heralded a fiery trial, the location of the affected areas became as ambiguous and mobile as the correspondents themselves. They reportedly spread from the dust bowl proper into dust bowls in the Dakotas, Iowa, and Minnesota. Reports led with exaggerated descriptions of fervent heat "rushing out of the furnace of the prairie dust bowl," which "blasted crops, sucked up rivers and lakes, and transformed the nation—from the Rockies to the Atlantic—into a vast simmering cauldron." In 1936, *Newsweek* considered the ordeal one of the most serious peacetime problems in the nation's history. The lucid if sensational coverage sounded the alarm of "an American Sahara," warning that "deserts mark the homes of forgotten civilizations." Across fallow fields once cultivated, then, the "marching sands of the desert point the finger of guilt at man, not weather."[27] Although hope remained, time was running out.

An article by A. B. Macdonald of the *Kansas City Star* discerned "a hopeless desert." He witnessed "fields thick with hummocks of earth blown there by the winds and no vegetation except weeds anywhere in sight." He found that "wherever the gray skeleton of a tumbleweed had held its ground there stretched from it a drift of earth." Mindful that "rains would surely come," he found residents who claimed harvests would inevitably "blossom like the rose and give them big crops and prosperity again." Wait until next year, they admonished the downtrodden. Even in despair, folks suggested that "seven years of drought and hardship would be succeeded by seven prosperous years." The story cited various examples of how nature maintained a cycle of "seven good fat years" and "lean years," as if the country had "ended a dry cycle" and stood "on the threshold of a cycle of fine wheat weather again." After interviewing Ida Watkins, dubbed the "Wheat Queen" of southwestern Kansas, the reporter offered her words of counsel: "I guess the good Lord is going to lead us out into the promised land again. . . . For five years we have been living here in the desert of the dust bowl and the abundant rains have taken us up into a high mountain and shown us close ahead the bounteous land of Canaan, blossoming with wheat and new prosperity."[28] However romantic, crop failures and dry winds continued to disturb the order of things.

Ernie Pyle, the most famous investigative journalist of the period, arrived during the abysmal summer of 1936. He observed "the saddest land I have ever seen," which at that time seemed "a mild form of desert, and hence rather sandy." During his trip through "this withering land of misery," he recounted the "day upon day of driving through this ruined country," which "gradually becomes a sameness that ceases to admit a perspective."[29] After blistering in the sun from the Dakotas to Kansas, Pyle lamented the social consequences: "I saw not a solitary thing but bare earth, and a few lonely, empty farmhouses. . . . There was not a tree, or a blade of grass, or a dog or a cow, or a human being—nothing whatever, nothing at all but gray raw earth and a few farm houses and barns, sticking up from the dark gray sea like white cattle skeletons on the desert."[30] Pyle's popular dispatches, syndicated in Washington, D.C., and national newspapers, depicted a fall of unparalleled proportions.

Passing through potholes and beside buttes, Pyle beheld the desolation of "the drought bowl." Homesteaders, in his estimation, had received "a onetime paradise" and turned it "into a whirlpool of suffocation." In this haggard state, citizens and farmers were forced to "accept it as a vast land that is dry and bare, and was that way yesterday and will be tomorrow, and was that way a hundred miles back and will be a hundred miles ahead." While such judgments portended ill for government measures to irrigate fields and to plant trees, Pyle observed "the whole backward evolution into oblivion of a great land, and the destruction of a people." Clearly, the misfortune produced "long years on end without privilege for those of the soil." Before hitting rock bottom, the lost souls confronted their fall with "the horror of a life started in emptiness, knowing only struggle, and ending in despair."[31] While these dispatches announced bad news for locals, they produced stories for distant audiences with only a limited appreciation of the landscape.

The poet Archibald MacLeish offered an extended essay in *Fortune* magazine on the bad news. In "the living and the dead land," the poet protested the ultimate sacrifice of the soil. The literary prose described permutations of "dead quarter sections with the hardpan clean as weathered lime and the four-room flimsy ranch houses two feet deep in sand." The windswept grasslands were exhausted, according to the poet, distinguishing a place of devastation with "stock tanks brimming full but not with water, trees dead and a raven's nest of fence wire in the branches—these the dust did."[32] MacLeish's lines traced the ruins of civilization, thereby producing a secularized jeremiad.

Of course, the poet conflated the sites of ruins. "The city of Antioch was a rich and dissolute city in the days of Paul," scribed MacLeish with the authority of a lyrical apostle, but "today Antioch is a miserable Syrian town of 30,000 and the archeologists who excavate its ancient stones may shovel through some eighteen feet of mountain-washed detritus." Dust, whether in rural North America or in some distant lost city, produced the same cataclysmic end because "deserts look like deserts" wherever the sands swirl. Looking across the sifting dunes, he discovered "no philosophic difference between the fate of Antioch in Syria and the possible fate of Garden City in Kansas." That is because mankind, the "greatest of all abraders of the earth's hide," had learned over the interval to "destroy his planet with an amazingly increased dispatch."[33] During a modern age, he opined, Depression America appeared to be on the downward slopes toward the abyss.

MacLeish expounded on this theme in a pictorial poem, *Land of the Free,* published in book form in 1938. When the frontier beckoned Americans ever westward, there "was always the grass ahead of us on and on Father to father's son." But now "that the grass is back of us: back of the furrows: Back of the dry-bone winters and the dust: Back of the stock tanks full but not with water: Back of the snakeweed greasewood ripgut thistle," free land for settlement had disappeared. The crash left Americans wandering the countryside. While writing from the vantage of a field in Massachusetts, he protested that "the land's going out from us" just like "the dry wind in the wheat." The nation should "wonder if the liberty was the land" and if the grasses had been "grazed beyond horizons." The misery taught everyone a lesson, he concluded, while the "dust chokes in our throats and we get wondering." With the play on the word "wondering," the poet meandered into a reflective mode of cultural lament.[34]

Other poets of the 1930s reflected on the days of judgment, and these efforts confirmed the aesthetic of a wasteland. In a sense, poetry, unlike the landscape itself, sustained notable productivity in verse. "Song of the Buffalo-Wallow" gazed upon the "shaggy beards of buffalo" in a dustwhirl, suggesting a poetic justice for slaughtering the great beasts. Other eddies loathed the profound despair of "a dirty faced world," "ultimate darkness," "the long and listless plains," and the "grey, discouraged endlessness." Phrases such as "the bone-bare field" often interpolated dread about a "drought of heart" or comparisons to "the end of the world," and "Hell" denoted punishment for the guilty.[35] Julia Lott, for instance, penned a poem titled "Drought Survivors," which appeared in *Kansas Magazine* during 1936. She wrote:

> The creek bed, white with quicksand in the sun,
> Companions fields from which no wheat was binned . . .
> But yucca spikes are blooming, one by one.
> Oh for the racing shadow of a cloud
> To resurrect again this stricken plain!
> Hot winds are scorching through a land unplowed,
> Awaiting still the healing of the rain.[36]

Fearful of the fall, poets cultivated the dust bowl with their prose in the hard times.

Kenneth Porter in "Dust Cloud over Kansas" expressed a similar fear about the fall. With the disappearance of the bounties of the harvest, the appearance of a desert loomed in the wake:

> A chaotic chimaera, they trampled and horn one another
> as they rush through the land, over watered fields planted to
>   wheat
> or alfalfa; the towns and their people are lost in the smother
> and choke of parched panting breath, shedding hair, flinty feet.
> Behind is a desert; plantation and street
> are swept by brown fire which no breaking can stay. . . . [37]

According to the poet's dirge, discouragement and despair were culminating experiences for generations guilty of exhausting the soil.

Elmyr Doran Warren of Texas penned a poem titled "The Dust Storm," which discerned a supernatural origin for the punishment of the guilty. Published in 1936, the poem mourned:

> How long, Oh God, we pray Thee,
> Must we pay this terrible price
> For wheat thrown into an Ocean
> Or burned—what a sacrifice!

We know that Thou art ruling,
We can not read Thy plan;
In darkness, like children we pray Thee—
It is hard to understand.

We ask Thee, Heavenly Father,
To be with us through this hour
That all might know Thy wisdom,
That all might feel Thy power;
Give us hope on through this pall of dust,
And strength to say "Thy will be done,"
Yes God, we know we must.[38]

The onslaught of dirt, much like the drought and depression, represented another test of faith.

Poetic license extended to headlines and features, even after the most gruesome conditions subsided. George Greenfield authored an article in 1937 for the *Reader's Digest* observing "a Great American Desert in the making." While dramatizing "a dying land," he romped through "a flat Sahara," except that the ground was hard and brown and not rolling and sandy white. Consider his evocation of travel literature to some exotic realm. Greenfield found that descriptive "words are vague until you actually see what waste and greed have done to our land—actually see it blowing away under your eyes, piling up in mounds that make you think of the Gobi Desert." As he encountered the prevailing winds, in a country of busted sod, he claimed to see the "cold hand of death" moving over the wasteland. On the road, he beheld dreary dunes and degraded homesteads.[39]

The stories told from the vantage of the road gave readers a sense of a passing landscape. Francis Flood in one 1937 article for the *Oklahoma Farmer-Stockman* considered "the ghost cities of lost civilizations in other lands." If civilization became "buried beneath the follies of its builders—betrayed and forgotten by man, shamed and scourged by nature," then the rising dunes foreshadowed a burial in disgrace. He recounted: "I crossed the Sahara once—it took me a couple of months—and I don't recall seeing a more barren land in all the Sahara than the bleakness of that stretch of the panhandle." In the deluge overwhelming the wheat fields, Flood observed that "every tender shoot that stuck its tip above that no man's land was mowed down by the biting dust and sand barrage, and its roots were gone with the wind." The dust bowl was no lost cause, however, as his account testified to its eventual taming.[40]

The testimony of visitors turned more promising by the end of the decade. John Collins, who visited the region for the *Christian Science Monitor,* claimed to witness the "revival" of the Great Plains. The dust bowl "is slowly being wiped off the map," especially after "realization had come that this section was, in fact, headed toward that fate which once had been predicted—a return to the Great American Desert." Furthermore, Mark A. Dawber, reporting for the *Missionary Review of the World,* confessed that "large portions of the inland United States will doubtless go back to desert." He observed multitudes leaving their homes, remarking that "farm machinery left behind was still buried in the dust." The visitation overwrought fields "barren and desolate in the drought and dust for five years," but he also found plots of land "lovely in the green of the grass and the gold of the wheat crop." Faced with stark limitations, he announced that "the stewardship of the soil is a religious responsibility."[41] As rain fell on landscape, a recovery appeared to loom on the horizon.

Even with the rainfall, though, the recovery of heretofore dreadful sections remained precarious. Ward West in the *New York Times Magazine* concluded that "hope springs green in the dust bowl" but warned of possible permanent diminution. In 1939, he spent three hours in a car "speeding across what the maps once called 'the Great American Desert.'" Now, he crossed only a bad place on the nation's mental map—regardless of precise boundaries or actual weather. To the outsider, he admitted, "it is still pretty much desert, but for one who grew up on those plains there are always memories of endless grassland." While pondering the flush times of his childhood, he infused his recollections with contemporary references to restoration. Indeed, the return of harvests suggested that "the cycle is rounding out," and "Nature has forced the play and man can only stand patiently by and follow nature's lead."[42] After mapping the extremes of the country, journalists such as West were awed, if not humbled, by the graphic scenes from the fall.

A number of fascinating artistic renderings enclosed the fall in aesthetic form. Regionalism, for instance, highlighted natural, simple, and evocative landscapes, while social realism portrayed human suffering with grim accuracy. Both movements characterized the art of William Gropper, Joe Jones, and George Biddle, whose collective imagery reached audiences across the United States. Federal government programs, while patronizing artists during the 1930s, commissioned public art in murals depicting aspects of rural America. In Chicago, the Art Institute's Forty-Sixth Annual American Exhibition of 1935 included representations of the miserable realm. Portraits of the crisis graced New York at the A.C.A. Gallery, the Whitney Museum of American Art, the Museum of Modern Art, and the World's Fair of 1939. They also appeared at the 1939 Golden Gate International Exposition in San Francisco. The America Today exhibition, which opened in 1936, traveled to more than thirty cities and displayed prints of regional and realistic landscapes. Clearly, visual artifacts focused the mind's eye on the dust bowl.[43]

The son of a Missouri minister but a longtime resident of Texas, Alexandre Hogue produced a host of visual artifacts. A jeremiad took shape in his erosion series, which he began crafting in 1932. Influenced by his encounters with Taos artists, his sympathies remained with what he called a "crucified land," a message communicated in artistic "sermons on conservation." According to a review in *Life,* the Texas artist unveiled how "desert conquers Texas prairie" with his surrealist technique of "psychoreality" and by placing forms together in geometric patterns. His work castigated humans for "persistent mistakes" in relation to the environment, which, in effect, limned a desert more or less iconographic.[44] Of course, he considered his subject to be relevant not only to local audiences but also to distant observers.

The artist conveyed a narrative of a population abandoning its vanishing homesteads, leaving only rickety buildings, foreboding vultures, eroded soil, and an emaciated cow beside a dust-filled water tank. In one particular oil on canvas, *Drouth Stricken Area* (1934), a dust-covered road disappeared into the horizon to suggest a hazardous trail of escape from an American scene. Furthermore, in *Drouth Survivors* (1936), a painting destroyed by a fire striking the Jeu de Paume of Paris in 1948, the elements of Hogue's iconography sharpened. The devastated landscape, of course, sifted over fences that divided up the range. While a rusted tractor rested motionless amid hundreds of acres, a gaunt pair of cows stretched out in the fore. The stillness of the cows and the tractor, iconic of the two main activities in the region—cattle raising and wheat production—became unnerving when contrasted with the animation of the prairie dog and the rattlesnake, the only survivors. Across the frontier, in other words, he composed an image to reveal the desecration of a rural arcadia.[45]

End of the Trail (1938), the only lithograph of the erosion series, translated the particular elements of the frontier into black-and-white terms. Although the space depicted in the drawing appeared less vast than in Hogue's oils, the proximity of lines implied encompassing dunes that surrounded an isolated barbed wire fence, plow, and cow skull. His eschatological impressions bundled together modern technology juxtaposed with the lifeless signs of exhausted soils. The bondage reproduced a scene of humiliation and pain, which manifested in contrasting tones and subtle shading. Even if the trail in the lithograph denoted a generalized place, it signified the remnants of the American dream. In his limning, the trails westward no longer led to a home on the range but to a land of the lost.[46]

One of the sensual oil paintings of the erosion series, *Mother Earth Laid Bare* (1938), displayed Hogue's philosophy about nature's forces with full effect. Here, the deserted farm decomposed in the background once again, but the central feature of the picture formed an enormous female figure that sprawled along an eroded foreground. The pale colors and plumes of sand marked the vignette as characteristic of the anguish, but a stray clump of grass and clear stream of water suggested more than an act of wind erosion. Erect nearby, an agent for destruction—the plow— evoked the power of the phallus, and so a fallen landscape was assaulted by technology and laid bare. A great feminine figure, if resting just beneath the surface of a homestead, represented fertile energy. While commenting on his evocative technique, Hogue traced the inspiration to his gardening mother, who told the youth a fable about "mother earth" that became the basis for the portrait. Perhaps the reproductive capacity of the soil had been exposed to the sun after systematic acts of violence. Perhaps the perpetrators of the injustice fled the premises, leaving the victim and the weapon at the scene of the crime. Whatever the fantasy, the psychosexual complex testified about the rape of nature and the guilt of a brigand.[47]

Through the permutations of landforms, cultural narratives reconciled a nation to calamity. Across the Great Plains, the signs of the fall appeared quite upsetting to the order of things. Americans gazed into fields where crops had fallen under the withering circumstances; they read the news headlines and features about tempests blotting out the sun. The stories stirred feelings of utmost horror, associating powerful emotions with the words on each page. Stirring the soul, imagery of the end reflected the perspective of intellectuals responding to the worst of times. A tragic plot presented a repository for anxieties in that moment, especially as passages left behind an elaborate and prolonged cautionary tale—an ecological jeremiad. It featured artifacts of agrarian grief, filthy homes, barren landscapes, dying livestock, abject poverty, and lost opportunities, even if it did so in decidedly cultural-bound terms. What appears critical, then, is not only what Americans during the 1930s found in the dust bowl but also the ritualized expression of their findings.

The ritualized expression informed the trauma of recovering from the Depression, although it was not a new story. According to the historian Carolyn Merchant, the end drama of environmental alarmism, in effect, reverses the plots of land from a Judeo-Christian teleos. It eventually predicts a restoration of health, reclamation of abundance, and return to innocence, but it begins with a tragic story about the fall.[48] The beginning of the fall during the dirty thirties set the backslide, which placed the dust bowl at the end of a story of declension. Divine visitations followed from the sins of humanity. While sloping downward through discourses constituting the ecological jeremiad, the fall of the narrative projected descending lines of an event. The event was coherent therefore because of the discerning tendencies of a recovery narrative.

Chapter 3

ADJUSTMENT

During the farm crisis of the 1930s, the United States established production controls, direct payments, and price-support loans for agriculture. The Agricultural Adjustment Administration, created in 1933 under President Franklin D. Roosevelt's New Deal, attempted to balance production with consumption. Though doing so was ostensibly voluntary for farmers, crops and animals were destroyed to bring about a desired balance for farm commodities, and in subsequent years, penalties were imposed for overproduction. In addition, the Drought Relief Service aided farmers and ranchers in distress. The Taylor Act, moreover, discouraged continuing deterioration of grazing ranges. The Resettlement Administration and its successor, the Farm Security Administration, purchased submarginal acreage, while the Civilian Conservation Corps and Works Progress Administration provided temporary employment. Whatever the intention, the New Deal precipitated an evolutionary shift for American agriculture, albeit an unfinished one.[1]

The New Deal for agriculture laid the foundation for the subsidies that have uplifted generations of farmers. In 1936, the Supreme Court ruled that adjustment remained a local matter for state rather than federal agencies, declaring the first act unconstitutional because it included a processing tax. The Soil Conservation and Domestic Allotment Act of 1936, however, paid farmers for reducing acreage and for adapting certain soil-conserving practices. Since soil-depleting crops were cash commodities, this act was a stealth mechanism to sustain federally mandated production controls. Written as a soil-conserving measure to circumvent objections, the Farm Act of 1938 extended voluntary enrollment through acreage allotment and marketing incentives.[2] During the dirty thirties, the adjustment policies secured a position of special interest for agrarianism—an ideological commitment to stimulate the political economy of agriculture.

Agrarianism constituted a powerful ideological force to rationalize unprecedented government measures for assisting farmers. In 1931, Wilburn Cartwright, a member of the United States House of Representatives from Oklahoma, pleaded to Congress on behalf of drought relief for suffering toilers in his state. His statement, reprinted in several state newspapers, warned that "the greatest emergency that ever faced this country in time of peace is confronting it now." The farmers "have suffered one crop failure after another due to floods, hail, boll weevil, and drought, and as a result are without anything with which to subsist." Since the scale and scope of the upheaval overwhelmed Red Cross relief, Cartwright's plea on behalf of "the honest yeomanry of the country" called for federal government actions. "The drought has withered the plants in their fields," he continued, causing the devastation "over which they have no control." The virtuous, if blameless for the state of nature, were victims of an unforgiving environment. Confronted with blight, those in the "common walks of life" were forced into "looking hopefully to their government to aid them when nothing else under Heaven will aid them."[3] According to the message, a crisis necessitated that the federal government rescue the agricultural economy of the Great Plains.

That message for agrarianism was expanded in the calls for comprehensive efforts by 1933. Harold Ickes, secretary of the interior, considered new policies to curb overproduction on marginal lands. He questioned old policies that encouraged agriculture on the "edge of the desert" while "having farmers in the old-established agricultural belts plow under standing

crops." In the Great Plains, for instance, a "sizable proportion of our farming population struggles in vain to make a decent livelihood." While relief
measures remained costly, he complained about "the selfish and short-
sighted influences" creating the problems of surplus commodities and
falling prices. Speaking about the entire West, he reminded that Thomas
Jefferson—the founding father of agrarianism—suggested that it would
take civilization one hundred generations to march from the Appalachians
to the Pacific. Yet after just one century of farming and ranching in the
public domain, Ickes lamented "the evils that have followed," especially the
"millions of acres rendered unfit to support human life decently." Even
though drought acted as an effective means of crop control, the interior
could not be abandoned to chaos. He stopped short of blaming farmers for
maladjustment but called upon the government to adjust the agricultural
system on a national level.[4]

As the federal government sought a solution to the problems, few observers agreed initially on the proper course of action. R. V. Smrha, an engineer, proposed one solution to the Kansas State Board of Agriculture in
1933. Despite the extreme aridity, new irrigation projects might function to
"supplement rainfall during periods of drouth" and thereby provide "crop
insurance" against potential famines. He complained that "irrigation has
not received the attention which it merits as an accessory to economical
crop production."[5] N. E. Hansen, a horticulturalist at the South Dakota
State College and vice-director of the local experiment station, offered one
alternative "to the primeval wilderness." In lobbying on behalf of farmers,
he concluded with confidence that "we can conquer the great American
desert to a much greater extent than has heretofore been the case."
Through a concerted effort by local, state, and federal planners, farming
could be sustained with the importation of crested wheat grass and the raising of Siberian livestock. Hansen recalled that "thousands of eager settlers
have come in high hopes to settle these regions," only to be "beaten back"
by a series of drought years and by grasshoppers.[6] The disruption of farm
productivity threatened to undermine the Jeffersonian ideal of yeoman independence.

The future for farmers, however, looked bleakest when conditions
worsened. An editorial in *Collier's* during the drought of 1934 surmised that

individual farmers "in the seared districts have been the victims" of neglect in the past. "Years ago," explained the editor, the area between the Rocky Mountains and the Pacific Coast was considered a wasteland, where unlimited expansion brought disaster "in the Great American Desert." In another editorial, the line continued "that even though nature never intended the land west of the Mississippi to be a great American desert, unrestrained individualistic farming can quickly destroy the fertility of good lands." The underregulated and overworked fields seemed "destined to be desert," or so the tragic plot suggested. This danger called for a new era of "intelligence and courage of a high order" and, for the first time as a nation, an attack on maladjustment along a broad organizational front.[7] The upheaval presented a grave danger, which jeopardized the place of the farmer in the order of things.

Clearly, the farmers were hit hard by the double impact of drought and depression, and new policies were needed to engender equilibrium. The *Literary Digest,* for instance, pleaded for innovative government provisions to accommodate through the "lean years" and to assist tillers with their stress. With "the mercury rising to more than 100 degrees in some places, even trees began to wilt," or at least the few still standing. Nature, "red in tooth and claw," appeared bent on "making another American desert," where the unfit had little hope in a Darwinian struggle for survival. Indeed, civilization "must provide for the lean years from the surpluses of the fat years," borrowing a "method of ancient Egypt."[8] Moreover, the journalist Margaret Bourke-White called for emergency initiatives for victims, predicting that the dust would pile ever higher and leave "a steadily increasing number of deserted farmhouses." In her view, the "half-buried plowshare, a wheat binder ruffled over with sand, the skeleton of a horse near a dirt-filled water hole" provided stark evidence of "the meager life, the wasted savings, the years of toil that the farmer is leaving behind him."[9] The climatic perils required a greater level of bureaucracy and a better organization of commodity production.

In the search for order, the *Farm Journal* presented stories about the dangers of "flirting with famine." Bernard W. Snow wrote that these "current moisture conditions in the south-west stand as a definite sign post," warning against the "danger of further experimentation with programs of deliberate effort to reduce bread production in this country." In fact, he pointed out that in 1929 practically 31 percent of the wheat area in the United States lay between the 100th and the 105th meridians, even though "the American Desert in that year produced 226 million bushels of wheat." Despite the drought, high levels of production, if carefully managed, remained possible.[10] H. L. Freudenberger, in contrast, surmised that the establishment of a planned system of agriculture offered "the only way to reclaim this man-made desert, once called 'the Breadbasket of the Nation.'" While the voices for agrarian interests warned about famine, they associated the absence of order with the presence of hazards.[11]

The initial attempts to address agrarian interests, in fact, prompted a few critics of the New Deal to speak against crop reduction. Leland W. Mann in the *Christian Century* discovered that a host of ministers in rural isolation, along with agricultural middlemen, interpreted a prolonged drought as a divine will punishing producers. Accordingly, the Almighty had demonstrated his power by "parching the ground" and "scorching the verdant crops" across the country. Soon, livestock commissioners and meatpacking representatives, who possessed their own malevolent purposes, told farmers to recall "the story of Job." It reminded the victims of drought that "God will punish you," they claimed, "if you set yourselves up to control production." Equating an administrative bureaucracy with malevolence, middlemen told agrarians "plainly that this drought was sent by God to punish us for interfering with the normal process of sowing and reaping all we might." The author, though, raged that this "attempt of the packers to theologize for the farmer during this crisis is consistent with the many tricks used by the trader class to thwart every effort of cooperative action born of the soil."[12] It remains impossible to determine exactly who opposed curbing production, but the Agricultural Adjustment Administration faced spirited resistance.

During 1935, the Reverend Buren Sparks of Texas complained that husbandmen were sacrificing their principles for the sake of returning prosperity. He assessed "the depression, the drought, falling prices," which made small farmers "broke like all the other big ranchmen." He compared the "lost in a sandstorm" to the "lost in hell," linking them to government efforts to stop overproduction. Destroying livestock was "contrary to the teachings of the old Book," he opined. Joseph, for example, refused to destroy any of the crops in Egypt during bumper years but stored the surplus for dry years ahead, or so the story claimed.[13] If farm programs produced such disasters as the dust storms, then the tillers of the soils needed to revive their faith in an invisible hand.

No respondents to the programs for planned scarcity reacted more negatively than the Reverend Gerald Winrod, a minister from Wichita, Kansas. He sulked that the country seemed "gripped by a cataclysm in nature," which included such disturbances as "eruptions, famines, tidal waves, floods, earthquakes, dust storms and drouths." Focusing on the fate of husbandry, he decried "America's present departure from her historic moorings," a backsliding analogue to the "the fatal mistake which ancient Israel made in renouncing her God-given government under the Judges." Furthermore, Winrod compared "Joseph of Egypt and Wallace of Iowa," charging that Secretary of Agriculture Henry Wallace had failed to study the Bible. In Scripture, Joseph warned the Pharaoh about "seven prosperous years" followed by "seven years of drought and famine." Whereas Joseph prepared for it by storing crops, the "brain trusters" wasted the land, making "one blade of grass grow where five grew before."[14] With soils descending into an abysmal state, the radio crusader offered a sermon on the drought: "And years of famine, depression and dust storms came to the land of America and 22,000,000 people were on public relief rolls because Henry [Wallace] had ordered the destruction of the food supplies of the people instead of giving the farmer's surpluses unto the starving people. . . . One of the qualifications for office of all future secretaries of agriculture should be a sworn adherence to the agricultural program of Joseph, son of Jacob and Rachel."[15] According to the reactionary persuasion, hard times worsened with the intervening hand of the federal government.

Few critics of agricultural programs carried the argument to such an extreme, but local voices sounded cautious about the New Deal for agriculture. *Capper's Weekly,* a newspaper published by Kansas Republican Senator Arthur Capper, obtained a great deal of popularity among agrarians during the 1930s. Capper considered the precedent of "a season of plenty in Egypt," where the government "wisely built granaries and stored the surplus against the seven years of famine and pestilence which they knew surely would come." Living on the edge of a desert, when the "Egyptians had seven years of plenty, they didn't get excited and put a crop curtailment program into practice, they just kept on producing and storing." While he suggested that such a wise policy succeeded in regulating distribution, he reminded that "the Egyptians didn't have any Chicago Board of Trade" either. Just as the tyranny of evil men enslaved God's chosen people, so, too, were farmers during the Great Depression in search of "freedom from bondage in Egypt." Continuing this line of argument, he admonished progressives in Kansas to envision "the wild land of Canaan as the Promised Land." Even though "the white man brought civilization and intelligence to North America," he added later, the loss of fertile acres would leave it "an uninhabitable desert." While ambivalent about the rational organization of production, the calls for deliverance demanded that Congress initiate a new farm bill.[16]

While headlines and features raged against nature, the discourses on agrarian reform continued to express the fears about famine. During the worst years of sandstorms, T. A. McNeal offered commentaries in the *Kansas Farmer* about agricultural crises past and present. He used the biblical tale of Moses in the deserts of Egypt to illustrate his point in an editorial titled "New Crop Pest Visits Egypt." Although the Pharaoh had his "bureau of magicians and soothsayers," they were no match for the Children of Israel, when an "unusually dusty year" produced dirt storms that turned into lice. In this allegory, the Pharaoh and his advisers refused to free those in bondage, and so Moses reportedly declared: "What you have suffered in the farming business isn't a marker to what you will see." The next insects, he mused, will be "Kansas grasshoppers," bragging, "when you see these hoppers you will know that you have never seen any hoppers before." Although the homespun yarn conflated impoverishment with enslavement, it characterized the plight of farmers as worse than that of any other group.[17]

Some essayists made farm programs something akin to holy work. Alva Johnston, writing for the *Saturday Evening Post,* considered the need for adjustment a paramount issue for the country. Although "here and there was an oasis," much of "the land was barren, dusty, and drought-bitten" because of the decline. In some sections, he wrote, "it is feared that the drought not only destroyed last year's grass crop but killed the roots of the grass," and large areas "may be useless for pasture for years, until vegetation is restored." In the states between the Mississippi and the Rockies, the "authorities on the transformation of a desert into a paradise" continued to promise that if "there is only rain, the dust deserts are to become Edens." He feared that, if the dry cycle continued to worsen, the emergency relief agency "will probably throw good money after bad until the country can no longer maintain vast regions of stricken land." The agricultural economy appeared undisciplined, or at least it needed to adapt to the contingencies of an arid domain. While the desert threat to the environment remained serious, he explained that nothing less than reform would vindicate the cultivation of the soil.[18]

From the perspective of agrarianism, the dust bowl evoked fears about the impact of technologies on cultivation. Joseph Fichter in "A Comparative View of Agrarianism," which appeared in the *Catholic World,* used the troubling scene as a metaphoric prop for his message about the dangers of industrial farming. For example, industrialization in such unforgiving places as Nebraska transformed the family farm into "a mechanized factory." Indeed, corporate farms evident in the heartland conflicted "with the elemental interests of individual and State by attempting to grow rich where others attempt to grow produce that is sufficient unto the day."[19] Ernest Dewey in 1938 lamented the devastation in the pages of *Commonweal,* warning that large-scale extensive agriculture created dust bowls everywhere. He waxed nostalgic: "Time was when fertile Kansas fields were something solid to plant your feet upon." With "once-fertile soil rendered sterile" and "wheat fields with tender plants either shredded by impact of tiny cutting particles or smothered under a blanket of lifeless dust," the country collapsed under the weight of modernity. Government intervention, though, promised to reverse the winnowing of producers, the mechanization of living, and the consolidation of wealth.[20]

Henry Wallace, secretary of agriculture for the Roosevelt administration, explained that virtue alone would not help producers. Wallace, an agricultural fundamentalist, exhibited a unique combination of naive mysticism and rational liberalism in his defense of rural life. His support of agricultural prices promised to enhance the purchasing power of the farmer, hopefully pushing the country toward recovery. According to his assessment of the situation in 1934, the nation no longer possessed enormous, unexploited natural resources "awaiting only the touch of young and vigorous hands to be transformed into fabulous, individual wealth."[21] Instead, he envisioned:

When those forty thousand undisciplined slaves, the Children of Israel, left Egypt, it was possible for them to reach their promised land within a few months. But they were not fit to march a straight course, enter and take possession. . . . Before the promised land could be attained it was necessary for the younger generation, hardened by travels in the wilderness, to come to maturity. . . . They had put behind them a vague, nomadic wandering, but they still had to adapt themselves in some measure to the commercial features of the Canaanite civilization. Their old frontier was gone. They had to work on new frontiers.[22]

Wallace not only recognized the threat to agrarianism posed by maladjustment but also cast the crisis in mythic terms.

Wallace outlined for the *New Republic* and *Literary Digest* a vision of specific if voluntary farm policies to reflect this government-directed agrarianism. "When the frontier was open . . . worn-out land could be exchanged for new," he noted. Although expansion of agriculture into marginal lands created opportunities for social mobility, the nation developed "bad habits of forest devastation, overcropping, destructive grazing and soil mining." Unfortunately, the wilderness "won from the frontier began to blow away in dust storms, and to wash into the sea." With these signs marking closure for an era of unbounded expansion, he believed that "an ever-normal granary is necessary," at least while famine threatened. Since "we cannot foresee the weather, the bugs, and the pests, it is essential to provide against market contingencies by setting up reserves which can be held in such a way as to protect the consumer, but not harm the farmer."[23] As the New Dealer recognized the permutations of the crisis during the 1930s, he called upon the federal agencies to help rationalize agriculture.

Rexford Tugwell, administrator of the Resettlement Administration and collaborator with Wallace, explained in 1935 how irrational agriculture had been disastrous for thousands of producers. The Depression resulted from overproduction in agriculture, Tugwell insisted, and the government could underwrite a recovery with programs to subsidize farmers who left their fields fallow. No sooner had the farmer "plowed under the wild prairie grass than the wind began its destruction," observed Tugwell. With one drought year following another, "the wind has lifted the top soil—his capital—and blown it away," leaving little hope for returns. Agrarian hopes now lay "in drifts and dunes in once grassy fields," which left the tillers with virtually nothing. Although this was a problem for hardscrabble home-steaders, it also presented an opportunity for the advancement of civiliza-tion itself. Instead of rejecting the story of expansion, he punctuated it with a reminder that the "free land of the boundless West" expressed a "national dream from the dawn of our history on this continent." If "the frontier has gone" with the wind, then the destiny of the country appeared in jeopardy. The federal government thus inherited a "duty to end what might be called human erosion—the wasting away of millions of our people in a hopeless struggle to earn a living from lands which will not support life."[24] If the value of land declined, then the foundations for rehabilitation would de-mand organization for support.

Rehabilitation through organization, at least for Tugwell, turned the tragedy into a triumph. The eloquent New Dealer described "broad acres, burned with drought and swept by high winds, vanishing in the black, choking clouds of dust storms." He added that these "farmers have lost their land," and their "barren farms" were compounded by the absence of capital. In effect, those "who staked their life savings on the chance of farm-ing dry land" inherited "little but dust." They failed to achieve "a new econ-omy because the theory of non-cooperative individual control . . . has broken down before the hard facts of dry land, sparse grass, and limited water." He surmised that the Depression generation stood at a crossroads between the future and the past. If Tugwell and the New Dealers failed to correct maladjustment, "we shall go the way of Mesopotamia, Egypt, and China, and part with our collective birthright for a mess of individualistic pottage." Programs for rehabilitation, however, would save the farms and thereby raise the standard of living.[25]

Nonetheless, this propaganda on behalf of rehabilitation continued to tell a conventional story about the trajectory of civilization. "When the first settlers came to this country there was plenty of good land," began a 1936 pamphlet for the Resettlement Administration. Since "there are no new frontiers" for resettling, a crisis began in agricultural areas, "where dust storms and drought have ruined the land for farming." When traditional means failed to save the family farm from degradation, the "Federal Emergency Relief Administration fought off starvation" temporarily. Year after year of losing ground, though, tended "to make large areas of this region an arid desert," compelling the Resettlement Administration to buy up "dust-burned farms." Note in the narrative the heroic positioning of federal agencies, which saved the family farm from its arch nemeses—"parching sun" and "sweeping wind." Terms such as "barren living," "wreckage," "desolation," "trapped," and "farm debt" defined a "land tragedy." Strategic placement of photos and captions limned the descent into the "lands of the Dust Bowl region," which was followed by a recovery of "the Nation's future" through government action. Through the programs for "rural rehabilitation," the New Deal was "giving the farmer a chance to get off his barren acres and to earn a living on more fertile soil." Simply put, the discourse on adjustment elevated the commitments for reaching a higher stage of development .[26]

Discourses on adjustment, in fact, articulated stories about social relations, power, and dominion. According to the historian Frieda Knobloch, a narrative for colonization circulated through the literature on agriculture. The literature portrayed civilization as the emergence of a potent, stratified, and bureaucratic existence rising from a primitive and unruly nature. Nevertheless, the practices for cultivation and improvement assumed the guise of progress. Whatever the guise, a cultural narrative mapped a linear movement across the continent and erased subsistence modes of production. From the wild to the domesticated, from the natural to the cultural, the local became ever more entangled with the stories about organizational complexity. They analyzed the farm crisis in ways that considered rationalization not only desirable but also inevitable. By accepting government designs to rescue agrarianism, they ignored the paradox of want amidst plenty.[27]

When explaining the paradox, though, the federal documentary record tended to accentuate the movement of agriculture. Pare Lorentz, with the sponsorship of the Resettlement Administration, made history when he produced and directed a motion picture in 1936 as an official document placed in the congressional archives. *The Plow That Broke the Plains,* which appeared in over three thousand movie theaters across the country, began with a panorama of lush, verdant grass and ended with the symbolism of a dead tree. According to a review by *Time,* the farmers were "surrounded by the sun-baked desert." With few words but many images of a sandscape, a narrative voice in response to fifty years of toil warned on one occasion: "Plow at your peril!" Accompanied with mournful music by composer Virgil Thomson, the montage depicted a morbid "American desert," calling it a "Sahara."[28] The footage, although shot on location in the worst-impacted areas, complemented numerous newsreels and shorts. With the scene projected on a wide screen, documentary expression provided an animated reality as a visual artifact.

During 1936, photographers from the Farm Security Administration, including Arthur Rothstein, Dorothea Lange, and Russell Lee, also captured visual artifacts. Commandeered by Roy Stryker, the cohort between 1935 and 1943 obtained over 270,000 pictures, some of which documented the agony of the region. Among the most striking, Rothstein's *Fleeing a Dust Storm, Cimarron County, Oklahoma* portrayed a farmer and a boy dashing through a tempest toward a half-buried cellar. Others pictured several rows of turned-over fields, dust-covered farms, rusting disc harrows, abandoned machinery, and, of course, the legendary plow. In contrast, *Stock Watering Hole, Cimarron County, Oklahoma* and *Top-O-the-World Farm, Coldwater, Oklahoma* featured only emaciated cattle. The absence of an agrarian presence illustrated the need for reform, as image after image provided a vignette of oblivion. Even as they documented the spectacle, they evoked the imagery of a republic in peril. While pictures reproduced for newspapers, magazines, pamphlets, books, and exhibitions focused on human pathos, these government-supported photographers spun a story that extended the tale of the Old West.[29]

Chester Davis, administrator of the Agricultural Adjustment Administration, echoed this tale in his call for "planned harvests." With "cattle bawling into the dust" and "grain and pastures withering away," he reminded the administration that "civilizations have been checked and the destinies of nations changed by droughts." Before the dirty thirties, the administrator believed that the tiller "was forced to quit farming, as he knew good farming, and go into business of mining his soil instead." While cultivating for subsistence, farmers in marginal areas were forced to excavate and to exploit resources from the earth. Sodbusters "came and plowed," urged at first by unusual opportunities and later by sheer economic pressure, but they abandoned their homesteads and "left drought, dust storms and idle acres behind them." Note the irresponsibility associated with the unregulated farmer, who represented a public enemy.[30] The lack of responsibility required New Dealers to devise practical instruments for adjustment.

However subtle, the adjustments presumed the plot of the frontier. In an article titled "Lost Acres," Davis explained that agriculture was "carving out of the heart of our land a monument to national folly." The text explained that through severe sandstorms Nature offered "her protest" to misuse on dusty walls, on the desks of government officials, and in the food bills of consumers throughout the nation. He pointed, too, to the startling precedent of a China where peasantry "passed on to future generations the burden of paying for their intensive cultivation and exploitation of agricultural lands." Likewise, dry weather, dust blowing, and overproduction withered the farm belt, where twenty-five thousand square miles of land was "practically a desert—largely because man has made it so."[31] Because the absence of rational farming had devastated the soils, it was time for the federal government to act.

The Great Plains Area Drought Committee in 1936 echoed this sentiment, promising to uplift the nation's breadbasket. The group, which included Wallace and Tugwell, resolved that "activities for permanent rehabilitation and reconstruction already undertaken must be speeded up and expanded if the Great Plains area is to avoid a worse disaster than has yet befallen it." After sketching the situation, one report pointed out that the dust storms of 1934 and 1935 provided visible evidence to farmers living in the shadow of the Rocky Mountains that "something is seriously wrong." It meant that "the practices which have destroyed the sod and des-

iccated the soil" must, for the good of the society, be changed or abandoned. "We endanger our democracy if we allow the Great Plains, or any
other section of the country, to become an economic desert," directed the
committee. The landscape ostensibly threatened to unmake civilization, as
the narrative assigned the role of agency to a collective "we." It praised "the
courage and endurance of the people of the Plains," recalling their privileged position in the narrative about colonization and conquest.[32] The
place was a mess, to be sure, but the job to fix it assumed a team-building
process between husbandry and the state.

Assistant Secretary of Agriculture M. L. Wilson, who initially devised
the voluntary commodity reduction scheme, insisted that adjustment policies eased the farm crisis. Again, China provided a striking model of what
happened when a country continuously misused its land. In comparison,
the United States "has been moving in that direction at a rate probably
faster than that which led to the devastation of so much of China's soil."
The threat of "famine," in fact, continued to represent a threat to social security. The yeomen faced "the end of frontiers," wherein "moving away to
virgin lands" could no longer be allowed. Under the New Deal, however,
reform provided "plenty without waste," or producing within rational limits. Thus Wilson entangled a tragic plot of land into the fabric of a romantic
tale about progress. Pulling together, "future generations, whose interests
society exists to protect, will inherit fertile fields and forests rather than
eroded slopes and barren plains."[33] The level of cooperation among farmers with bureaucratic entanglements indicated that the information campaign was effective in a moment of urgency.

In fact, the federal agencies primarily responsible for disseminating the
information magnified their responsibilities. Joseph L. Dailey, assistant administrator of the Resettlement Administration, asked in 1936: "Are deserts
on the march, driving man out of the Great Plains?" He believed that it "is
unscientific today to assume that the West is turning into a desert," although the drought "has been an ordeal by fire for many thousands of dry
land farmers." Calling for rationalization, the essay considered the dust
clouds a natural consequence of uncoordinated tillage. They developed
after the occupation of "drought-burned farmland in the West," which
yielded "lessons in land use which Nature has taught us during the last six

years."[34] With the endorsement of volunteers and the payments from the government, the rationale for farm aid rested on a story about an old system of agriculture dissipating under a blistering sun. The modern support system, then, appropriately adapted to the extremes.

The extremities of the climate, nevertheless, required the regulating hand of government to prevent disaster. P. H. Stephens of the Farm Credit Administration explained in an article for the *Journal of Farm Economics* in 1937 that "we have no indication of a permanent change in climate," although "there is no indication that the end of the present drought can be accurately forecasted."[35] E. D. G. Roberts, chief of the Land Policy Section for the Bureau of Agricultural Economics in the Department of Agriculture, asserted that the variable climate demanded uniform vigilance. He identified "wide areas unfit for agricultural pursuits of any kind," where yields would not return without "re-seeding and mechanical assistance." The threat of dirt and winds made voluntary incentives for crop reduction seem insufficient. Invested with new claims to authority, the administrators of ongoing federal correctives became crucial for sustaining growth.[36]

With an indefinite extension, the Bureau of Agricultural Economics transformed into a central planning agency. By 1938, L. C. Gray of the bureau summarized the tentative success of strategic planning in combating the devastation. He recalled that for "more than a century the United States was dominated by a pioneer attitude toward natural resources." Again, the fresh but familiar version of the narrative followed the imperial march across the continent. The husbandman, wrote Gray, endeavored to "destroy the wilderness in order to live," at least until faced with ruin. As generations learned from each setback, they "settled the American continent and converted its natural wilderness into a civilized place of abode." The future of farming necessitated the development of new methods to "prevent dust blowing." According to Gray, the "intelligent use" of the region contained "the silt, sand, and dust that injured other lands and created great discomfort" for the cultivators.[37] Abandoning the policies of the bureau, in effect, presented a slippery slope for those farmers living on the edge.

The Southern Plains coordinator for the Department of Agriculture, Roy I. Kimmel, also underscored a cautionary tale for farmers. Beyond sterile fields and behind dust-covered masks, "the land and people are deeply scarred," whereas "fifty years of exploitation and seven years of drought have left their mark." He observed that fences remained "buried under drifts of wind-blown soil, here and there abandoned houses stand with vacant windows and sand-blasted walls, fields lie deserted." Since they provided "omens of ruin" for the homestead, they would forever remain "symbols of defeat for men who live by the land." Nonetheless, the "acute human suffering and living conditions of almost intolerable hardship" prompted those who were determined not to repeat the errors of their ways to change. Collaborating with the administration, producers learned "to prevent the kind of abusive land use that caused the Dust Bowl" and, in reversing the trends, began the organization of "farming that will make it once more the 'bread-basket.'" Participants in farm programs "can work for their own salvation," while the federal government and other agencies assisted them with regularity. Although Kimmel acknowledged fears that portions of the Great Plains were an actual desert, he declared that "a united front to reclaim the Dust Bowl" would turn the country around.[38] According to the narrative, the momentary lapse set the stage for the domestic allotments of the New Deal.

Clearly, the sweeping claims for rationalization made recovery for farmers seem inevitable. Herbert C. Hanson, president of the Ecological Society of America, in 1939 warned that "large portions of the western half of the United States are showing the serious, far-reaching consequences of grasshopper infestations, droughts, and various kinds of misuse, such as overgrazing, misplaced plowing, and improper irrigation." Even though farmers embodied an "industrious, enterprising people," the majority, according to his story, needed aid and comfort. That was because they were caught in "the meshes of disturbed equilibria," at a time when the "United States is passing from its pioneering stage into more advanced stages." Advancing cultivation with the organization of producers, he reasoned, adjusted the markets. Passing from risky agribusiness practices to working "intelligently" with the government, the administration promised "to secure balance and stabilization." In the process, a structure essential for the attainment of the "abundant life" and the building of "a culture far beyond our present dreams" was erected.[39] With a system of modern agriculture erected, then, the promises of unlimited bounties were secured for the next generation of agrarians.

As the decade ended, stories about farming hazards justified continuing the system. R. S. Kifer and H. L. Stewart in 1938 authored a volume for the Works Progress Administration that explored what happened to "counties laid waste by drought and its attendant disasters." The document warned that farmers remained endangered by "the climate of the region—the light and variable rainfall, the wide fluctuations in temperature, and the recurrence of severe drought—and from the failure or inability of Great Plains farmers to adjust their farming systems to natural conditions." Thus, improving the situation required surveillance by watchful extension agents.[40] Likewise, Bushrod W. Allin and Ellery A. Foster considered the fate of farmers who "traditionally depended upon the frontier in time of economic crisis." Investigations into "once-fertile lands" now revealed places with "fertility washed or blown away," where multitudes "either clung on in poverty or drifted away to relief rolls in the towns or to live as vagrants on the highways."[41] Under the guise of progress, the new establishment extended the domain of costly programs beyond the initial terms of adjustment.

The terms were established in reference to eviscerated acreage, extreme temperatures, and economic uncertainty, which devastated farmers during the 1930s. When anxieties about vast agricultural areas heading toward destruction manifested, a national conversation about relief, reform, and recovery began. The conversation considered the dust bowl symptomatic of a lapse toward famine, making corrective measures, at least under the direction of federal government agencies, the rational response. Therefore, following the lines of the frontier led to institutionalized authority and to reinforced discipline. While the ecological disaster presented problems that demanded innovative solutions, agricultural adjustment became a story about the decline of the homestead but, when regulated, the eventual uplift of husbandry. It is remarkable not that state expansion to rationalize crop production occurred but that it occurred without changing the basic values of the culture. The farmers became the beneficiaries of catastrophe.

That is because the position of farmers, even if challenged by the searing heat and blowing winds, remained privileged in the discourses on ad-

justment. While referencing the story of westward movements and unbounded freedom, they retained what the historian Henry Nash Smith
called the nation's master symbol—the yeoman.[42] The mastery of his domain, though shaken, became reaffirmed in upgraded versions of a social
drama featuring the policies of the New Deal. While forging a collective
bargain between farmers and the federal government, the stories did so in
ways that never challenged basic assumptions of the Jeffersonian ideal. Stories about improvement and cultivation proliferated with the dirty thirties,
underscoring the movement toward an organizational synthesis in agriculture. Glossing over the anxieties, the plane of myth accommodated modernity without disturbing the underlying order of things. It is no coincidence, then, that farm subsidies and costly programs tax a society driven by
its vision of maladjustment.

Chapter 4

CLIMAX   On 14 April 1935, blue skies darkened over communities from Lubbock, Texas, to Topeka, Kansas. The air turned cold, and the heavens filled with birds fleeing from an unseen force. An awesome cloud rolled over the horizon, laying a blanket of dirt across the landscape. Visibility declined to zero, while the atmosphere charged with static electricity. Before the dust storm subsided late in the afternoon, cars stalled, homes shook, and soil blew.[1] That month, a United States Senate committee in Washington, D.C., heard testimony about black blizzards from Hugh Hammond Bennett, head of the Soil Erosion Service. As he crusaded against destructive farming and ranching practices, the room darkened; the air filled with topsoil arriving from over two thousand miles across the continent. Bennett delivered the message: "This, gentlemen, is what I have been talking about!" On 27 April 1935, Congress enacted Public Law 46, creating the Soil Conservation Service.[2]

The dust bowl of the 1930s forced the nation to assume a deeper and broader responsibility for soil conservation. According to the science of soil conservation, the controlled use and systematic protection of natural resources managed what the historian Richard White called "a paradise before labor."[3] Before nonindigenous agricultural laborers entered a pristine grassland, the ecosystem had presumptively reached a final, mature, stable, self-maintaining, and self-reproducing culmination to plant succession.

The contemporary theories for ecosystem organization called this culminating sere the climax community. When a human community began to overwork the soils, a disclimax interrupted the pastoral. The discourses on imagined ecological communities made climax the order of things, then, representing the alternative to the disorderly nature of the other. While the stories about order conferred greater legitimacy to conservation methods, they also privileged management over labor in the process. Through the application of scientific management, conservationists claimed to lay the dust storms and to sustain the climax community.

The theory for the climax community was grounded in the research of Frederic E. Clements, a Nebraska scientist and fellow of the Carnegie Institution. Clements's writings from 1916 to 1941 informed the science of conservation with a homology between the naturally and the socially constructed. The succession of plants related to the advance of the frontier, that is, organismic stages of development advancing upward from simpler to more complex entities. The ruderal species prepared the ground for new waves of vegetation, and the perennial grasses adapting to the macroclimate stabilized the flux. This evolutionary process, of course, complemented the discourse on the human community maturing from fur trappers to modern urbanites. Clements claimed, however, that nature developed vegetative reproduction in a balanced ecosystem until human invaders upset it. The basic point, then, was that internal colonization into the grasslands interrupted an even flow toward climax. Maintaining the climax, in effect, required an offsetting power to check the presence of toilers.[4]

Clements puzzled over the dilemma that their presence in the Great Plains posed for the climax community. Drought, he knew, arrived with "climatic cycles" and forced multitudes to adapt or to suffer the consequences. He explained that in times of low rainfall, "vegetation catches and holds soil particles" and "keeps the wind from picking them up to form soil-drift or dust-storms." Without the culminating sere of pastures, soil drifting produced deposition and built dunes until it buried windbreaks and fences and overwhelmed the advances of settlement. Settlers who held on recalled "the account of a climatic cycle and its effects which appears in the Book of Genesis," with the "seven fat years and the seven lean years" of an Old Testament landscape. They actually coincided with a sun-spot cycle, he continued, ranging between ten and fourteen years. A population out of sync with the cycles, he cautioned, faced "rainfall and drought," "plenty and famine," and "abundance and want." To regularize the effects of the cycles on settler societies, Clements called for the application of science to land management.[5]

Likewise, Roger C. Smith, professor of entomology at Kansas State Agricultural College, opined in 1932 that management respected the cycles of the grasslands. When colonization came to the area of the "Great American Desert," the newcomers intended "to establish homes and to wrest a living out of this virgin soil." The monoculture of crops, however, increased the local entropy of the ecosystem. The increase "upset the age-old balance of nature," and an outbreak of pests and the exhaustion of soils followed. Smith warned that "insect and plant disease problems are actually increasing, both in number and severity," and a landholder "will have to employ artificial control efforts for a long time, or be seriously handicapped in his labors." Arguing for greater control over the countryside, Smith depicted the environment as "a complicated and delicate machine in which a slight misadjustment of a part affects all the others." If experts managed the flow of production in a mechanistic nature, then the vigor, hardiness, and resistance of the sod would revive in the process. In theory, the scientific management of ecosystems became commensurable with a gospel of efficiency.[6]

Climax theorists also included John Weaver and Evan Flory of the University of Nebraska, who extolled their gospel in 1934. Facing a grim scene, they determined that the "great dust storms are an increasing menace and give cause for reflection." Because of the imprudent actions by "sodbusters," generations of settlers plowed up the grasses and left the soils exposed to the wind. With "the millions of acres of bared soil" spreading across the locus, the exposed layers furnished "tons of dust that are carried in the atmosphere for miles and finally deposited in neighboring states." Dirt devils had long existed in the region, to be sure, but "not clouds of dust that darken the sky!" A native vegetative state composed harmonious interrelations of water, humidity, temperature fluctuations, and other critical factors of both air and soil, which contained "Nature's plan of a stable environment." Weaver and Flory called for scientists to intervene "before the opportunity with the destruction of the natural vegetation has forever passed." Science offered a way out of instability, they argued, by measuring the degree of departure from the ecosystem of pastoralism.[7]

Returning to the ecosystem that constituted the climax became the objective for conservationists. "Unless something is done," warned the associate chief for the Forest Service, E. A. Sherman, "the Western plains will be as arid as the Arabian desert!" He illustrated "the way deserts start," usually with "excessive grazing, which destroys the protective vegetative cover and permits the ground to be trampled into dust." With the protective turf removed, "desert conditions will begin, and once established, these lands can never be reclaimed." The management of trained experts, he advised, held out the last hope for preventing a cataclysm. With an ounce of prevention, "thousands of years from now our nation will not be 'as Nineveh and Tyre'; but that under the care of a wise and intelligent people its fields will prove as enduring as the eternal hills."[8] Before the most dramatic dusters, though, the conservationists were unable to remediate wasteful land-use practices on a significant scale.

With the creation of the Prairie States Forestry Project in 1933, the Civilian Conservation Corps participated in the damage control. Clyde M. Brundy wrote "Trees for the Prairies" in *American Forests,* which explained how "reforestation is one of the most outstanding phases of the 'new agriculture' in the western territory." With new lessons acquired from combating heavy winds, sudden changes in temperature, drought, and other adversities, farmers and ranchers learned that "reforestation is meeting its real test." Broken sod caused the topsoil to blow away, but the introduction of shelterbelts would secure the verdure from disorder. Furthermore, the coming of sylvan groves transformed "weary sameness" into "inviting farms." By planting forests in strips running from Texas to North Dakota, the project began the drive to restore an idyllic landscape.[9]

In 1934, Ellsworth Huntington, research associate in geography at Yale University, minimized the benefits of the tree-planting scheme. He explained that "droughts, together with locusts and other misfortunes, prevent the crops of western Kansas from affording a satisfactory living." Wherever nutritious grasses grow admirably, the crop-raising laborers "incur debts in dry years and cannot pay them during good years." The best-case scenario for the shelterbelts, even with the greatest care in choice of seedlings, seemed "slow growth and an extravagant percentage of deaths among the trees." Huntington, however, desired to study the possibilities of vegetative growth by means of small experiments. Moreover, he suggested converting the region into "a safe and prosperous cattle country" by promoting the repair of the ranges. Because of environmental constraints, scientific techniques could create tree plantations only at great costs. Droughts would in due time kill a large share of the groves, but President Franklin D. Roosevelt continued his support for the plantations—one of his favorite projects.[10]

Raphael Zon, director of the Lake States Forest Experiment Station, expected an aesthetic improvement to result from the president's advocacy of the shelterbelts. Transplanted across the North American interior, arbors added "much needed variety to the monotonous prairie landscape." According to his projections, "the still primitive and hazardous existence in the plains region will be raised for thousands of settlers to a higher level of permanence and stability." The plantations, in effect, promised to create "the amenities of a higher cultural life."[11] By displaying the sylvan fantasies of a culture alien to grasslands, the president attempted to affix his signature upon the landscape through the shelterbelts.

Business Week, in particular, praised Roosevelt's expenditures for the shelterbelts. On 28 July 1934, the weekly asserted that America "must restore ground cover and windbreaks," or "our central plains will become as the central desert of Asia."[12] One editorial explained the situation:

It was recognized that this year's drought is not a casual affair, likely to be remedied by good rainfall next year, but that it represents fundamental climatic change, or rather, it demonstrates Nature's response to man's tampering with delicately adjusted natural balances—and no emergency measure will suffice to solve the problem. Scientists in government employ have been predicting the disaster for years. Nobody listened. Today, they get attention. They utter the solemn warning that millions of acres must be abandoned to trees and grass if we are not to have a great desert in the plains. . . . It has been described in Washington as "reconquering of the plains" which, won to civilization nearly a century ago, have been all but taken back and converted to desert by the drought.[13]

Even though the nation was losing ground, scientists gained the leverage to introduce small-scale forestry experiments.

Wilson Compton in *Forum,* however, dismissed the Prairie States Forestry Project in a 1935 article, "Government versus Desert." When foresters introduced "a grand army of trees into the hostile near-deserts of the West," the act offered false hope for abating the erosion. What happened in desolate lands such as Syria, Palestine, and North Africa happened in America, where "desert conditions have naturally resulted" because of the exposure of fertile topsoil. Grass-planting—not tree-planting—remained more appropriate to "the cattle country." While critical of the shelterbelts, a host of advocates for soil conservation preferred government actions mindful of the climax.[14]

Although government actions occurred haphazardly, landholders were the beneficiaries. The *Kansas Farmer* in 1935 declared: "Drouths and soil blowing are not new in the Great Plains region." The editor bragged that no one knew "how many successive 10-year layers of vegetation have been buried in the 150 feet of fertility" under the surface, and so it remained "idle to speak of the region as returning to desert conditions." While claiming that "no other land on earth can be damaged less by occasional losses of top soil," he feared a lack of water "could make Western Kansas a desert" in the future. Instead of resisting the efficiency experts, longtime residents shared with conservationists a passion for grass. Imbued with "a fascination in living on the Plains," the seasoned toilers "will stay and oppose the dust-storm menace and by opposing it will end it, using such methods as have been here outlined." Damage control included land retirement, controlled grazing, diversification, building ponds, strip cropping, terracing, listing, and restoration of hardy cereals and native grasses.[15]

Damage control required a greater sense of urgency, though. J. N. Darling, chief of the U.S. Bureau of Biological Survey, declared in 1935 that Americans had become "desert makers." With the black blizzards spreading, he asserted that the "next generation of American youth will be born into a continent well on the downhill side of those gifts of Nature which make living splendid and fortunes easily won, and which made our forefathers prosperous." In fact, corrective measures would catch up with soil depletion only in "ten million years, say, after agriculture in the U.S.A. has reached the productive level of the Gobi Desert." Curiously, he inked a political cartoon with a caricatured Indian standing in the midst of a "Kansas Dust Storm" and calling out to Columbus: "Hey! Where Yu Goin'?" Observe an inversion of ascensionist plots for colonization. Rather than abandoning the occupied lands, they offered an inscrutable call to arms for the conquerors of Indian country. Without questioning progressive assumptions, the conservationist's line was a modern expression of imperialism.[16]

Consider the imperialism accentuated by Stuart Chase, an economist, who coined the term "New Deal" for Roosevelt's bold initiatives. In the 1936 book *Rich Land, Poor Land* he beheld a rolling duster as "an awful warning that the earth has literally lost its roots." Once upon a time, the nation began to build "a vast, rich empire, home for millions of Americans and tens of millions of domestic beasts." Because of the recklessness of sodbusters, though, "we have a raging desolation of dust when the winds begin to blow, and ultimately—desert." The fields of grain degenerated into a "grim, lifeless desert, ribbed with drifting dunes." He noted that labor took the soil down to hardpan, thereby destroying a pristine place. A legendary if not fictional "first white male" appeared as a culprit in this cautionary tale, assuming his position as the primary source for the social drama. Overcoming primitive instincts for isolation, the fight against erosion "must be collective, not individual."[17] Chase summarized a plea for restoration of the pastoral:

North America before the coming of the white man was rich with growing things, incredibly beautiful to look upon, wild and tempestuous in its storms and climatic changes, and perhaps the most bountifully endowed by nature of all the world's continents. Today, after three centuries of occupation, the old forest, the old grass lands have almost completely disappeared. Desert lands have broadened. A dust desert is forming east of the Rockies on the Great Plains where firm grass once stood.[18]

In this nostalgic yet poignant narrative, the absence of order turned a rich country into an impoverished one.

Rexford Tugwell, economist and head of the Resettlement Administration, summoned his cohorts to restore order to the grasslands. He presented this summons on one occasion in the form of a journal from a hypothetical expedition into the "Great Desert of the Plains" in the year 2235 A.D. He mused: "This week we have crossed the Mississippi River and have journeyed in our high-wheel motors deep into the great desert. . . . There now are only moving pieces of dust for hundreds of miles." He and his fellow travelers noticed the remains of a fictive metropolis, which included "skeletons of twisted steel." The source of the dusty trails "was the exposure of the plains to the wind," which left "no living thing" as it blew away the roots of life. While his story suggests the tragic sense of ruin, it nevertheless underscored the need for a new regional planning agency comparable to the Tennessee Valley Authority. In fact, he expressed hope and resilience in the voice of the scientist, planning a "study of the records" to begin to solve the problems. Claiming authority through science, he intended to analyze "the soil of this desert, measuring, as well as we can, the climatic changes since vegetation disappeared, and collecting specimens of various remains."[19] Undaunted by the disorder, he saw the dust bowl as a place to begin anew.

Tugwell, like other conservationists, outlined a strategy for that new beginning. He called on federal agencies to "launch at once numerous soil-erosion projects to protect from further ruin about a million acres which are washing or blowing away." The wealth of nature was at stake, he observed, requiring "a gradual resettlement of America" to conserve "great stretches of our country now bare and unfarmed." The outspoken if idealistic administrator believed that planting belts of forests and grass helped break the wind and temper the climate. As a result of scientific practices, he posited, the "country will be better looking." If a fresh sense of national purpose emerged from efforts to conserve the soil, "America will turn in a new and more promising direction" after its days of descent. Ostensibly, "this depression will not have been endured in vain." The battle for democracy required changes in the land, or at least in the policies to manage it.[20]

Tugwell asserted that the time had come for national policies on behalf of soil conservation. Clearly, the government had for too long ignored the exhaustion of acres "subject to great extremes in rainfall, with adequate moisture sometimes for several years in succession, followed by extreme drought for a term of years." Since the destruction of the native vegetation, wind and water erosion had intensified. He identified "an area of many hundred square miles" where debilitated farmers and ranchers lacked control over their fates. They no longer possessed a land providing "traditional rural stability and peace," because "all that has been lost." Though concerned about the environment, Tugwell made the case for conservation an economic one. Since he considered the fecundity of the earth the ultimate source of wealth, he assumed that a civilization negligent of it eventually "decays." The destruction was accelerated by the declining yields and falling prices of the Depression. A generation overreaching its limits was forced "to conserve what is left and to build up the land to its former fertile state."[21] Although the nation had learned a painful lesson, it had come at the costs of undermining the economy.

Rather than ignoring the costs, the federal government underwrote a range of expensive programs. Morris L. Cooke, administrator of the Rural Electrification Administration and chairman of the Mississippi Valley Committee, cried out to the public: "I believe that at our present rate of soil erosion this country of ours has left to it less than a century of virile national existence." As the yields of the soil declined, he related, "the morale of the people also will ebb." Awakened by "the smell and the gritty taste of prairie dirt," the nation realized that it faced the horrors that destroyed "scores of civilizations which have arisen and flourished and disappeared." After abusing the soils for too long, the "acres—dead acres—will still be here as monuments to the folly of 'educated' man." Techniques for soil conservation, however, sustained the "high undreamt adventure" and rebuilt the "foundations in this country." The disaster presented an inverted tale of the frontier, but conservation repaired a pastoral refuge.[22]

Henry Wallace, the secretary of agriculture, described this pastoral refuge in his call for "new frontiers." He entreated the government to begin "putting our lands in order" before they vanished. If they vanished, future generations would inherit a wasteland "even worse than the Chinese, because we made no real effort to restore to the soil the fertility which has been removed." He complained that too many landholders refused to improve their techniques and practices. "Human beings are ruining land," he groaned, and "bad land is ruining human beings, especially children." To avoid the breakdown of society, "it will be necessary to get more and more of our people thinking seriously about the continuously balanced harmonious relationship which I call the Land of Tomorrow." He recalled the harmony of a lost "Golden Age," suggesting that areas ill suited to the hand of labor "might be best restored to wild life, including antelope, deer and buffalo."[23] To end overgrazing and overcropping, Wallace pleaded for a return to pastoralism.

On behalf of pastoralism, Wallace spoke of regulating the activities exhausting the fields where grasslands once prevailed. In the dust bowl, "rich soil in moderately dry areas" decomposed "into regions of marching sand dunes." He added that each "little dune so formed represents a small area of desert" and warned that if "we cannot stabilize them with some practical covering of vegetation, they will grow larger, join together, smother great areas of now useful land, and perhaps become altogether unmanageable." Note the panic about a subversive plot to overthrow and thus destabilize an orderly regime. Such disorder produced "waste and ruin," according to scientists, who found "in this rich new land of ours conditions which already suggest conditions like those bordering the Sahara." Wallace called on scientists to help the government stop the rising black blizzards on the horizon.[24]

No conservationist more eloquently articulated the fear of black blizzards than Paul Sears, a botanist at the University of Oklahoma. In a 1935 text, *Deserts on the March,* he explored the disaster that culminated in the abominable sandstorms. "Mechanical invention plus exuberant vitality have accomplished the occupation of a continent with unparalleled speed," wrote Sears, "but in doing so have broken the gentle grip wherein nature holds and controls the forces that serve when restrained, destroy when unleashed." Irrational exuberance among sodbusters thus produced terror in the heartland. The labors of "the white man in a few centuries" released "deserts, so long checked and held in restraint, to break their bonds." On the edge of vast pastures, the "girdle of green about the inland deserts" gave way and the "desert itself [was] literally allowed to expand" unchecked. Loose, sandy soils blew and drifted until "a temporary desert" formed around the little houses on the prairies, where "a child has been found stifled in a window of dust." The roller clouds sounded the alarm about a menace to society.[25]

According to Sears, the advance of civilization had created the menace. The deserts on the march signaled "the wrath that is brewing against our western civilization unless we mend our ways." Clearly, the warnings about the emergency came in the form of raging dusters, which arose from "the destruction of the living sod which alone can bind the looser soil types of the semi-arid plains." He feared that the nation was "headed at full speed on a path that has brought destruction to others as well-meaning and as energetic as ourselves." In the "Great American Desert," generations of farmers and ranchers faced a "long period of beating back" until they abandoned their property. He admonished that "North America, like other continents before it, is drying out."[26] The occupation of the land overturned the order of things, and putting a genie back in the bottle, so to speak, presented a problem to be solved by the luminaries of science.

The occupied realms lapsed, at least temporarily, because of the wasteful exploitation of resources by the unenlightened. Sears called upon "white civilization to retrieve itself and justify its name" by a return to the climax.[27] For the botanist who later lauded ecology as a subversive subject, successive stages of struggle culminated in the pastoral:

The plains are the classic ground for last stands—bison, Indian, bad man and cowpuncher having in turn faced their final destiny here. And now the dry farmer, represented at the Governor's conference, finds himself in the throes of a deadly struggle to survive. Perhaps we shall understand this situation better if we look into another contest—agelong—which has been set in this theater. I refer to the struggle between grassland and desert. The scanty, irregular rainfall of the plains, the high, drying winds and the rapid fluctuation between blistering heat and paralyzing cold make this region the climatic borderland of the desert. Only by dint of countless centuries of effort is anything better than desert vegetation present.[28]

Sears invoked venerated traditions of suffering, sacrifice, and competition, suggesting that hard labor had produced a stillborn beast.

Not all research on conservation arrived at the same dreadful conclusion, though. Johns Hopkins University geographer Isaiah Bowman expressed less concern about "our expanding and contracting desert" than some of his cohorts. He questioned the "assumption running through our present discussion of submarginal western lands that we have definitely and permanently destroyed large parts of them." If this, indeed, was the case, then "the earlier maps showing 'Great American Desert' written across the plains of western Kansas, Nebraska, and Texas" represented the "more nearly permanent condition." Even if "we are now in process of returning to the desertic conditions that once prevailed," he contended that the cycle was only temporary. He added that "all our climatic belts expand and contract," but more climatological evidence was needed to understand the freakish nature of the dirty thirties. In fact, in individual years of severe drought, Bowman found that "a third of the United States may be 'desert.'" Therefore, the geographer planned to intensify research and record keeping of rainfall, groundwater, streamflow, glacial discharge, snow cover, and dendrology before resigning the soil to a tragic fate.[29]

Whatever the conclusions, conservationists found the public receptive to scientific management. *Science* in 1936 compared the unclaimed area to the "parched land of Canaan," where exodus and hardship for colonists seemed endemic. In modern times, however, engineers mitigated the consequences of drought by building dams and diverting waterways. One author opined that "the present drought, like its predecessors, will spread this gospel mightily among such as are still unconverted." In full effect, the wonders of engineering not only promised to conserve water but also to save the country from the "curse" of soil erosion.[30] William E. Warne, director of information for the Reclamation Service, elaborated on the power of new technology to accomplish miracles. He reminded readers that "a desert is a barren tract incapable of supporting any considerable population without an artificial water supply and almost destitute of moisture and vegetation." Irrigation became essential to those bad places where "the Great American Desert" had expanded. If the worst ravages continued, then the creation of new federal irrigation projects promised to reclaim arable land from blight.[31]

Commissioner for the Reclamation Service John C. Page made a compelling case for new projects, too. He recalled that the "receding frontier" had brought the present generation to the arid and semiarid West, although past generations had "passed rapidly over its deserts." These newcomers "crossed miles upon miles of arid land, hoping to find fresh fields." Eventually, however, they realized that "it was upon the foundation of this desert that the permanent civilization in the West must be built." To aid in settlement, the agency inherited a mission to secure this soil from ambushes by dusters. Where adequate irrigation systems had been built and remained in operation, only 5 percent of the taxes were reported delinquent, while in many counties adjacent or nearby where no irrigated fields existed, tax delinquencies amounted to 95 percent. Furthermore, the appraised value of irrigated fields generally reached more than ten times as high as that of dry farming and grazing lands. Without irrigation enterprises, Page concluded, "the very governmental structure of the West, as we know it today, could not exist." Soon, reclamation projects boosted the use of the Ogallala aquifer by the proprietors of the region.[32]

The research of the National Resources Committee, which later became the National Resource Planning Board under Roosevelt, attempted to project future land-use needs. This group suggested that "most of the territory occupied by the United States is not naturally suited for a permanent civilization." The committee, then, compared the occupied territories with those "of the Mayas of Yucatan or the land of Babylon—a rich country where civilization can flash into a blaze of glory and then collapse in a few generations into ruin." Without soil conservation in the exhausted sections, the "splendor of our bankrupt cities will become a ghastly joke" after the unrelenting "scourge of wind and flood." Assessing the environmental risks, they cautioned that a "nation whose land naturally tends to turn into desert must either take measures to preserve the land or it will surely die." Through the dissemination of reports, the committee devised a rationale for resource management.[33]

The Future of the Great Plains, authored by the Great Plains Committee assembled by Roosevelt, in 1937 submitted a comprehensive and sweeping report on resource management in the region. The report set a scene of waste and positioned "the white man" in the lead. Following his path, it depicted "foothills shorn of timber" and soil degradation after "unwise cultivation." Sliding down a slippery slope, the earth "drifts with wind in sand hills and in dust clouds." Cattle grazed "scorched roots," while the streams and the groundwaters irrigated poor fields. Worst of all, "men struggle vainly" for a living, because "the plough ignores Nature's Keep Off signs." Note the psychosexual innuendo of the phallus dominating the "virgin soil." As a consequence, forlorn communities decomposed through "poor schools, shabby houses, the sad cycle of tax sales, relief, and aimless migrations." Therein appeared generations of paupers accompanied by a staggering burden of mortgages, debts, and foreclosures. While "steady progress" seemed "to reverse itself," lamented the committee, the descent afforded "a test for American ways of dealing with matters of urgent common concern." Whatever the merits of the report, it presented a gothic landscape in the grips of peasantry.[34]

The report to the president, in fact, offered a regressive analysis based on the frontier. The pedantry of the narrative, moreover, assumed that the landholders were "socially degraded" and needed contact with "higher civilization." It punctuated an environment of poverty, where the people became resistant to change, fatalistic, suspicious, and distrustful. The "Plainsman" must realize, announced the report, that he cannot "conquer Nature—he must live with her on her own terms, making use of and conserving resources, which can no longer be considered inexhaustible." Of course, the metaphors denoted a domestic relationship. The feminine earth was depicted as both wife and mother, but the masculine husbandry endeavored to conserve her bounties. The report recommended that the producers "make the most of what Nature has to offer," even if "large areas were decreasingly productive even in good years" and "tended more and more to lapse into desert." With domestic order the goal, however, the "land may bloom again if man once more makes his peace with Nature."[35] Through the implementation of conservation programs, the state possessed the capacity to recreate the pastoral.

Even when the drought ended, conservationists continued to uncover evidence of a clouded future. When the American Association for the Advancement of Science sponsored a symposium in 1938 titled "Scientific Aspects of the Control of Drifting Soils," M. M. Leighton of the Illinois State Geological Survey resolved that, without soil in a stable condition, "civilization can not exist." In addition to the serious damage to the soils, he complained that "dust storms have brought tragedy and loss to human be-ings" for too many years. Once unregulated laborers broke the sod, the act had begun to "diminish plant growth and adversely affect weather condi-tions," observed the geologist.[36] The *Science News Letter* opined that "it will be a long time before all traces of the years of the Great Thirst, 1934–1937, will have vanished from the grasslands of the West." Although the rainfall began to return, "a complete resurrection" of the short-grass prairies neces-sitated more scientific research and development. Going forward, author-ities planned to make conservation a high priority.[37]

In 1939, G. V. Jacks and R. O. Whyte in *The Rape of the Earth: A World Survey of Soil Erosion* examined disclimaxes of ecosystems around the globe. While surveying the persistent hazards stemming from negligent practices, they also featured "a record of struggles" against the ongoing "desiccation of agricultural land." Ostensibly, the grasslands of North America were "reduced to a state of desolation and poverty by the hand of man more than by climate change." The "man-made desert in the United States," they observed, "was not a transitional zone on the fringe of an existing desert." Rather, "an almost desert-like state" resulted from the "over-cultivation of the original semi-arid grasslands," which was an act tantamount to a crime. Their story unveiled evidence about crimes against nature, making the case for a cadre of experts to police the danger zones across the earth and to arrest environmental abuses.[38]

Despite the expertise of science, Raymond J. Pool of the University of Nebraska remained worried that the abuses of the environment would con-tinue. He wrote: "We have boasted too much of our inexhaustible supplies of earth's native goods, and of a growing mastery that gave us every right to win in the conquest against nature and time." With the impression left by the dust bowl, the "nation is just now learning that white man has also con-tinued to function as the blatant beast of the wasted prairies." Note the re-versal of civilization and savagery here, even as the subtext continued to denote coincidental lines of race and gender. Although the pastures de-clined in density and virility, Pool proclaimed, "Mother Nature is not a nudist by choice." The imprudence of the proverbial "white man," in fact, had disgraced the nation by removing the ground cover. Increased government funding for conservation programs, though, might prevent future generations from lapsing in judgment.[39]

No one worked more vigorously for conservation programs than Hugh Hammond Bennett, who earned acclamation as a "Messiah of the Soil" but more modestly preferred the sobriquet "Big Hugh." Bennett headed the temporary Soil Erosion Service and became the director of the Soil Conservation Service after 1935. His reforms included the creation of self-governing districts for landholders, who consulted the Soil Conservation Service for advice and support. He lauded the democracy of an advancing civilization, but he called for wiser management of soils. Unrestricted abatement produced "a condition equivalent to skeletonized land," he complained. The precious humus accumulations of millennia will be exhausted, and "there will be nothing left to save." Failure to curb "this insidious process," he observed, toppled unstable regimes. Underneath rising sands, "magnificent temples are being dug from beneath the products of erosion in regions where land is all desert," indicating that "civilizations have disappeared" as a result of declining yields. "We are not merely crusaders," he told his corps of conservationists, "but soldiers on the firing line defending the vital substance of our homeland."[40]

Bennett seized every opportunity to extend the lines of his corps. He referred to the negligent toiler as the "Highwayman of the Fields" and lamented "that this country has been more wasteful of its land than any other nation in the history of the world." For generations, "the white man" destroyed "virgin soil" by breaking the fertile slopes of prairie earth, and "with plows we have laid the soil bare to the wrath of the heavens."[41] The pastures "seemed doomed to desert conditions," where "dust storms were ripping the plains to pieces." He found that "the recently-created desert areas are still drifting in dune conditions," which produced "land instability and worthlessness." Furthermore, he reasoned that "highly erodable areas will have to go back to grass," that is, the climax community conservationists were duty-bound to protect. Too many landholders, according to Bennett, ignored "omens of potential desert and permanent ruin." The New Dealer warned of black blizzards overtaking America unless the science of conservation prevailed.[42]

With the support of Congress, Bennett expanded the capacity of the government to conserve precious topsoil. Each blowing dune area, he alerted agents in 1938, represented "the equivalent of an area of desert sand which will advance upon and at least temporarily cover good land to its lee." The disorder suggested "conditions which prevail in parts of the Sahara border," threatening to swallow up the heartland with darkness. Considering such a possibility, he feared the worst: "If we fail to stabilize the dunes in time and permit them to coalesce and cover townships, counties or groups of counties—no exceptional vision is required to perceive the land anarchy which will follow the probable eastward march of sand across extensive areas of presently productive farms." Although drifting might "reach Nigerian proportions" and ebb across the interior, federal demonstration projects determined that "blowing can be largely, if not entirely, controlled by practical farm and range methods and that young dunes can be halted by vegetation." With genuine concern about an emergency situation, extension agents such as H. H. Finnell, an Oklahoma farmer, administered federal aid and managed government projects. The projects could not miraculously change the climate, but they enabled communities to begin to uplift themselves.[43]

The relative success of the projects prompted Bennett in 1939 to publish his magnum opus, *Soil Conservation*. The tome resonated with nostalgia, asserting that "transplanted Europeans" encountered "a vast wilderness teeming with apparently inexhaustible stores of game, fish, fur, timber, grass and soil." Regrettably, lush stands of native short grasses winnowed with "shifting sands left in the wake of dust storms." The widening swaths of erosion contained "a record of man's efforts to wrest the land from nature," and far "too frequently man's conquest has been disastrous." He found that "over extensive areas, his culture of the earth has resulted in extreme impoverishment or complete destruction of the very soil resources upon which he is dependent." The irregular recurrence of severe drought, the susceptibility of bare or scantly vegetated land to wind currents, and the general failure of laborers to amend hazardous conditions "are chiefly responsible for the peculiar problems and economic maladjustments that characterize the Great Plains." Conservation techniques, however, reformed a landscape; the tillers of the soil were managed by experts. Bennett committed his service to restoring a delicate balance.[44]

Committed to that goal, conservationists of the soil made a compelling case. One passage of Bennett's work delivered the message:

Recent archeological evidence indicated that erosion doubtless played a large part in undermining and obliterating many ancient civilizations in Africa, in Near Asia, and in Central Asia. . . . Now, man must move rapidly over this diminishing area in order to clear away not trees or prairie grasses but old methods of wasteful land use and substitute therefore new methods of conservation that will provide security for the soil and for those living by the soil.[45]

His story about conservation, in effect, climaxed in romance.

Conservationists during the 1930s mixed messages for the scientific management of natural resources. The discourses refined the violent language of sodbusting by deploying the progressive language for discipline, balance, and regulation. Through narrative, theories for the climax community provided an emotional basis for recognizing the fantasized harmony of nature before civilization. The socially constructed terminology, however, continued to make nature a resource for mastery and for control. That is because this kind of domesticity channeled assumptions of a psychosexual complex. At its core lay a masculine yearning to know and to respond to the landscape as feminine, that is, the pastoral impulse. According to the literary scholar Annette Kolodny, the pastoral impulse expressed the thrust of a movement back into the realm of rebirth. It also related an attempted movement out of that containment to experience the self as independent, assertive, and active. Finally, it aroused a sense of guilt about the conflict between the desire to see nature as bountiful and the desire to dominate it and to make it more bountiful. While legitimating conservation programs, patriarchal norms remained bound to the subjugation of nature.[46]

The nature of science, of course, cannot know and make known its specialized knowledge without resorting to cultural narratives. If narrative and science represent different language games, then the moves and the rules of one cannot be judged by those of the other. As a modern institution spawns competing theories, it nevertheless appropriates narrative strategies in disseminating information and submits likely stories authorizing its own legitimacy. The bureaucratic state invests vast sums of capital to pass itself off as a metanarrative on the grandest platform, for its potency and authentication require the consent of the experts if not the governed.[47] When expertise insinuated a drive for restoration, it was premised upon the controlled yet sustainable use of natural resources. Pastoralism, in other words, turned the misadventure of the frontier into a project for management.

A plow in the sand after a dust storm, Oklahoma,
c. 1930s. (Farm Security Administration photo.)
Courtesy Carl Albert Center Congressional Archives,
University of Oklahoma, Helen Gahagan Douglas
collection, photo #434

View of a dust storm, 1930s. *(Photo from U.S. Soil Conservation Service report.) Courtesy Carl Albert Center Congressional Archives, University of Oklahoma, John "Happy" Camp collection, photo #957*

*Dust storm in Lamar, Colorado. (Photo by J. H. Ward,
Resettlement Administration.) Courtesy Carl Albert Center
Congressional Archives, University of Oklahoma, Helen
Gahagan Douglas collection, photo #379*

Dust cloud rolling over the western Kansas prairie,
February 21, 1935. Courtesy Carl Albert Center
Congressional Archives, University of Oklahoma, Elmer
Thomas collection, photo #1687

Sand whirling around a house and barn, Cimarron County, Oklahoma, c. 1930s. (Photo by Arthur Rothstein, Farm Security Administration.) Courtesy Carl Albert Center Congressional Archives, University of Oklahoma, Helen Gahagan Douglas collection, photo #369

*Barn hit by dust storms, 1930s. Courtesy Carl
Albert Center Congressional Archives, University of
Oklahoma, Page Belcher collection, photo #203*

Oklahoma sharecropper and family entering California,
February 1937. (Photo by Dorothea Lange, Farm Security
Administration.) Courtesy Carl Albert Center Congressional
Archives, University of Oklahoma, Helen Gahagan Douglas
collection, photo #427

Worn-out land and abandoned cabins, Newport,
Oklahoma, June 1937. (Photo by Dorothea Lange,
Farm Security Administration.) Courtesy Carl Albert
Center Congressional Archives, University of Oklahoma,
Helen Gahagan Douglas collection, photo #419

Downtown Caddo, Oklahoma. (Photo by Dorothea Lange, Farm Security Administration.) Courtesy Carl Albert Center Congressional Archives, University of Oklahoma, Helen Gahagan Douglas collection, photo #407

Chapter 5

SURVIVOR "No cracked earth, no blistering sun, no burning wind, no grasshoppers are a permanent match for the indomitable American farmers and stockmen and their wives and children, who have carried on through desperate days and inspire us with their self-reliance, their tenacity, and their courage." Thus spoke President Franklin D. Roosevelt during a fireside chat broadcast from Washington, D.C., on 6 September 1936. After a campaign swing that took him through nine states experiencing drought, Roosevelt witnessed firsthand fields blasted with heat and the "forgotten Americans" faced with blowing winds. While surveying the dreadful scene, he pledged to fight on behalf of federal programs to assist the down but not yet out. Roosevelt expressed solidarity with folks in no ordinary time, then, as his moving rhetoric elevated the plight of afflicted residents struggling against forces beyond their control.[1]

His story of the dust bowl recognized the struggle of the people as heroic, if only for a fleeting moment. The historian James Gregory explored how this struggle resonated with working people who saw themselves as victims of the Depression. The Depression generation socially constructed an obsessive devotion to stubborn determination and physical courage, that is, the "cult of toughness." Group identity was expressed by a willingness to fight against the powerful forces of nature. It composed a hyper-masculine, neopopulist style, which became quintessential for an "Okie" subculture and for "Plain Folk Americanism." The style was indicative of a sense of exceptionalism, as people found inscrutable faith in the belief that they shared a special fortitude for overcoming loss.[2] Grounded in hard times, the survivors fashioned a modern identity as rugged as the environment itself.

John L. McCarty, who edited the *Dalhart Texan,* wrote about the ways that the land and the people had become inseparable. In 1935, the irascible McCarty organized the Last Man's Club, whose hundred or so members pledged to remain in the dust bowl "until hell freezes over and skate out on thin ice." His fellow Dalhart boosters hired Tex Thornton, an explosives expert and self-proclaimed rainmaker, to detonate TNT and solidified nitroglycerin jelly on a day with low cloud cover. After the rainmaking venture, dirt blasted into the air and mixed with the winds to exacerbate the discomfort of a blowing duster. Although some broken residents limped out of the blight, McCarty and his cohorts gestured to the skies and admonished them to fight with brute strength: "Grab a root and growl!" They raged against the woebegone reports of journalists and the horrifying paintings of artist Alexandre Hogue, complaining that the scenes of deserts ignored the stories of success.[3]

In some sense, the rhetoric of the Last Man's Club appealed to a collective outrage over the discouraging words of the Depression. In one stirring rant, "A Tribute to Our Dust Storms," McCarty captured the cult of toughness in a most compelling form:

Let us in stentorian tones boast of our terrific and mighty sandstorms and of a people, a city, and a country that can meet the test of courage they afford and still smile. Let us humbly and in shame admit our part in the rapacity our land has suffered at our hands, but vow, with the raging winds of the prairies, that we will with God's help carpet our lands once again with grass and vegetation and with our heads unbowed, our spirit undaunted, view the majestic splendor and beauty of one of the great spectacles of nature gone rampant—a Panhandle sandstorm—and smile even

though we may be choking and our throats and nostrils so laden with dust
that we can not give voice to our feelings.[4]

Across the Great Plains, editors extolled the virtues of those who never gave
up or never gave in when facing defeat.

Editors, moreover, spun tall tales about the virtues of the country. Eugene A. Howe, the editor of the *Amarillo Globe* of Texas, preferred the pseu-
donym Kernal Erasmus R. Tack in his whimsical column "The Tactless
Texan." Without superficial sophistication, the column featured self-
deprecating humor accentuating bad weather, local customs, and the "Old
Woman"—Howe's denigrating euphemism for the Texan's wife. When
receiving letters about a divine curse placed on the region, "Old Tack" with
tongue in cheek asserted: "I can't believe He would select the very best
people for punishment when there are others so much more deserving of
His wrath." In another yarn, he joked that the billowing sandstorms provided higher levels of "Vitamin K," claiming that "we've never been fatter,
healthier, or dirtier." With his idiomatic buffoonery, he added: "And the
women folks have never been jumpier." Howe's parodies repeated other
homespun anecdotes, including one about a man discovering a cowboy hat
on a sand dune. Under the hat appeared a cowboy's head. The cowboy
claimed to be doing fine, although he quipped that he was on horseback.
The diversions of the Tactless Texan encouraged the forlorn to grimace at
their misfortune but cling to their homeland.[5]

Clinging to the homeland, then, constituted a revered subject for editorial cant. The editor of the *Earth* answered the "erroneous impressions"
of the dirty thirties "as temperately as a Western man could," reporting that
the multitudes "through years of trials and tribulations have wrested from
the wilderness" a region intolerant to "quitters."[6] In the *Kansas Farmer,* an
editor announced: "I pay tribute to real courage." While blistering in the
sun, the "common man" contended against "not only a rising tide of cost
of government and rising cost of living" but also the "forces of nature"
allied against him.[7] The *Daily Oklahoman* also mused that "truly we have
wrested a realm from the primitive raw." The hardy boys "have brought order
and law into a region where the jungle law had been the only limitation of

conduct." The "last frontier is still ours," claimed the vignette, as the raw materials of "The Land of the Fair God" awaited "the magic touch of toil and intelligence to make them bloom like the rose." Newspaper columns highlighted a special place demonstrating with full effect the will of the people.[8] In particular, stories praised the stubborn resolve of the "stickers," that is, those who stayed despite the tempests.[9]

Stories about women who stuck through hard times displayed this resolve in peculiar ways. Caroline Henderson, a graduate of Mt. Holyoke College, a farmer's wife, and an Oklahoma resident, composed a series of letters printed in the *Atlantic Monthly*. She shared worrisome lines about her family's hardships in a "No Man's Land," where dust obliterated the dreams of the faint of heart. "Our little locust grove which we cherished for so many years has become a small pile of fence posts," Henderson mourned. "With trees and vines and flowers all around you, you can't imagine how I miss that little green shaded spot in the midst of the desert glare." With undaunted courage, she and her husband, Will, refused to leave the spot because their "twenty-seven years of life together" were forever "bound up with the little corner to which we have given our continued and united efforts."[10] Observe her blending of hearth and nature, which oriented her perspective upon tragedy.

As the Oklahoma woman gazed upon the dying wheat fields, she reflected on her sorrowful state. The country, Henderson observed, was "lying asleep like the princess in the fairy tale." She pined with a "painful longing" that soon the "enchantment may be broken, that the deliverer may come with the soft footfalls of gentle rain and waken our homeland once more into gracious, generous life." In romantic tones, she imagined the teasing of a suitor who brought water to arid landforms. Nevertheless, the woman farmer wondered if barren fields, ruined pastures, buried fences, dead trees, abandoned wells, and desolate homes reflected the insensitive pride of foolhardy gamblers. On days when there was little more than dust to eat, Henderson questioned whether "the traits we would rather think of as courage and perseverance are not actually recklessness and inertia." Under the guise of gender, she associated surviving with the ability to shoulder burdens, to withstand pain, and to persevere through tribulations.[11]

Narratives in magazines contemplated surviving as well. Lawrence S. Morris, for instance, suggested that problems for drought-stricken farmers began with Adam and Eve, when from "a world of plenty they were driven straight into the bleakest scarcity." Toilers unhappily ever after were destined to struggle "against drouths, frost and cloudbursts, insects, and hunger with its accompaniment of human exploitation." Paul C. Ellis claimed that "our garden spot was almost a desert," yet the human acts of "courage and spirit are tremendous national assets." Buren Sparks offered a parable titled "When Rain Came to the Desert," in which a modern Elijah prayed with congregations for a cloudburst "until it looked like the whole country was a sea instead of a desert." J. S. Ploughe worried about "going back to desert" but pleaded for resilience. They survived the worst, asserted Ploughe, because "the true westerner has his roots deep and can't be driven out by dust storms and drought." Most significant, the allegorical language fashioned a new Adam "neither defeated nor discouraged" rising "out of the dust" of a Great American Desert.[12] The episodic failures, then, recalled familiar parables and refashioned them as a literature for self-making.

Even the mass media presented episodic failure as part and parcel of an epic conflict. *Time* in 1935 reported that frustrated folks "in ten Midwestern States had sand in their beards, in their hair, in their ears, in their eyes, in their mouths, in their pockets, in their pants, in their boots, in their milk, coffee, soup and stew."[13] Asserting that the sweltering heat "blackened" the earth, *Newsweek* depicted legions of doom "traveling with herds like nomadic biblical tribes." One dispatch compared the refugee exodusters—those provincials displaced from their land—to "Israel's eleven sons," who likewise "trekked somberly through parched lands." In a country with "dried-out alkali lakes" and where "sloughs lay white as buffalo skulls," a "caravan of derelicts" limped westward. Coughing up clods of dirt, their ranks included "thousands of weary farmers, victims of recurrent cycles of droughts, poor crops, low prices." They looked "to Washington for some Joseph to load their sacks with grain and money against seven years of famine when all the plenty shall be forgotten in the land of Egypt."[14] Alarmed by the Depression, the bearers of bad news highlighted a diaspora of rural Americans.

H. L. Mencken, one of the most noted and notorious journalists of his time, complained in the *American Mercury* about that diaspora. With his signature wit and sarcasm, Mencken in 1936 described the dust bowl as "the very Zion of the eternal but bogus Farm Problem. Here is the Holy land of locusts, droughts, whirlwinds, and big freezes." The landscape contained the "bogus farmers" who were responsible for creating the costly disaster. Land speculators and suitcase farmers pervaded the agricultural system there, at least "unless and until the whole region is emptied of its present hopeless population and turned back to the Indian and the buffalo."[15] With hyperbole and exaggeration, such stories focused on a place remote from the personal experience of urban readers as symbolic of national ills.

Mencken, of course, earned a national reputation for his caricatures of rural simplicity during the roaring twenties, but he was no less iconoclastic during the dirty thirties. He charged that "no farmer of any sense could ever have been tempted into that harsh wilderness, with its murderous climate, its thin and fugitive soil, and its remoteness from good markets." Why, he asked, did those "unhappy herds of Ishmaelites flock into the desert," dragging their "helpless wives and children"? Ignorance, he answered. These drifters "pushed their blundering way into the wilderness, scratched casual and meager livings from its unwilling soil," but by the mid-1930s, "it lay too far buried in primeval chaos for civilization ever to overtake it." In that "bleak country," his commentary concluded, the rabble constituted a peasantry reduced to "natural barbarism" and clamoring at the gates of the metropolis.[16] Mencken opined: "They lack the hard diligence and pertinacity that are needed to wring a living from the earth, either where they languish or elsewhere. They are not conquerors of Nature, but puerile parasites upon its bounty. . . . Their movement is backward toward the stage of the first pioneers of desert nomads just come to the grasslands. They are on their way back to the Stone Age."[17] Mencken ridiculed the unsophisticated, and his findings challenged the popular appeal of contemporary back-to-the-land movements.

With greater sympathy for the tormented, Sherwood Anderson descended into the dust bowl for a 1935 book titled *Puzzled America*. The picaresque account assessed a netherworld, where "man's eternal struggle" and "tragic war with nature" continued "to be seen, in the raw." Anderson, too, described a hell-bent personality in the region. "I walked around the country church," he wrote with sadness, and there found that the "long dry year just passed had done its work well." The searing temperatures "had curled up the boards covering the sides of the building so that you could look through and see the daylight streaming in from the opposite side." He imagined a religious service in the midst of the drought with "sun-burned people, men and women" arriving from distant farmhouses. They plodded "past their own fields, where the corn is shriveled away to nothingness, the fields their own hands have plowed, planted, and tended only to see the crops all burn away to a dry ash of dust." The author pitied a fool's paradise, for the poor devils were near their end. "Now it may all blow away," explained a country newspaperman to the author. "They have got this notion of dry farming in their heads. It's dry all right."[18]

The travel literature of Walter Davenport uncovered malapropism, violence, and insanity among the woebegone he encountered. He scoffed at the speeches of rainmakers promising, in exchange for proper compensation, an "end of the gr-r-rea-a-a-at American desert." Clearly, such hucksters lived in a landscape where only "the homely cactus and the scraggy Joshua tree could thrive." In a 1937 narrative of a journey, "Land Where Our Children Die," Davenport encountered "Paw, Maw, and two babies" living where "they've perverted Nature until she too has gone crazy." Scary and incestuous forms of "suckers" and "open-mouths" lived off "a nice crop of subsidies," but infantile dependency was the result. Lacking maturity, these nascent beasts from the fields appeared arrested in development and required a paternalistic government to nurture them. While the government prepared the "dead lands" for their deliverance, the "hapless farmer" for "dust-minded reasons" objected to reform "so hotly that his beard has caught fire."[19] Davenport set the scene with a meandering sketch of life and death in the dust bowl:

We were to see the wretched, naked desert the winds had left behind; the ghost villages, once the silvery ballyhoo of real estate racketeers; the abandoned farmhouses, buried to the eaves in eddying dust; the corroded tops of farm machinery, deserted in what had been fields and now buried in sand with only levers and rods protruding from their graves, like pitiful arms thrust upward, beckoning for help. . . . On our six-hundred-mile ramble from Amarillo to Denver, keeping mostly to the dusty back roads that we might see the bald clay, the dust dunes, the drifted houses, the abandoned farms and the government subsidy farmers, we heard all of the inevitable shifting of responsibility. Preachers hurled Scripture and the Gospels at us.[20]

Davenport's tragedy degraded the wind-blown pedestrians, but his impressions reinforced prevalent assumptions about the misery of the most unfortunate ones.

The unfortunate ones, of course, became the concern of social workers who were both participants and observers. Traveling Great Plains Schools, organized in the late 1930s by rural social scientists, studied impoverished people devastated by the blight.[21] The stories of Josephine Strode, for example, illustrated "manifestations of Dust Bowl courage" in 1936. The social worker dignified the poor, who exhibited the ills of Depression America. She told of a "crippled old woman left on a wind scoured farm with two small grandchildren" pulling herself about on the floor and crawling on hands and knees. She told of another woman, Liz, who lived in a dugout with two small boys. There was a one-room prairie shack housing eight people and a homesteader and his family living in a patched-up henhouse. Kansans greeted social workers with defiant slogans interpolated with environmental references—"It takes grit to live out here," "We may be dusty but not in the head," "Weak in crops but strong in spirit." They said, too, that folks "know ways to take a dust storm. They can take it on the chin, in the eyes, ears, nose and mouth, down the neck, and in the soup." The veracity of the stories seemed less important than the underlying values they expressed for group identity. Even the social worker claimed a common pioneer stock, acting out the symbolic order of the frontier in her tenacious endeavors to uplift the downtrodden.[22]

Paul S. Taylor of the University of California collaborated with his wife, Dorothea Lange, on a study of rural poverty, *American Exodus* (1939). Seeking to demonstrate poverty and despair, they provided "a record of human erosion." Taylor found that black clouds of dust were "leaving land and life impoverished," while a "shifting of human sands" evoked the imagery of the covered wagon as jalopies sifted down the highways. Featuring "white Americans of old stock," a social drama detailed by Taylor placed "long, lanky Oklahomans with small heads, blue eyes, an Abe Lincoln cut to the thighs, and surrounded by tow-headed children" in the lead. "God only knows why we left Texas, 'cept he's in a movin' mood," moaned a wife when forced to accept a husband's decision to relocate. Ultimately, the poor family was forced to "grope for help" in "squatters' camps and rural slums." Taylor concluded: "Thus the refugees seeking individual protection in the traditional spirit of the American frontier by westward migration are unknowingly arrivals at another frontier of social conflict."[23] This uprooting of society, however, made the narrative primarily a tale of woe.

Woe punctuated a short story about the uprooted, "Dark Retreat," which appeared during 1937 in *Frontier and Midland.* Eric Thane, the author, wrote about a family escaping from a wrecked homestead in the "lousy dust bowl of hell." Unable to find "El Dorado" where the "Injuns' an' buffalo" roamed, "great granddaddy Riggs" rode in an automobile passing "dust duned across the road" and "intermittent waves over a tumbleweed-choked fence of which only the post tops were now visible." The author made the landscape a simile for aging manhood, limning "a grey, grey waste, twisting, writhing in tortured folds under the scourge of the wind." "It's terrible!" explained the grandson who rescued the old homesteader from self-destruction. "The Great American Desert, grandpop! Dust Bowl is right!" The younger generation, then, led the old-timers away from a tragic rural life that "was reaping the whirlwind."[24] Instead of the vigorous moving westward—a long-enduring tradition in American fiction—Thane's "Dark Retreat" reversed the lines in the face of the landscape. Nevertheless, the story retained the symbolic order of character development, albeit moving in a refractory direction.

No better illustration of character development exists than in Morrow Mayo's caricature of "the man with a tractor." In a 1938 story for *Harper's,* he followed the unbroken routine of a panhandle wheat producer named Sank, "just an ordinary-looking man, just an average-looking farmer, with arms and legs, a mouth and eyes, a wife and two children." Appropriating the tools of modernity, the lonesome rider "looked like a product of a more advanced civilization," even if "some horrible, sightless, anthropoidal thing

with a snout." Preparing for toil, he "oiled and watered and fueled the tractor and lubricated both tractor and drill." While he planted hybrids in the
soil to create "the staff of life," the mechanized warrior raised the discs out
of the ground and drove his tractor over the "impregnated earth." Wet with
moisture that washed away a dusty film, "he sat erect in the tractor seat,
steering the juggernaut to the house." Clearly, the author blended the phallus and the machinery, referencing the metamorphosis of Millet's man with
a hoe. "Driving that tractor," observed Mayo, "Sank didn't look like a
humble and degraded tiller of the soil." Moreover, he no longer resembled
"a hay-chewing rube with chin whiskers, or a dunghill yokel, or a peasant
without thought or hope." In fact, futuristic technology transformed "a
farmer from a clod into an operator" and "from a dumb brute into a me-
chanic." Whereas poverty degraded the weak, Sank rose from abysmal conditions endowed with optimism.[25]

John Steinbeck's classic novel *The Grapes of Wrath* endowed the populace with little more than optimism. This 1939 novel electrified the nation
with its fictive tale of one "Okie" family, the Joads, driven from their
shanties. The story's main theme of collective resistance obtained the fullest
development in the far western "factories in the field." Steinbeck, a resident
of California's Salinas Valley, sought to expose the conditions evident in
these migrant camps; the dust bowl offered a dramatic setting for introducing characters in terrible misery. One Oklahoma congressman, Lyle
Boren, called the opening scenes "dirty, lying, filthy," as he ranted: "I
would to Almighty God that all citizens of America could be as clean and
noble and fine as the Oklahomans that Steinbeck labeled Okies." To be
sure, the tragedy of sharecroppers and tenant farmers reflected more
accurately the economic structure of the American South than of the
Great Plains. Moreover, the fictional account confused the location of the
decade's severe weather by describing blowing sand along the corn and cotton fields of eastern Oklahoma. Nevertheless, the book featured ordinary
folks not only caught up in a struggle against nature—the droughts and the
floods—but also raging against a mechanistic order.[26]

The story of life's most adverse conditions began in deserts across the
continental interior. Steinbeck revealed a "a thin hard crust" on the surface,
and as the "sky became pale, so the earth became pale, pink in the red coun-

try and white in the gray country." Herein appeared a parody of the Old Testament creation account. When the dust blew, the "dawn came, but no day," for in "the morning the dust hung like fog," and the "sun was as red as ripe new blood." The country thus created primitive Joads, Oklahoma tenant farmers facing restless days when "the dust sifted down from the sky, and the next day it sifted down" until an "even blanket covered the earth." In the beginning, Steinbeck blended culture and nature into deformed hybrid beings as desolate as the dust bowl itself.[27]

Moving in a slowed motion, a drifter offered signs of life in these scenes. Into this empty wasteland, Tom Joad, paroled from a McAlester, Oklahoma, prison, "turned about and faced the dusty side road that cut off at right angles through the fields." When he took a few steps, "the flour-like dust spurted up" in front of his new yellow shoes, even as the yellowness disappeared "under the gray dust." He did not walk alone for long, though. Jim Casey, a former preacher, fled from the dark recesses of a "wilderness" with the seeds of a spiritual union planted in his mind. When offering baptism for human salvation, the evangelist "used to get an irrigation ditch so full of repented sinners half of 'em like to drownded." Water represented a privileged signifier in Steinbeck's narrative, and its absence in the agricultural fields denoted the presence of a malevolent system. With Casey as the voice crying out from a wilderness and Joad yet unconscious of his mission, the dynamic duo awaited a baptism by a fire for social justice.[28]

Crossing the deserts, Joad and Casey searched for their calling among sharecroppers and tenants who trekked westward. As the Okies walked "toward the horizon," the "dust road stretched out ahead of them, waving up and down" into the distance. They noticed the smell of "burned dust" in the dry air, which kept "mucus in the nose dried to a crust, and the eyes watered to keep the eyeballs from drying out." According to Steinbeck, an evil force with its tractors and machines brought the agony, when the "land bore under iron, and under iron gradually died; for it was not loved or hated, it had no prayers or curses." Forged from the landscape, the working people appeared grotesque and disembodied. Beginning their quest for a new field of dreams, the Okies as Americans writ small clung to a vintage of paradise lost.[29]

The quest insinuated a theme in another novel about surviving hard times, *The Golden Bowl*. Frederick Manfred, while working as a reporter for the *Minneapolis Journal*, wrote his first draft of the tale in 1937. Manfred traveled, lived, and worked among the populace about which he wrote. During 1939, he rewrote the narrative as a play for the local Federal Theater Project, and the social drama of fear and loathing in South Dakota appeared in book form in 1944. His setting of barns and silos was "deserted," while a "gray dust films everything, even the moving things." Rotting bodies of dead animals lay facing empty water tanks, and skeletons of farms remained in "a dusty slumber." Accordingly, "dust beat on the grain and killed it. Dust beat on the animals and choked them. Dust battered the barns and the houses." Throughout a series of vignettes, the "wind drove and the sun burned, drying and cracking and breaking the land."[30] Descending into the mythic bowels of the earth, the living took a beating.

Celebrating the spirit of the rainmaker, Manfred's novel emphasized the human will to resist fate when faced with awesome challenges. The Thors, a valiant family adhering fiercely to a plot of land, refused to abandon their homestead. Of course, Manfred invoked the name of the mythic Norse god of thunder as their patron. The wandering protagonist of the novel, Maury Grant, who rejected farming and nature as evil, in one early scene proclaimed: "I don't know what's wrong with you, but I know fer sure that I ain't workin' in a desert."[31] In contrast to the young Maury's wanderlust, Pa Thor demonstrated a profound sense of place, one of affection for the soil despite its barrenness.

Maury, who desired to be "free as the wind," left the blighted domain to chase the illusion of wealth in the gold mines of the Black Hills. Nevertheless, the odyssey ultimately led him back to the Thor home and to the fertile Kirsten—the family's young daughter. Despite the infertility of the landscape, the family stayed in the fields and continued to hope for a return of rain. Manfred's concluding chapter unfolded as diabolical forces assaulted them, with "the great earth dying" while "the drouth wrinkles the skin of the old creature." Sand dunes "rise and billow," he limned, and drifts "move slowly in the lee of the boulders and the posts and the stones, back and forth, beside and above the buildings and the machines and the graves of men. And then a desert drifts where once a home had been tucked away in a valley."[32] Maury accepted his unforeseen destiny, then, and assumed the lead in coaxing moisture from thin air.

Coming back to the place of the story's beginning, the return of a warrior king promised deliverance. Wiser and stronger, Maury rose at dawn to confront an enshrouding storm at its height, to wrestle with nature, and to protect the pregnant Kirsten. Manfred set the scene: "Dust charged the mountains, fell upon the gutted prairies, droned across Colorado and Nebraska, tumbling, twisting, cutting, spilling, over the knolls and buttes, stirring the silt of the Dakotas." With the nature of the story against him, Maury believed that "it wasn't a wind they were wrestling with, but a malevolent being, and one of such unmatchable size that, if it wanted to, it could kill them all." After he "bound up his wounds against the dust," the virile youth surveyed a stillborn countryside with extended drifts and dunes—rising, falling, billowing. What failed to kill the toiler only made him stronger, he affirmed, refusing to bow under the physical pain inflicted on him. Renewing the cycle, the living embraced a long-suffering quest for a mythic golden bowl.[33]

The quest for a better place also figured prominently in Woody Guthrie's *Dust Bowl Ballads,* but the unsettling landscape stuck with him as he roamed across it. During the dirty thirties, Woodrow Wilson Guthrie, whose permutations included the "Dustbowl Troubadour" and the "Okie Balladeer," began to evolve from a restless saloon singer into a visionary folk musician. With a great deal of wanderlust, he envisioned himself as "bound for glory" and with a mission to preach the restoration of community and democratic fairness. After experiencing firsthand the dusters that hit Pampa, Texas, he left his family and took to the road in 1937 for a pilgrimage to the "golden state," California. The boom in country music on the radio had brought folk ballads to KFVD in Los Angeles, and listeners enjoyed Guthrie's folk songs depicting a distant homeland and "cornpone" philosophy. He evangelized his audiences about the exploitation of the Okies by a system of greed and corruption. With his own restless sense of place, the balladeer adhered to the drama of dust as a lyrical setting, developing songs about class consciousness.[34]

While reciting experiences seemingly long ago and far away, Guthrie's lyrics captivated his audiences with ditties about hard luck. Guthrie recalled that he watched the black blizzard of 14 April 1935 hit his home "like the Red Sea closing in on the Israel children." He complained about "teachers, preachers, screachers" unable to comprehend "such awful and terrible dust storms . . . and you might be able to stand the dust, if it was the dust alone."[35] In the "Dust Storm Disaster," he sang of their fear "as a curtain of black rolled down." Sitting helplessly in isolation as "the worst of the dust storms that ever filled the sky" appeared, folks "thought the world had ended, and they thought it was their doom." While he sang a chorus refrain, "so long, it's been good to know you," people ran for cover, usually to their neighborhood church. With frightened ones seeking answers about the upheaval, Guthrie wailed the line that this "dusty old dust is a-getting my home, and so I got to be moving along."[36] The ballads depicted the desert as a dramatic background for the laborer's passage to freedom.

Ranging from whimsical to sober, Guthrie's ballads revered the toughness of working people refusing to quit. In "Dust Can't Kill Me," the unfolding tragedies were contrasted with the coda "It can't kill me, Lord." "End of My Line" told of "a devil of a fix," as he mused that "there aint no country worth a dime if I'm just a mile from the end o' the line."[37] The balladeer identified with the "Dust Bowl Refugees" of the era and, in effect, reinvented himself as a member of an extended family. He reminisced with the audience of "a little farm and I called that Heaven," at least until the dust "turned my farm into a pile of sand." In "Blowin' Down the Road," the uprooted were "goin' where the water tastes like wine" only to tumble into more misfortune in each verse. In a parody of a jolly Baptist hymn popularized by the Carter family, he wrote "I Ain't Got No Home" to describe his outrage when "my brothers and my sisters are stranded on this road" and impoverished in "this wide wicked world." The ballad "Do Re Mi" further illustrated a bum's rap, as gangs of Okies were searching for "a paradise to live in"; the underclass arrived where "you won't find it so hot, if you aint got the do re mi."[38] Crafting the traits of a rural proletariat, Guthrie's musical narratives revealed the people's ordeal by fire.

Guthrie hoped that socialism offered solidarity for this proletariat, even while he sang about a primitive rebel in a nascent state of consciousness. In the ballad "Tom Joad," Guthrie narrated the plight of an ex-con escaping injustice, calling on "workin' folks" to unionize and to create "one big soul." The outlaw "Pretty Boy Floyd" appears as another working-class hero in the collection.[39] Perhaps Guthrie's social bandits traveled with him in the classic anthem "This Land Is Your Land." He personalized the experiences of the Okie, who viewed endless vistas, natural wonders, and new worlds. In the original version, he "roamed and rambled" in search of refuge until he heard the voices of his fellow travelers:

> When the sun come shining, then I was smiling
> In the wheat fields waving, and dust clouds rolling
> The voice was chanting as the fog was lifting:
> God Blessed America for me.[40]

In the spirit of the land, the dispossessed would ultimately inherit the earth.

In *An Empire of Dust* (1940), Lawrence Svobida depicted his own dispossession as a wheat farmer in Meade County, Kansas. "From my experience I have written a true, inside story of the plight of the average farmer in the Dust Bowl," he wrote, where "an area extending over the greater part of ten states is rapidly becoming depopulated and appears doomed to become, in drear reality, the Great American Desert shown on early maps and so described by writers until less than eighty years ago." An agricultural march into the modern era sounded "the death knell of the Plains," which arrived with the adoption of powerful tools for extensive farming. According to Svobida, the whirlwinds and dunes devastated the homesteads.[41] In confessing the sins of his generation, he contemplated the errors of his youthful, ambitious judgment.

While many local and national leaders denied a sense of guilt about the permanent devastation, Svobida provided a depressing account in his apologia. The drought might have been only a temporary setback to the region as a whole, he suggested, but "the winds began to attack the soil which was no longer anchored by the grass roots." Furthermore, "the black clouds of dust that blot out the sun, cross half a continent, and travel far out to sea" left behind the remnants of "the new Great American Desert." A desolate scene appeared when the storm lifted, as "cattle had huddled in fence corners, by trees, in ditches, behind steep banks," but "they were all dead." While ranchers buried the "decaying carcasses," he believed that wheat farmers were "coming to the belief that it may already have become established beyond the knowledge and skill of the Government conservation experts to restore the wasted land, or even to check seriously the processes of destruction now in operation in the Great Plains." Even the fleet-footed jackrabbits succumbed to the sand, although many of them were slaughtered by hunters.[42] Despite the disappointments, Svobida resolved to save the wheat kingdom.

The transplanted Kansan felt as if nature toyed with him, even while the dusters deflated his buoyant resilience. With a consuming desire to make the prairies produce, he became bitter and weak with "dust sickness." He lifted himself with humor and faith, but his heart fell to "the depths of utter despair."[43] During an encounter between a service station attendant and a tourist in Liberal, Kansas, Svobida observed his quandary: "The tourist stated with emphasis: 'Why, this country is nothing but a desert!' The filling station attendant, resentful of this remark coming on the heels of the visitor's impressions of Death Valley, retorted: 'You went through worse desert back there in California.' 'Yes, that is true enough,' the tourist agreed with a smile, 'but there aren't any fools out there trying to farm it!'"[44] Svobida persisted through the terrible year of 1935, as he witnessed men and women suffering starvation and disease, frustrated by a future without hope.

At the end of his tale of woe, there was no place of grace in a troubled country once known as the national breadbasket. The self-destruction left behind a population of fools going adrift and committing suicide. With no work available, the proverbial Job observed fields "completely bare, unprotected from the sunrays, which they absorbed like fire brick in a kiln, creating the wind which, in turn, brought it to our land, to the destruction of our growing crops." While making a "last stand in the Dust Bowl," another resident considered commitment "to an asylum." The "greatest desert in the United States" generated hot winds blistering the face so that "the skin peeled off." Despite "heroic efforts to stop the march of destruction," Svobida concluded that the "whole Great Plains region is already a desert that cannot be reclaimed through the plans and labors of men."[45] With a poignant mea culpa, the narrator left the dust bowl behind after 1939.

Revisiting a community he had studied fifteen years before, Thomas Alfred Tripp narrated the "Dust Bowl Tragedy" for the readers of the *Christian Century* in 1940. The population changes amazed him, for he noted that the "weaker ones were weeded out," while the stickers "hate the place and long to escape it." Unmarried professional women, for instance, told him: "There is no chance to progress in this dried-up, God-forsaken hole." The visitor drifted across unmarried men "loafing about the streets, slovenly dressed, drinking and telling unprintable yarns in the pool halls and taverns." He also uncovered anecdotes about sexual irregularity, clandestine affairs, and partner swapping. While blaming "the drabness of the dust laden surroundings" and "the drudgery of the harsh existence" for moral decline, he mused how religion uplifted the collective spirit. "Class differences are deeper," he confessed, accounting in part for the growth of evangelical "Holy Rollers." In his nostalgia, Tripp recalled "a lesson from the frontier days," when "the best side of human nature in the local folk" enabled them to endure loss. Despite the losses, he revered the community's determination to survive.[46]

With the end of the Depression one popular magazine sanctified the survivors. Don Eddy in *American Magazine* summarized the war versus "a savage enemy" in the "gaunt, gray wilderness," where the perils of the climate threatened to erase "new farms from the desert." The "men of God" possessed a divine conviction of their ordination "to subdue the wilderness." As underdogs facing an inferno, they battled with great severity against "drought, grasshoppers, tornadoes, crop blights." Against all odds, they had overcome. In Eddy's victory parade, a tour of duty through the fecund fields affirmed American strength "stirring deep in the dust of the Great Plains." With true grit, the cultural narratives displayed the vital signs of heroism.[47]

As the country seemed to melt down into a hot, arid, lifeless desert, the rise of the cultural hero appeared crucial for the vitality of communities. A hero possesses a thousand faces, explained the anthropologist Joseph Campbell, but only a limited number of responses to the riddles of life. The archetypal form, nonetheless, symbolically expresses desires to transcend human weakness and frailty. With a world turning upside down, stories about heroes seductively fuse sacred and secular codes into a recognizable mask for the observer to don. Escaping from the Depression, audiences recognized it in the humorous facade of Will Rogers, a celebrated Cherokee satirist from Oklahoma. They recognized it in the celluloid of Cecil B. DeMille's *The Plainsman* (1937), or at least as Gary Cooper playing Wild Bill Hickok. The hero was there in two of John Ford's classic films, *Young Mr. Lincoln* (1939) and *The Grapes of Wrath* (1940), in both of which actor Henry Fonda played the lead role. Clinging to a self-image insinuating bravery and innocence, modern societies no less than ancient ones have imagined heroes for their sense of exceptionalism.[48]

Indeed, the popular view of President Roosevelt tapped into this conception of heroism. Perhaps the physical debilitation of polio, which required him to use a wheelchair and to wear leg braces, made him a potent symbol for communities disabled by hard times. Delivering a speech at Devil's Lake, North Dakota, in 1934, he told the crowds there that they were "up against the forces of nature." Praising their spirited resistance, he admonished them to "keep up that courage and, especially, keep up the faith." The local pundits called him a rainmaker, that is, one who lifted the spirits of drought-stricken villagers by delivering federally funded relief. When he was on a campaign visit to a sultry Amarillo, Texas, in 1938, rain fell on the president as he rose to speak about the "battle" against the dust bowl. Although the effects of blight lingered for another year, folks took the patrician's words to heart as they donned their gauze masks to fight the dust.[49] Through radio addresses of the decade, he spoke in flattering tones about fortitude to the down though not out in a plain, friendly, and direct voice. In homes across the country, moreover, they hung his portrait next to a picture of Jesus or the Madonna. People beheld a survivor, who noted no fear but fear itself.[50]

Through a kind of liminal mimesis, Depression America socially constructed a cult making people more powerful than the circumstances confronting them. Mustering physical courage and determination through stories, folks knocked down by the blows of disaster resolved to get up again. Even if the experience scarred them, they tended to discount the assistance of modern mechanisms. The survivors resented the intruding presence of the modern state, although the visible hand of federal government agencies making a New Deal relieved thousands of Americans in the dust bowl. The inconsistency between faith and practice permitted the selective thinking that glorified rugged individualism but accepted bureaucratic dependence. The Tactless Texan undoubtedly found solace in the cult of toughness: "But folks, at least we have a real he-man in the White House and he has a backbone of corrugated iron."[51]

Chapter 6

LEGACIES Although Frederick Jackson Turner died in 1932, the popularization of his thesis has reigned over historical fields for generations. Amateur as well as professional historians generated newspaper and magazine features, books, and journal articles that continued to elaborate on the Turner thesis. On the one hand, romantics attributed much of what appeared desirable in American life and character to the significance of the frontier. On the other hand, tragedians tended to renounce its consequences and to seek its reinterpretation. Both rescued artifacts from deadly antiquarianism, recycling them in highly circumscribed forms of historical narration. A narrow and unimaginative cast of mind may condemn narratives to what the historian T. Jackson Lears once labeled "dust bowl empiricism," prompting scholars to dismiss fresh evidence. The dust bowl of history, however, was situated within a lineage that revised the legacies of conquest.[1]

Historians during the 1930s began to revise the legacies by looking backward, envisioning a line between the experiences of the Depression generation and those of venerated ancestors. By extending the line back to the frontier, they communicated a sense of continuity in the present tense. The ordeal was a catalyst for scholarship, but it also shaped scholars' general frame of reference. To be sure, not all of the accounts reported good news while unearthing sacred grounds. A few found the ghostly sites from the usable past to be nothing if not significant. Even in the wake of whirling winds and blistering temperatures, though, the tales recalled a social drama with more than coincidental significance. However provincial, the legacies made universal history in ways configuring a definitive heritage for civilization.

In the beginning of the Great Depression, the provincial plots were on line with the challenges of universal history. One celebration of Old Settlers Day in the *Amarillo Sunday News Globe* hailed the pioneers who "blazed the path of progress from the staked plains to the Amarillo of today." In the panhandle of Texas, "boundless plains" enriched the meek who inherited the earth. Those with "far-seeing vision and high courage" faced "savage Indians," "hunger," "thirst," "desolation," "hardship," and "weary months of toil" while creating "the civilization we have today." Seth Holman, farm editor of the newspaper, insisted that the region would "weather" the storms, recollecting that the stockman was "tried in the crucible of bitter experience and strong in his self-reliance and resourcefulness."[2] The claims to history reflected traditional premises about the genius of the pioneer, adding local color to polemics for expansion.

Such polemics appeared in the *Earth,* a magazine published by the Santa Fe and Topeka Railroad. F. D. Farrell, the president of the Kansas State College of Agriculture, declared in 1931 that "Kansas is a desert—a blooming desert." Kansans, in fact, descended from a "queer people" who demonstrated "the habit of paying their debts." Portraying able-bodied occupants in conventional tones, he contrasted early settlers with "the wandering and uncivilized aboriginees of the country." Most of the sons of the pioneers, he continued in his fable of scarcity, lived by the "quaint Puritanical ideal that human slavery should be abolished."[3] One editorial lauded "our forebearers, the brave pioneers," who came through perils with "faith, hope, and courage" and established a beachhead in dangerous territories. "They expect us to be worthy of them," he admonished, for "our time of stress and trial" offered no solace for "whimperers." Despite misfortune, they adapted to a "desert oasis" and built an empire along the railroad company's routes. Indeed, native sons were descendants of founding fathers who colonized the arid regions of the earth.[4]

In 1931, Walter Prescott Webb published a classic narrative about one arid region a few years before the impact of localized drought and dust storms became a national concern. With unabashed regionalism, his story, *The Great Plains,* identified climatic characteristics of the physiographic province as a source of distinction. What distinguished the stubborn soil was a "deficiency in the most essential climatic element—water." In this dry land, the Texas scholar explained that the level surface, treeless landscape, and subhumid climate marked an institutional fault line, where "ways of travel, the weapons, the method of tilling the soil, the plows and other agricultural implements, and even the laws themselves were modified." The Great American Desert existed in the public mind, he claimed, because explorers and scientists found the interior "a desert, wholly uninhabitable with the methods and the implements and the instruments of pioneering which had been previously used east of the ninety-eighth meridian, and wholly undesirable." The absence of resources limited national expansion and frontier settlement for many decades in the nineteenth century.[5]

The nineteenth century posed peculiar problems, some national and some sectional, and Webb explained how the United States experimented to resolve them. Adaptation and accommodation marked the history of the Great Plains, especially in regard to the innovations necessary for civilization to emerge. In overstating the barriers to transportation across the continental interior, he asserted that the climate "demanded a reorganization of the United States army and the adoption of a military system resembling that used by the French in the deserts of Africa." Obtaining disproportionate power, the federal government attempted to control "the transportation routes across the desert." Even Secretary of War Jefferson Davis in the 1850s did all he could to provide such means and methods of transportation through the wasteland. To solve the transportation problem temporarily, Davis imported "camels for use in the desert."[6] Unfortunately, such folly blurred the lines of distinction within the region, conflating the prairies of Nebraska with the dunes of New Mexico. Nevertheless, the narrative denoted aridity as a worthy antagonist.

Aridity, the primary feature of Webb's native grounds, made economic and social development all the more miraculous, since the sultry landscape undermined the practices appropriate for more humid regions. The environment informed what the Texan called the "mysteries of the Great Plains in American life." Here, the geophysical resonated with the spectacular and fanciful elements of the social, providing further evidence of his claims. "Desert countries," he observed, represented "fertile sources of inspiration for literature." They sustained "a mysticism and a spiritual quality which have found expression in the lofty and simple teachings of Jesus and Mohammed, both of whom lived in a region so like the Great Plains that the similarities have often been pointed out." Whatever he meant by the comparison, Webb hoped that these mystical and spiritual elements might contribute "much to a civilization that thus far is notorious for its devotion to material things." His "history of the white man in the Great Plains" presented "a land of survival" as ethnocentric as Webb himself. In contrast to the people without history, a host of regional ideals and rural virtues were legacies of pioneering folk.[7]

One eminent geographer, Isaiah Bowman, observed additional legacies in a 1931 volume, *The Pioneer Fringe*. He argued that in this "western zone of experiment," a "frontier or pioneering people could not survive if it refused to experiment." Instead of stabilizing social and economic life and adopting sound agricultural practices, though, the primitive community remained in "a state of unsettlement." In the arid zones such as the Great Plains, populations were forced to adapt to the land or move on. He reminded: "'This is our earth, friendly and fair,' was written for quite another rainfall zone." In the areas of frequent drought, the frontier never closed as new waves of settlement confronted scarcity. Bowman cautioned the reader about a record of failure that began with the lawlessness and social conflict of the nineteenth century. This kind of analysis of the past, however, made the pioneer symbolic of the initial stage of colonization.[8]

The ghost of the pioneer haunted the writings of regionalists seeking the native glamour and glory of the Old West as well. The *Kansas Farmer*, for instance, also recalled how dry lands had long made the arid region distinctive. One editorial in 1932 compared the blight with those in the past and explained that Americans "will meet problems and difficulties, even as those brave souls who made up the caravans of old that threaded their way across unbroken prairies, pushing the frontier westward." As in the past, the vignette promised that "somehow the soil repays in many ways the investment of responsibilities that men make in it." In another editorial, "Better Times on the Way Back," the leader of the farm bloc in Congress, Senator Arthur Capper of Kansas, reminisced about landscapes of yesteryear creating "the Slough of Despond." Dust and drought "put lines in men's faces and in women's too, that would not have been there" if not for a rugged country, but at the same time it "has aroused the pioneer fighting spirit in them and so given them courage to go on."[9] On an unbalanced scale, regional boosters weighed in to illuminate the greatness of their traditions.

Likewise, the greatness of their traditions appeared in lines of poetry. Hazel Barrington Selby, for instance, wrote "Dirge for a Pioneer" in *Frontier* in 1932. The poem depicted the grief:

> If these plains shall ever bloom,
> Recking [*sic*] not their pain or doom
> Pioneers as he must leave them
> Bones and flesh and will unbeaten,
> Stubborn land to save and sweeten . . .
> Dust is death and death is dust:
> Let the dusty earth receive him.[10]

Such poetics offered the sterile soils as a challenge to the trailblazers and scouts, even recalling the persistence of ancestors for those in the present contemplating a move.

Persistence remained a common thread in the recollections. The *Clark County Clipper* of Kansas printed an article in 1934 contending that the "sturdy pioneers who settled this country were not 'leaners,'" a label used disparagingly against those people who accepted employment in the Works Progress Administration or Civilian Conservation Corps. Instead, saints of the past were "helping themselves" when "they needed water to make crops grow." Rather than complaining about dry weather, they dug "irrigation ditches and built their own dams." Since they designed the infrastructure, "many of us are now enjoying blessings that came through the ability of those pioneers to help themselves."[11] Faced with the blistering heat and the blinding dust, the *Amarillo Daily News* explained that "sturdiness, rugged-ness, fortitude, and courage were bred into the plainsman." The terms "bred" and "stock" appear commonplace as legacies, denoting a local idiom derived from the work culture as well as a nativist appeal to ethnocentric pride. They told of honorable folk who "lived a hard life"and "fought bit-ter fights." Ostensibly, "the fighting kind" civilized the frontier and made it prosperous.[12] Inspired by the forbearance of the past, the romantics re-called tales about a land where proverbial giants once walked.

William Wells's *The Desert's Hidden Wealth* (1934) represents a typical version of this kind of tale, complete with pictures of sod houses and In-dian chiefs. His modest first-person history proposed to be about "a man of the people" who transformed Kansas from "Desert to world-granary." Wells came with his parents and siblings to the "great American desert" in 1868, but his parents divorced soon thereafter. He stood by his mother, who kept their farm, preserving their little house on the prairie. He even killed a buffalo—the ritual of an authentic frontiersman. Upon reaching the age of twenty-one, he homesteaded along the Solomon River and then married in 1880. His story continued to unfold in a state containing "one-eighth of the desert," where his Spring Creek farm prospered and elevated his prospects so much that he became a member of the Kansas state legislature of 1906–7. Looking backward from his point of view during the 1930s, Wells in retirement remembered sacrifices rendered in a difficult country.[13]

As a social drama, the long and winding roads to the present touched those experiences saturated with pain. The droughts, dust storms, and hard times demanded courage of men to stand "out on the edge of civilization," or so Wells claimed. He remembered the changes in climate that made agri-culture possible along the Solomon River, where the "desert was trans-formed" from hot winds and short buffalo grass to bluestem, wheat, corn, and alfalfa fields. Suggesting a kind of magic, the testimonial involved a symbolic repertoire that subtly blended pagan and Judeo-Christian motifs. The martyrs of his generation forced the desert to "yield up its long-hidden treasures," which fulfilled the "work of the white man and God, or Na-ture."[14] Telling a story for a regional or local audience during the 1930s, the tome celebrated a triumph of the will over nature.

The point is that Wells's traditional story situated a localized experience within the sweep of a metanarrative. Because his tale has little significance in its particulars, the nature of a grander story was woven into personal remembrances. While envisioning the time and the place, he ordered the past, the present, and the future with the changes in the land. As the fittest to survive, Wells invented himself:

I wish to show how it was that this great, once-desert plain, once called the Great American Desert, was transformed into the greatest granary of the world during my lifetime. . . . So I write this, that these truths may not pass on with me, but that the present and coming generations may know the story of this vast empire, once known as the Great American Desert, which Time and the toil of men have effaced from the maps familiar to the present generation.[15]

While accentuating the legacies of conquest, the rise of civilization shaped a narrative relevant to the anguish of the Depression generation.

John Piquet in *Scribner's Magazine* deliberated over the anguish from "our unconquered frontier." According to his 1934 essay, the "best example of our land settlement follies is found in the great agricultural territory that stretches for a thousand miles between the Mississippi River and the Rocky Mountains." While generations of pioneers endeavored with futility to domesticate that soil, "Nature herself had never been successful in growing anything but short grass on these treeless plains." The emptiness exacerbated the evolutionary dead ends and culturally inferior forms, he believed. Across the desert "roamed the most savage Indians in America, nomadic tribes never able to develop the villages and agriculture common elsewhere." Furthermore, the "summers were burning hot" with "great armies of locusts or parching droughts," and these conditions aroused "powerful dust-storms that in some places ripped the top soil and young crops clear off the premises." Even so, the "greatest drought and dust storm in twenty years" demonstrated for Piquet that "the frontier still howls around us." It remained, in other words, to be conquered through a concerted effort by the next generation.[16] The ravages thus set another stage for American history.

While the stage was set for a conflict between Americans and nature, a few versions of the past underscored a mood of pessimism. Margaret Bourke-White in a 1934 *Fortune* article offered a "post-mortem" on the dust bowl, identifying "the piteous meager sweat on the air, and the earth baked stiff and steaming. . . . And the land lay long past death all around you." She understood the frontier as the bleakest country, emplotting tragedy for the westward movement so famous in the nineteenth century. In any arraignment of the weather and climate, she indicted the patriarchs as co-conspirators. The "sun's right hand man deserves mention," which included "the man whose father or whose grandfather, encouraged by your government, staked out a Dakota homestead, tore away the buffalo grass, drained the lowlands, and over-planted the country that maybe never should have been cultivated."[17] Reversing the course of history, in effect, might arrest the downward slope toward mortification, but the author was not particularly hopeful.

With the clarity of hindsight, the course of history illustrated the pitfalls of a fatal environment. In the *Warsaw Times,* a Missouri newspaper, a front-page editorial about bad places in Kansas, Colorado, Oklahoma, and Texas reminded readers that "old geographies printed 100 years ago and even later marked this section as the Great American Desert, inhabited by wild Indians." Millions of beasts grazed and roamed from the Rio Grande on the Mexican border and over into Canada on the north, at least until land speculators arrived. Soon, "a wild era in speculation [and] in town building" ended with a great crash. Ghost towns littered the landscape as reminders of the "gullibility of the land hungry" after breaking up millions of acres of buffalo grass. As a result of greed and ignorance, the "Great American Desert with its lack of moisture and prevailing high winds have made this a desert in fact, a barren waste, that will never come back." The newspaper solemnly concluded: "Civilizations in the past ages have been forced to migrate or die of starvation due to changing climatic conditions and unless some grasses can be found to take the place of the buffalo grass, this will again become known as the Great American Desert."[18] What otherwise represented senseless tragedy, in fact, was condemned to play the role of a bad land.

Reclamation Era, a publication of the federal Reclamation Service, demonstrated how tragedy enabled the government to accentuate patriotism. In 1935, it opined that as "a result of this vision pioneers under the protection of the Stars and Stripes forced their way through hostile lands." While enduring privations and suffering unspeakable hardships, they "lived in constant fear of massacre from unfriendly Indians." The fears laid the basis for enterprise, which "has built a new empire, and has carved from a wilderness a new civilization rivaling the one established at Plymouth Rock." Federal programs reclaimed "worthless deserts peopled only by jackrabbits and prairie dogs," transforming expanses into "an empire with an assessed valuation of nearly one billion dollars." The new lands carved from "these barren wastes" were necessary for "increasing the financial stability of both State and Nation." In other words, the power of the bureaucracy—not the virtue of the individual—inspired a new age of progress.[19]

The *Sooner State Erosion News,* likewise, celebrated the progress of extension service programs. "New frontiers challenge the best efforts of all men," opined an essay in 1935 titled "Declaration of Independence." The narrative remembered that "our forefathers built from a wilderness a nation of home-loving people," but the "conquering" of the original frontier opened up unanticipated problems for descendants. With shadows cast over the region, "out of the chaos of present economic and social disturbances must come order, security, and happiness." Whereas soil wastage defeated the Chinese, sending millions of inhabitants to starvation, "it will never defeat America" because "home-loving, peace-adoring Americans have ever blazed trails, conquered enemies, and prospered." Because the Union endured hardship, each generation "holds sacred the foundation of national security—the soil." Erosion will be defeated, admonished the *News,* and the champions will reserve for posterity "the land of the free and the home of the brave." The local agency used the past to promote bureaucratic extension of its ideological commitments to freedom.[20]

Although railroad pamphlets never reached the level of promotion common during industrialization, accentuating their commitments to expansion remained self-evident. *Western Agriculture and the Burlington,* one pamphlet written in 1938 by O. O. Waggener of the Chicago, Burlington, and Quincy Railroad, attempted to record crucial phases of his railroad's development of "a wild, uncultivated region." He reminisced about a region that "was classed by geographers of the time as a great American desert capable of sustaining no permanent agriculture of a more intensive nature than the production of range cattle." Undaunted by naysayers, the "builders of the Burlington found a waste prairie populated largely by buffalo and Indians" and provided it with transportation, which in turn brought to the frontier "a sturdy race of pioneer farmers." Through a tenacious campaign for the improvement of the environment, they and their beneficiaries "played a major role in transforming it into the beautiful, fertile and productive area it is today." While praising the quality of life, his story taught that "a restless but co-operative spirit" built the steel rails that materialized a "benevolent abundance of nature" in a land that was once lost.[21] When nature presented adversity, the lessons of the past provided models for the continuing advance of civilization.

Using lessons from the past, histories great and small retold traditional stories during the unsettling years of the 1930s, but the discourses did not delineate radical departures as much as derivatives of a singular historical consciousness. That is because modernity dissolved contingency into an ideal continuity, moving a part of the story through a teleological whole. The whole constituted a one-dimensional linear domain assembled from linguistic landmarks and reference points. Without a language for complexity, histories of events discerned an epistemological world reduced to primary causes, essential traits, and final meanings. According to the philosopher Michel Foucault, the rationalist understandings of universal history flatten "a profusion of entangled events" into straight ideological lines.[22] Ideological lines follow recurrent paths that yield predetermined outcomes and prevent modern storytellers from breaking their attachments to tragedy and triumph. When narrators and audiences returned to these paths in retrospection, they became tethered to the frontiers of American tradition.

Consider the semibiographical retrospection of John Ise, who published in 1936 an account of his Kansas homesteading ancestors titled *Sod and Stubble*. This personal yet popular narrative unfolded to reveal the characteristic resilience of immigrant sodbusters who battled for twenty years against drought, grasshoppers, prairie fires, dust storms, and depression. The imagery was not alien to an audience of the dirty thirties, especially when he described "roaring winds, swaying cottonwood trees, flying sand, rattling shutters and creaking doors and screens." While discouraged settlers trekked away from their bleak sod houses like the "retreat of the defeated legion," the homestead endured, "standing out on a treeless and fenceless expanse of waving grass—bare and lonely." In the hagiographic tale, a pioneer encountered "a world rapidly shedding the wildness, the raw, savage loneliness of the uninhabited prairie." After years of turmoil, it eventually began taking on the "habiliments of settled and orderly civilization." In that kind of desert, then, the ordinary acts of everyday persistence seemed extraordinary.[23] Because the courageous souls of the past willingly left a part of themselves in the fields, Ise testified that their presence improved the land.

That improvement required the presence of women as well as men, suggested Edith Kohl's mixed autobiography and novel. Published in 1938, *The Land of the Burnt Thigh* underscored hardships experienced by pioneer women who homesteaded the Dakota wastes. In the preface, Kohl promised to tell "the story of the people, the present day pioneers, who settled on that part of the public lands called the Great American Desert, and wrested a living from it at a personal cost of privation and suffering." Her story, she noted, possessed relevancy because of "an infinite deal of talk about dust bowls, of prairie grass which never should have been plowed under for farming, of land which should be abandoned." She praised the settlers who "marched into the desert," facing fire and thirst, cold and hunger, staying against great odds to build up a new section of the vast empire in the West. Over thousands of acres, men and women continued to fight "to control that last frontier."[24] She detailed in the first person the events and emotions experienced by two sisters terrorized by uncivil places.

The sentimental account placed women in the midst of a less than respectable realm. Wherever the female homesteaders "proved-up" their claims, the process of domestication obtained significance in Kohl's narrative. To engender the value of cooperation, neophytes were pushed together in a setting where "hot winds swept the plains like blasts from a furnace." There was no shelter as far as the eye could see, she recalled, except "those little hot-boxes in which we lived." This shelter, then, was not for living alone but for nurturing relationships, sharing experiences, and feeling compassion. "It was a boundless territory," Kohl found, "which was once marked on the map as the Great American Desert," that is, until a gentle tamer pushed westward and civilized its bewildering nature. She observed: "A wilderness I found it, a thriving community I left it," thereby confirming the traditional role of wife and mother for the story about female settlement. In the end, she left the story open, even concluding with a quintessentially western refrain, "The sun was getting low and I had new trails to break."[25] A simple yet moving tale forged a view of the past that appealed to romantic sentimentalism.

Less prone to such sentimentalism, professional historians nonetheless accounted for the past with the environment in mind. In 1934, Bernard De-Voto, a distinguished scholar of the American West, described a "plundered province" where "the land is discovered to be what the maps label it, desert." The outsiders robbed wealth from the land and were responsible for the extraction of resources. In "sub-marginal land" and the "ultimate barrens," moreover, generations of reclamationists had failed "to enforce their will on the desert." Linking the past with the present, Louis M. Hacker warned that government resettlement and rehabilitation proposals "create a sheltered peasantry" and, if overextended, may indicate that "the United States has gone fascist." With an overview of the "conquest" of the prairies, Louis Bernard Schmidt announced that "the time has passed when the individualism of pioneer days is sufficient to overcome any difficulties that may be met." He decried the patterns of "peasant farming," where "the standard of living is extremely low."[26] Ranging beyond political, military, and diplomatic affairs, historians highlighted the social and economic legacies of regional development.

In particular, J. Evetts Haley, who joined the faculty of the University of Texas in 1929, ascribed the legacies in social and economic terms. While helping to establish the Panhandle-Plains Historical Museum in Canyon, Texas, he also served as historian for the Texas and Southwestern Cattle Raisers Association. Indeed, his biography of Charles Goodnight, published in 1936, told the heroic story of the "cowman and plainsman." Across the ranges, he observed solitude where "not a spear of green grass tempted a hungry cow; the weeds were burned to a crisp; the mesquite leaves hung slant-wise beneath a torrid sun that burned from a cloudless sky, and all day long the whirring of the locusts—the terrible symphony of the drought—beat in our ears with the bawling of starving cattle." He admitted that his native soil was naturally "poor and dry," yet Texans "have that pride in its possession that is to be expected of people who have for long loved and lived close to this soil." Ranching in the "desert country" encouraged the "feeling that ownership of land and settled life are stabilizing moral factors in a mechanical, mobile world." When used properly, "everything about this land of ours induces frugality."[27] On the frontier of Haley's imagination, then, dry land required a dogged nature that a generation under seige needed to revive.

Haley, who devoted his life to cattle raising and writing, became one of the greatest ranch historians of his generation. He explained that his home had been "lashed by the triple scourges" of depression, drought, and dust. Unfortunately, New Deal planners added to the nature of chastisement when "lands, stripped of vegetation by lack of moisture and by government decree, began to blow." That sacred space for Haley demanded a raw determination from its occupiers rather than federal government entanglements.[28] His naturalist view of life represented the outgrowth of a history defined by what might be called the "cowboy philosophy." With his retrospective gaze, he observed a direct relationship between arid conditions and "true Texas traditions":

Of deep psychological import and of wide social and governmental implication is the fact that the desert throws a man back upon himself and enhances his individualism and self-reliance. In the midst of some of these storms the water-barrel under the windmill cannot be reached; Austin is distant; Washington inaccessible. Life itself must be maintained at home. Out of the tragedy some are finding hope in the fact that Nature's ruthless lessons are being learned again.[29]

Clinging to the memories of hardship, Haley envisioned an unbroken bond with the past.

Rupert N. Richardson, a historian from Hardin-Simmons College and president of the Southwestern Social Science Association, highlighted other continuities. He published two regional works in the decade, *The Comanche Barrier to Plains Settlement* (1933) and *The Greater Southwest* (1934), which emphasized cultural, social, and geographic processes. While acknowledging that certain scholars warned that the region was "a desert in the making," he reminded that the notion was dispelled long before the end of the nineteenth century. The breaking of the sod in the western part of the region and its subsequent ecological hazards represented a twentieth-century development, which in turn threatened to create the fatal environment so long feared. Accordingly, the "conquest of the plow has been too complete; the eagerness of Plains farmers to utilize the rich virgin soils has defeated its own purpose." He warned that erosion affected as much as 80 percent of the land. Although the notion of an uninhabitable wasteland seemed exaggerated to Richardson, the recent history of environmental misuse threatened to force depopulation of the region.[30]

One of the region's most prolific sages, William Allen White, the editor of the Emporia, Kansas, *Gazette,* published *The Changing West* during 1939 as the anxious decade closed. He summarized not only his memoirs of a land beyond the Mississippi River but also his ruminations over the nation's metaphorical trek through time and across space. "Why," rhetorically asked White, was "that West which they made here in these wide valleys, across these bleak deserts . . . so different a civilization from that which the ancient pioneers established in the valleys of the Nile, the Euphrates, and the Ganges?" The answer seemed to be a matter of progress, according to White, since "millions of acres lying in what was once the Great American Desert" matured with intelligent efforts into "a brand new world."[31] That pilgrimage ended in success, though it was a success that first required persistence.

White's story did not end there, however, but continued onward to another chapter in his native land. The "grandson of the American pioneers" refused to assume "a peasant's status," he continued, and the resilient forefathers "who died in the last decade of the old century, if they could see us today, would behold here the Utopia of which they dreamed." Episodes of failure made a birthright all the more meaningful to posterity, opined White. He reiterated that what "man did with the fabulous increase in wealth that came with the settlement of the West, man can do now as he plunges into the new era." The soils, if prudently worked by the industry of individuals, still returned the bounties of nature. In the process of settlement, the descendants of pioneers became disciplined through hard experiences, educated and civil. In effect, they acquired "the two things that made the wilderness blossom as the rose: first, a neighborly faith in the decency of man; second, a never faltering vision of a better world." In a sense, he described the value of the frontier in terms of its embourgeoisement of life. A Protestant ethic of work and sobriety, in other words, assured a recovery.[32]

The dust bowl began to experience that recovery, although the memories of the hard years left scars. Alfred B. Sears, a historian at the University of Oklahoma, considered in 1939 the "desert threat" in the Great Plains. He complained that the historical profession appeared too "concerned with the deserts of the Orient rather than the Dust Bowl of today, with the poor whites of 1840 rather than those of 1940, and with the bread and circuses of ancient Rome rather than the bread and cinemas of the New Deal." In fact, he believed that the sandstorms and high temperatures of the dirty thirties might force a reexamination of the national past. He noted that the region of the Louisiana Purchase and north Texas had been regarded as largely a desert by most people east of the Mississippi River for the greater part of the nineteenth century.[33] Although the dangers were serious, there was still time to avoid the mistakes of the past.

Sears's history of soil exhaustion, if sweeping, overcast the future with modest predictions. The desert threat was real, he insisted, but the entire region need not be "destined to become a sandy Sahara." Modern methods of farming, ranching, and management promised to conserve the land and prevent the environment from worsening. Without reform, the region would "become so unproductive through misuse that it will have to be abandoned, even as parts of it already have been." Beyond this environmental waste, he also cautioned of agrarian discontent, continued social degradation, and barbarous dictatorships unless the nation came together to save the soil.[34] According to such relevant and pressing concerns, disorder represented a threat not simply to sustainable agriculture but also to civilization.

Frederick Lewis Allen, who wrote a timely history of the Great Depression, *Since Yesterday,* chronicled the threat of disorder in 1940. In a chapter named "When the Farms Blew Away," Allen explained that "the very land itself had risen in revolt." Following the nightmare that lasted much of the decade, "Oklahoma farms became great dunes of shifting sand." His narrative sympathized in lucid detail with the domesticated role of women. He portrayed housewives in horror scouring the windowsills, frustrated by dirt infiltrating the home through nooks and crannies. Although some of them tried to seal up every aperture in their houses with gummed paper strips used on wrapping parcels, the tormented females remained unable to check the "choking dust" that "filtered in and lay in ripples on the kitchen floor." According to Allen, the raging black blizzards "blew blindly across a No Man's Land."[35] His story of Depression America, then, featured inadequate shelter from the storms.

Whatever the terror in the heartland, Allen's history reviewed a tragic fall but eventual recovery for the nation. He described "roads and farm buildings and once green thickets half-buried in the sand," devastation that uprooted families. The narrator followed "the refugees from this new Sahara, as if obedient to the old American tradition that westward lies the land of promise." Land-hungry speculators irresponsibly encouraged "stripping off forests, ripping out minerals, and plowing up grasslands without regard to the long consequences." This greed imperiled "the men and women whose farms had blown away" and left them "wandering homeless through the land." The New Deal reforms, which he labeled "the new pioneering," developed measures to eradicate the conspicuous poverty. That is how the nation confronted the "hard fact that the days were over when Americans could plunder and move on," a hard fact confirmed by what had occurred "since yesterday."[36] In their miserable circumstances, Americans had acquired maturity.

The acquisition of maturity, moreover, laid the foundations for the greatest generation. Kunigunde Duncan in the *Nation* described how "pitted brain and muscle" liberated a country trapped between the blistering sun and hard times. As tensions mounted, the narrative limned the "final scene" of a "tractor-fought battle" against the elements. "The Dust Bowler," as he dubbed the reforming agent here, fought valiantly until burdened with "the mistakes of his predecessors," including but not limited to "financiers," "settlers," "cattlemen," "farmers," and "speculators." Behold the pantheon of frontier types, who were succeeded by the offspring of pioneering folk. Beset by sweltering heat, menacing grasshoppers, and suffocating dusters, the "fellow of the furrow kept both his head and his courage." Once he called "science to his aid," he became "grass-root conscious." His story, of course, turned in a crescendo of the New Deal and its mantra of experimentation.[37] Finally, he assessed the significance of the new frontier:

Thus is man winning his fight against the variability of that mighty star, our sun; against the carelessness and greed of those who preceded him and of his fellow in other parts of the country. . . . Women still seal windows against dust, clean house with shovels, not brooms, protect babies with wet sheets and endure a scourge more cruel than Indian raids, a scourge which can only be conquered by a courage and an endurance superior to that demanded of the early pioneers.[38]

Courage and endurance, if raised to an unprecedented scale and scope, uplifted the motifs of the story of victory.

On the eve of U.S. entry into World War II, Bliss Isely for *Nation's Business* told a story of victory titled "Unwhipped Dust Bowl Heroes Won't Budge." Accordingly, farmers and ranchers solved problems "in the self-reliant manner we expect of the descendants of those who rode the Santa Fe Trail" and "took homesteads on the Great American Desert, a land nobody else wanted." While he remained confident that they would not "reproduce another Libya or another Gobi," he compared their history to "when the children of Israel homesteaded the arid land of Canaan." In the course of his journey, the author blended legends of religion and science into a hybrid apotheosis. "Nature is cruel to the weak," he opined, but "nowhere is she more heartless than on the High Plains where only the fittest survive." In naturalist tones, he observed the "selection" of people just as the country "selects its crops and farming methods" for rational use. With uncommon valor in the dusty fields of battle, the "unwhipped survivors" lived on to fight another day.[39] Proclaiming no mercy for any foe of a great nation, a victory culture erased the disinherited from the environment and replaced them with the specter of saints.

The environment and the culture, then, were intertwined through narratives bound by the Turner thesis. Content and form became mutually constitutive; they revised lines of discourse for a usable past in retrospectives designed after the fact. A tragic line contained communities and families who failed during catastrophe, which offered a justification for the statist reforms sought by progressives. A romantic line, though, contained souls of undaunted courage and vigor fighting to break free from the history of their own making. The making of historical tropes represented a critical part of self-understanding and self-creation, as the process imparted a redemptive sense to the otherwise random follies of existence. However culturally bound, the genealogical traces recovered memories from the empiricist renderings of the American dream.

Memory, therefore, made Turner's thesis something both contemporary and alive. Because tradition involved vernacular forms of the past, civilization regenerated itself through its legacies cast in a familiar light. If the legacies illuminated ancestral realms, then the narrow and unimaginative cast of mind sifted through the fragmentary and the partial artifacts of a metanarrative. As a whole, the reconstructions claimed meaning not merely for each of the artifacts taken separately but also for the closure of the narrative itself. To be sure, narrators with distinct perspectives observed things from different points of view. That is because they glimpsed tragic and romantic plots with regard to their own values and concerns. Moreover, they mapped the historical markers of a culture obsessed with loss as much as gain. Furthermore, they revised a great story by finding new significance in its remnants. Ultimately, they recycled a usable past in the dust bowl of history.

Epilogue

Living on a reservation in South Dakota, One Bull, nephew of the legendary Sitting Bull, told his story about the dust bowl. During the 1930s, he wrote letters to Walter Stanley Campbell, a professor of literature at the University of Oklahoma. In agony, he asked that the professor return the Sioux *wotawe* to him. It was a sacred medicine bag that had belonged to the last *blotaunka,* or war chief. It contained a small white stone, human hair rolled into little balls, and bits of wood and shell. While protecting the bearer against enemies, it also allowed him to control the weather by conjuring storms of wind and rain at will. Once the old relic was repatriated in 1937, abundant rainfall returned the following year.[1]

Now a single, simple story may be dismissed as one of the minor absurdities of living, but stories about stories call attention to disconcerting patterns of probability. This book considers the ways and the means by which Americans understood the patterns during the Great Depression. The understandings of environmental phenomena recognized the dystopia of myth. Whatever their limits, myths that constitute an *epistimé* form in traumatic experiences and are ongoing in the life of an individual, a tribe, or a nation. They perpetually present binding assumptions for acquisition and deployment of artifactual knowledge, making it possible for subsequent generations to come to terms with constant change. With subtle charm, language fashioned containers for carrying lives through the angles of time and place. Thus, Depression America conceived the dust bowl as an episode of the frontier.

In fact, the dust bowl resurfaced in linguistic permutations during the "filthy fifties." While black blizzards swirled from 1950 until 1957, J. S. Russell, a member of the Soil Conservation Society of America, complained that subversive elements caused "the soil itself to be wasted and blown away." Containment required a new look at federal government policies to stop the spread of erosion, or so he opined. Planted from fencerow to fencerow, fields of hardy grains might be "heading back" to dunes in a domino effect. He rhetorically asked: "Do we want any part of the United States to get as bad as the deserts to be seen in Saudi Arabia or Pakistan or India, to mention only a few that are glaring examples of poor land use and neglect?" With the Great Plains pushed to the brink, he summoned scientists and government agencies to "conquer most of the ravages of unfavorable weather." Pleading for a soil fertility bank or a soil conservation acreage reserve, conservationists such as Russell imagined a threat to national security in their own fallowed backyards.[2]

Moreover, the modern environmental movement raised awareness about the potential for a worse nightmare. In 1987, Rutgers academicians Deborah Epstein Popper and Frank J. Popper mused "that over the next generation the Plains will, as a result of the largest, longest-running agricultural and environmental miscalculation in American history, become almost totally depopulated." Meditating on the gravity of global warming and corporate farming, the Poppers crafted plans for a "buffalo commons." It would allow people to rest in peace, they resolved, and prevent "inevitable disaster" by preserving portions of the short-grass prairie for the return of the bison. Otherwise, desertification would exhaust the dry lands once again. The greenhouse effect would produce a buildup in the atmosphere of carbon dioxide from fossil-fuel combustion, possibly warming the country by an average of at least two or three degrees. The Ogallala Aquifer, which provided a primary reservoir of water for irrigation, approached depletion, too. Unless modern agribusiness moved for a return of the great beasts, the environmentalists warned that the "rural Plains will be virtually deserted." Ironically, spirited resisters to the variations on a frontier theme park roared about their own "stubborn adaptability" and "ingenuity."[3]

Even as a place long ago and far away, dystopian motifs inspired the sorrowful songs of postmodern scribes. In 1989, New Yorker Natalie Merchant of 10,000 Maniacs wrote a seductive lyric about "more dust bowl days," which appeared in the album *Blind Man's Zoo.* One melancholy line on the culture of consumption wailed: "Pennies, nickels, dollars slip away—I've tried and tried but I can't save." Hugh Sidey for *Time* heard "echoes of the great dust bowl" in the cries from drought-stricken states in 1996, especially after the Freedom to Farm Act began phasing out commodity price supports and other agricultural entitlements. Mark Alan Hughes for the *Washington Post,* furthermore, lamented the "welfare dust bowl" created by the impoverishment of the rural underclass. Far more bleak, one *New York Times* headline on science announced: "Great Plains or Great Desert? A Sea of Dunes Lies in Wait." Appearing on PBS and its web site for the *American Experience* series, images from a documentary film in 1998 featured heartbreaking remembrances of sunburned, gritty folks.[4] At the end of an alarming millennium, then, cultural narratives continued to score a haunting tune.

Language, in effect, haunts the ecological imagination with what the geographer Yi-fu Tuan called "landscapes of fear." The word "fear" derives through Old English from the German word for "road" or "travel." Once upon a time, to be on the move in a strange country brought ambushes, death, or worse. Beyond the borders, people faced a no-man's land where danger awaited. Authorities cunningly used terms of terror to control subjects and to keep them close to a protected sphere. While civilizations promised freedom from fear, the terrified devised strategies for manipulating fabrications ranging from fairy tales to fencerows. Stories about dystopias will not fade away; the metropolitan psyche must come to terms with them. Articulating terms that retain codes, transfer metaphors, and accommodate ideologies reconcile anxiety about modernity. For populations occupying realms of uncertainty, the disturbances of metanarratives exist simultaneously in a world of sense and in one of fantasy.[5]

In frontiers made of sense and fantasy, the stories about drought, erosion, and disaster strengthen the interconnections between humans and the environment. When bundled together, they feature hybrid strings of parables, legends, lore, fables, ballads, allegories, poetry, and fictions. The discursive strategies, literary modes, and ideological investments of a metanarrative hold a fascinating range of possibilities, as do the circumstances to which they are applied and by which they have been generated. Cognitive anchors and ecological taboos, however, link to the chaos hosted in the dystopia of American mythos. Indeed, Americans ignore the myths at their own peril.[6]

Grasping a slender thread of myth, speculation on frontiers need not end in annihilation. Frontiers provide grounds for repatriation. Returning to a greater plane of myth once considered home, natives and strangers become entangled within the lapses, twists, and turns of our extraordinary earth. If the dust bowl forces each of us to dwell on the lows as well as the highs, then it reminds us of the historical dimensions present in the universe of sagas. Sagas will not hold water on the Great Plains, but they do teach us how we shall live here. We have learned about our own cosmic dance of creation and destruction, and that we are not separate from the environment but evolve with it.

Notes

Introduction

1. *Oxford English Dictionary,* 1961 ed., s.v. "dust," "bowl"; *Oxford English Dictionary,* supplement, 1972 ed., s.v. "dust bowl"; see also Floyd P. Gates, "Duststorm Words," *American Speech* 13 (February 1938): 71–72.

2. With the allure of postmodernity, the dystopian genre has gained aesthetic power. See David Sisk, *Transformations of Language in Modern Dystopias* (Westport, Conn.: Greenwood, 1997); M. Keith Booker, *Dystopian Literature: A Theory and Research Guide* (Westport, Conn.: Greenwood, 1994); Robert S. Baker, *Brave New World: History, Science, and Dystopia* (New York: Twayne, 1989); Lois B. Zamora, ed., *The Apocalyptic Vision in America: Interdisciplinary Essays on Myth and Culture* (Bowling Green, Ohio: Bowling Green University Popular Press, 1982).

3. There seems to be no consensus about what environmental histories entail, but for a particularly engaging approach, see William Cronon, ed., *Uncommon Ground: Rethinking the Human Place in Nature* (New York: Norton, 1996); Cronon, "A Place for Stories: Nature, History, and Narrative," *Journal of American History* 78 (March 1992): 1347–76; see also Harry C. McDean, "Dust Bowl Historiography," *Great Plains Quarterly* 6 (Spring 1986): 117–26.

4. An intriguing introduction to the relationship between phenomenology and environmentalism may be found in David Abrams, *The Spell of the Sensuous: Perception and Language in a More-Than-Human World* (New York: Random House, 1996).

5. James C. Malin, *The Grasslands of North America: Prolegomena to Its History with Addenda* (Lawrence, Kans.: James C. Malin, 1947); Malin, "The Turnover of Farm Population in Kansas," *Kansas Historical Quarterly* 4 (November 1935): 339–72; see also Allan G. Bogue, "The Heirs of James C. Malin: A Grassland Historiography," *Great Plains Quarterly* 1 (Spring 1981): 105–31.

6. James C. Malin, "Dust Storms," *Kansas Historical Quarterly* 14 (May–November 1946): 129–44, 265–96, 391–413; Malin, "Factors in Grassland Equilibrium," in *History and Ecology: Studies of the Grassland,* ed. Robert P. Swierenga (Lincoln: University of Nebraska

Press, 1984), 31–67; Malin, "The Grassland of North America: Its Occupance and the Challenge of Continuous Reappraisals," in *Man's Role in Changing the Face of the Earth,* ed. William Thomas (Chicago: University of Chicago Press, 1956), 364–67; see also Donald Worster, *Nature's Economy: A History of Ecological Ideas* (New York: Cambridge University Press, 1994), 242–53.

7. Donald Worster, *Dust Bowl: The Southern Plains in the 1930s* (New York: Oxford University Press, 1979), 2–8, 142, 231–43; Worster, "The Dirty Thirties: A Study in Agricultural Capitalism," *Great Plains Quarterly* 6 (Spring 1986): 107–16; Worster, "Transformations of the Earth: Toward an Agroecological Perspective in History," *Journal of American History* 76 (March 1990): 1087–1106.

8. Worster, *Dust Bowl,* 231–43; see also David S. G. Thomas and Nicholas J. Middleton, *Desertification: Exploding the Myth* (New York: Chichester, 1994); Gerald Thompson, "New Western History: A Critical Analysis," in *Old West/New West,* ed. Gene Gressley (Norman: University of Oklahoma Press, 1997).

9. R. Douglass Hurt, *The Dust Bowl: An Agricultural and Social History* (Chicago: Nelson-Hall, 1981); Pamela Riney-Kehrberg, *Rooted in Dust: Surviving Drought and Depression in Southwestern Kansas* (Lawrence: University Press of Kansas, 1994), 1–4, 165–81; Paula Nelson, *The Prairie Winnows Out Its Own: The West River Country of South Dakota in the Years of Depression and Dust* (Iowa City: University of Iowa Press, 1996); see also Paul Bonnifield, *The Dust Bowl: Men, Dirt, and Depression* (Albuquerque: University of New Mexico Press, 1979).

Chapter 1

1. "Pioneer Days Are Recalled by Byron Clark," *Custer County Chief,* 12 August 1930.

2. Ibid.

3. Mircea Eliade, *The Myth of the Eternal Return: Or, Cosmos and History,* trans. Willard R. Trask (1954; rpt. Princeton: Princeton University Press, 1991), 139–61.

4. Simon Schama, *Landscape and Memory* (New York: Knopf, 1995), 1–19.

5. Alun Munslow, *Deconstructing History* (London: Routledge, 1997), 1–16, 163–78; see also Kerwin Lee Klein, *Frontiers of Historical Imagination: Narrating the European Conquest of Native America, 1890–1990* (Berkeley: University of California Press, 1997).

6. The literature on American mythos is daunting, to say the least. The most relevant cultural studies for this chapter are Henry Nash Smith, *Virgin Land: The American West as Symbol and Myth* (New York: Vintage, 1950); Gregory H. Nobles, *American Frontiers: Cultural Encounters and Continental Conquest* (New York: Hill and Wang, 1997); John R. Short, *Imagined Country: Society, Culture, and Environment* (London: Routledge, 1991); and Frederick W. Turner, *Beyond Geography: The Western Spirit Against the Wilderness* (New York: Viking, 1980).

7. William Riebsame, "The United States Great Plains," in *The Earth as Transformed by Human Action: Global and Regional Changes in the Biosphere over the Past 300 Years,* ed. B. L. Turner II et al. (Cambridge: Cambridge University Press, 1990), 561–75; see also

Gilbert Fite, *Conquering the Great American Desert* (Lincoln: Nebraska Historical Society, 1975); Merlin P. Lawson, *The Climate of the Great American Desert* (Lincoln: University of Nebraska Press, 1974); W. Eugene Hollon, *The Great American Desert, Then and Now* (New York: Oxford University Press, 1966).

8. Elliot West, *The Way to the West: Essays on the Central Plains* (Albuquerque: University of New Mexico Press, 1995), 13–50; see also Roderick Nash, *Wilderness and the American Mind,* 3d ed. (New Haven: Yale University Press, 1982), 8–43.

9. Short, *Imagined Country,* 91–124; Hollon, *Great American Desert,* 33–87; John L. Allen, "The Garden-Desert Continuum: Competing Views of the Great Plains in the Nineteenth Century," *Great Plains Quarterly* 5 (Fall 1985): 207–20; B. H. Baltensperger, "Plains Boomers and the Creation of the Great American Desert Myth," *Journal of Historical Geography* 18 (January 1992): 59–73; Martyn J. Bowden, "The Great American Desert in the American Mind," in *Geographies of the Mind,* ed. D. Lowenthal and M. Bowden (New York: Oxford University Press, 1976), 119–47.

10. Fite, *Conquering the Great American Desert,* 1–20; Martyn J. Bowden, "The Invention of American Tradition," *Journal of Historical Geography* 18 (January 1992): 3–26; John L. Allen, "Horizons of the Sublime: The Invention of the Romantic West," *Journal of Historical Geography* 18 (January 1992): 27–40; Ralph C. Morris, "The Notion of a Great American Desert East of the Rockies," *Mississippi Valley Historical Review* 13 (September 1926): 190–200; Donald Worster, "Beyond the Agrarian Myth," in *Under Western Skies: Nature and History and the American West* (New York: Oxford University Press, 1992), 3–18.

11. Francis Parkman, *The Oregon Trail* (1849; rpt. New York: Signet, 1950) 34–35.

12. See Elliot West, *The Contested Plains: Indians, Goldseekers, and the Rush to Colorado* (Lawrence: University Press of Kansas, 1998); Richard Slotkin, *Fatal Environment: The Myth of the Frontier in the Age of Industrialization, 1800–1890* (New York: Atheneum, 1985).

13. Sir Richard Burton, *The City of the Saints and Across the Rocky Mountains to California,* reprinted as *The Look of the West, 1860: Across the Plains to California* (Lincoln: University of Nebraska Press, n.d.; originally published 1862), 8; Malin, "Dust Storms"; Smith, *Virgin Land,* 201–13; Richard White, *It's Your Misfortune and None of My Own: A New History of the American West* (Norman: University of Oklahoma Press, 1991), 150–54; Baltensperger, "Plains Boomers and the Creation of the Great American Desert Myth," 59–73.

14. Charles N. Glaab, "Visions of Metropolis: William Gilpin and Theories of City Growth in the American West," *Wisconsin Magazine of History* 45 (1961): 21–31; David Emmons, *Garden in the Grassland: Boomer Literature of the Central Great Plains* (Lincoln: University of Nebraska Press, 1971), 9–14, 35–37; Smith, *Virgin Land,* 38–46; West, *Contested Plains,* 335; Baltensperger, "Plains Boomers and the Creation of the Great American Desert Myth," 59–73.

15. G. Malcolm Lewis, "Regional Ideas and Reality in the Cis-Rocky Mountain West," in *The Great Plains Experience,* ed. James Wright and Sarah Rosenberg (Lincoln: University of Mid-America, 1978), 27–33; Hollon, *Great American Desert,* 120–80; Baltensperger, "Plains Boomers and the Creation of the Great American Desert Myth," 59–73; Smith, *Virgin Land,* 228–33.

16. Henry Nash Smith, "Rain Follows the Plow: The Notion of Increased Rainfall for the Great Plains, 1844–1880," *Huntington Library Quarterly* 10 (February 1947): 169–93; Emmons, *Garden in the Grassland,* 128–61; see also Clark C. Spence, *The Rainmakers: Pluviculture to World War II* (Lincoln: University of Nebraska Press, 1980).

17. Charles Dana Wilbur, quoted in Smith, "Rain Follows the Plow," 191–93.

18. James L. Haley, *The Buffalo War* (Austin: State House Press, 1998), 94–137; see also Dan Flores, "Bison Ecology and Bison Diplomacy: The Southern Plains from 1800 to 1850," *Journal of American History* 78 (September 1991): 465–85.

19. Frank Linderman, *Plenty Coups, Chief of the Crows* (Lincoln: University of Nebraska Press, 1962); Cronon, "A Place for Stories."

20. West, *Way to the West,* 51–84; Robert Utley, *The Lance and the Shield: The Life and Times of Sitting Bull* (New York: Henry Holt, 1993), 131–39; "Prophecy of Sitting Bull of a Disastrous Year," W. S. Campbell Collection, Box 104, Folder 18, Western History Collections, University of Oklahoma, Norman, Oklahoma. For a fascinating study of Plains Indian visions of the landscape, see Lee Irwin, *The Dream Seekers: The Native American Visionary Traditions of the Great Plains* (Norman: University of Oklahoma Press, 1994).

21. Malin, "Dust Storms," 129–44, 265–96, 391–413; Hollon, *Great American Desert,* 148; Richard Conrat and Maisie Conrat, "The Great Migrations into the Agricultural Lands of the West," *American West* 14 (March–April 1977): 33; Carl C. Rister, *No Man's Land* (Norman: University of Oklahoma Press, 1948), 3–77; Craig Miner, *West of Wichita: Settling the High Plains of Kansas, 1865–1890* (Lawrence: University Press of Kansas, 1986), 132–44.

22. James B. Kracht, "Perception of the Great Plains in Nineteenth Century Folk Songs," *Journal of Geography* 88 (November–December 1989): 206–12; Bill Malone, *Country Music, USA* (Austin: University of Texas Press, 1985), 32–135; Barre Toelkin, "Folklore in the American West," in *A Literary History of the American West* (Fort Worth: Texas Christian University Press, 1987), 29–67.

23. Frank H. Spearman, "The Great American Desert," *Harper's Monthly Magazine* 77 (July 1888): 232–45.

24. White, *It's Your Misfortune,* 227–32, 370–77; Hollon, *Great American Desert,* 149–51, 183–85; Garry Nall, "The Farmer's Frontier in the Texas Panhandle," *Panhandle-Plains Historical Review* 45 (1972): 1–20; Walter M. Kollmorgen, "The Woodsman's Assaults on the Domain of the Cattleman," *Annals of the Association of American Geographers* 59 (June 1969): 215–39; Richard Hofstadter, *The Age of Reform* (New York: Vintage, 1955), 23–130.

25. Hamlin Garland, *Jason Edwards: An Average Man* (Boston: Arena, 1892), 132–51.

26. Frederick Jackson Turner, "The Significance of the Frontier in American History," in *The Frontier in American History* (1920; rpt. New York: Holt, Rinehart and Winston, 1962), 1–38; see also Frederick Jackson Turner, "The West and American Ideals," ibid., 290–310; Gerald Nash, *Creating the West: Historical Interpretations, 1890–1990* (Albuquerque: University of New Mexico Press, 1991), 3–99; see also Allan Bogue, *Frederick Jackson Turner* (Norman: University of Oklahoma Press, 1998).

27. This critical analysis of narrative may be traced to Hayden White, *The Content of the Form: Narrative Discourse and Historical Representation* (Baltimore: Johns Hopkins University Press, 1987); see also Munslow, *Deconstructing History,* 140–62; Hans Kellner, "Language and Historical Representation," in *The Postmodern History Reader,* ed. Keith Jenkins (London: Routledge, 1997), 127–38.

28. Cronon, "A Place for Stories," 1347–76; David Demeritt, "The Nature of Metaphors in Cultural Geography and Environmental History," *Progress in Human Geography* 18 (June 1994): 163–85.

29. Timothy J. Rickard, "The Great Plains as Part of an Irrigated Western Empire, 1890–1914," in *The Great Plains: Environment and Culture,* ed. Brian Blouet and Frederick Luebke (Lincoln: University of Nebraska Press, 1979), 81–98; John Opie, *Nature's Nation: An Environmental History of the United States* (New York: Harcourt Brace, 1998), 309–31, 355–65; White, *It's Your Misfortune,* 401–6; see also Samuel P. Hays, *Conservation and the Gospel of Efficiency: The Progressive Conservation Movement, 1890–1920* (Cambridge, Mass.: Harvard University Press, 1959).

30. Steven F. Mehls, "Garden in the Grassland Revisited: Railroad Promotional Efforts and the Settlement of the Texas Plains," *West Texas Historical Association Year Book* 55 (1984): 47–66; Jan Blodgett, *Land of Bright Promise: Advertising the Texas Panhandle and South Plains, 1870–1917* (Austin: University of Texas Press, 1988), 1–85; Donald E. Green, "The Idea of an Inexhaustible Supply of Ground Water on the Texas High Plains: The Obstacle of a Myth to Water Conservation," *Proceedings of the Oklahoma Academy of Science* 50 (1970): 151–54; John Miller Morris, *El Llano Estacado: Exploration and Imagination on the High Plains of Texas and New Mexico* (Austin: Texas State Historical Association, 1997).

31. Donald E. Green, *Land of the Underground Rain* (Austin: University of Texas Press, 1973), 1–115.

32. "Transforming the Panhandle of Texas," *Earth* 3 (April 1906): 12.

33. Walter Prescott Webb, *The Great Plains* (1931; rpt. Lincoln: University of Nebraska Press, 1981), 322, 367–69; Mary W. M. Hargreaves, *Dry Farming in the Northern Great Plains, 1900–1925* (Cambridge, Mass.: Harvard University Press, 1957), 45–137; Malin, "Dust Storms," 391–413; see also David E. Kromm and Stephen F. White, eds., *Groundwater Exploitation in the High Plains* (Lawrence: University Press of Kansas, 1992).

34. *Free Government Lands in Nebraska, Wyoming, Colorado, Montana, South Dakota,* Chicago, Burlington, and Quincy Railroad, 1912, Val Kuska Collection, Nebraska State Historical Society, Lincoln, Nebraska; Garry Nall, "Panhandle Farming in the 'Golden Era' of American Agriculture," *Panhandle-Plains Historical Review* 46 (1973): 68–93; Nall, "Specialization and Expansion: Panhandle Farming in the 1920s," *Panhandle-Plains Historical Review* 47 (1974): 1–20; White, *It's Your Misfortune,* 435–39.

35. U.S. Department of Commerce, *Thirteenth Census of the United States: 1910, Population,* Vol. 1, Table 20 (Washington, D.C.: U.S. Government Printing Office, 1913), 700; *Fifteenth Census of the United States: 1930, Population,* Vol. 2, Table 17 (Washington, D.C.:

U.S. Government Printing Office, 1933), 148; White, *It's Your Misfortune,* 435–39, 464–65; Hollon, *Great American Desert,* 160–80; see also Carl F. Kraenzel, *The Great Plains in Transition* (Norman: University of Oklahoma Press, 1955).

36. Charles Moreau Harger, "The Next Commonwealth: Oklahoma," *Outlook* 67 (December 1904): 273–81; Harger, "The Passing of the Promised Land," *Atlantic Monthly* 104 (October 1909): 461–66; Harger, "The West's New Vision," *Atlantic Monthly* 120 (July 1917): 121–28.

37. Martyn J. Bowden, "The Invention of American Tradition," *Journal of Historical Geography* 18 (January 1992): 3–26; Baltensperger, "Plains Boomers and the Creation of the Great American Desert Myth," 59–73.

38. Frank W. Blackmar, "The Mastery of the Desert," *North American Review* 182 (1906): 684–86; Randall Parrish, *The Great Plains: The Romance of Western American Exploration, Warfare, and Settlement, 1527–1870* (Chicago: A. C. McClurg, 1907), 382; Charles Richard Van Hise, *The Conservation of Natural Resources in the United States* (New York: Macmillan, 1910): 270–79; Morris, "Notion of a Great American Desert," 190–200; Bowden, "The Great American Desert in the American Mind," 119–47.

39. Webb, *Great Plains,* 453–515; James Shortridge, *The Middle West: Its Meaning in American Culture* (Lawrence: University Press of Kansas, 1989), 27–66; Robert Smith Bader, *Hayseeds, Moralizers, and Methodists: The Twentieth Century Image of Kansas* (Lawrence: University Press of Kansas, 1988), 41–71; see also Diane Dufva Quantic, *The Nature of the Place: A Study of Great Plains Fiction* (Lincoln: University of Nebraska Press, 1995); Harold P. Simonson, *Beyond the Frontier: Writers, Western Regionalism, and a Sense of Place* (Fort Worth: Texas Christian University Press, 1989).

40. Bonnifield, *Dust Bowl,* 20–38; Nall, "Specialization and Expansion," 1–20; Leslie Hewes, "Agricultural Risk in the Great Plains," in *The Great Plains,* ed. Blouet and Luebke, 157–85.

41. Worster, *Dust Bowl,* 10–63; Hurt, *Dust Bowl,* 1–15.

42. David Wrobel, *The End of American Exceptionalism: Frontier Anxiety from the Old West to the New Deal* (Lawrence: University Press of Kansas, 1993).

Chapter 2

1. Lea Rosson DeLong, *Nature's Forms/Nature's Forces: The Art of Alexandre Hogue* (Norman: University of Oklahoma Press, 1984), 46, 100, 130.

2. My research indicates that Hogue's painting labeled the dust bowl as early as 1933, though other historians credit the label to a dispatch in 1935 from Robert Geiger, an Associated Press reporter. For a discussion about the origin of the term, see Worster, *Dust Bowl,* 28–31, 33; Hurt, *Dust Bowl,* 3; Fred Floyd, "A History of the Dust Bowl" (Ph.D. dissertation, University of Oklahoma, 1950).

3. Sacvan Bercovitch, *The American Jeremiad* (Madison: University of Wisconsin Press, 1978); see also Brad Lookingbill, "A God-Forsaken Place: Folk Eschatology and the Dust Bowl," *Great Plains Quarterly* 14 (Fall 1994): 273–86.

4. One of the more eloquent, if not ironic, jeremiads on environmental peril remains Lynn White, "The Historical Roots of Our Ecologic Crisis," *Science* 155 (10 March 1967): 1203–7. White blames the Christian dogma of "man's transcendence of, and rightful mastery over, nature" for placing civilization in peril.

5. "Drouths Within and Without," *Baptist Messenger* (Oklahoma), 21 August 1930; see also Paul Boyer, *When Time Shall Be No More: Prophecy Belief in Modern American Culture* (Cambridge, Mass.: Harvard University Press, 1992).

6. "Drouths Within and Without," *Baptist Messenger* (Oklahoma), 21 August 1930.

7. "Depression Tragedies," *Church Advocate and Good Way,* 25 August 1932.

8. "Haskell Joins in Appeal for 5 Million in Immediate U.S. Aid," *Sublette Monitor* (Kansas), 22 June 1933; "Embarrassing, But Necessary," *Sublette Monitor,* 22 June 1933; see also Earl H. Bell, *Culture of a Contemporary Rural Community: Sublette, Kansas,* Rural Life Studies 2, Bureau of Agricultural Economics, U.S. Department of Agriculture (Washington, D.C.: U.S. Government Printing Office, 1942), 89, 109–13.

9. M. E. Markwell, "Methodist Church," *Boise City News* (Oklahoma), 18 April 1935; "Methodist Episcopal Church," *Meade County Press* (Kansas), 28 February 1935; "Revival at Local Church This Week," *Meade County Press,* 21 March 1935; "Hodgeman Prayer for Rain Band Is Growing," *Dodge City Daily Globe* (Kansas), 29 March 1935; see also Worster, *Dust Bowl,* 170.

10. "Hodgeman Prayer for Rain Band Is Growing," *Dodge City Daily Globe* (Kansas), 29 March 1935; see also *Elkhart Tri-State News* (Kansas), 12 March 1936; Hurt, *Dust Bowl,* 49–66; Michael Parfit, "The Dust Bowl," *Smithsonian* 20 (June 1989): 46.

11. "Dust Storms in West Kansas," *Catholic Advance* (Kansas), 13 April 1935; "This Week," *Catholic Advance,* 14 April 1934, 11 May 1935, 11 July 1936.

12. "This Week," *Catholic Advance,* 11 July 1936.

13. "Agriculture: Mother Nature Lays Down a Withering, Calamitous New Deal," *Newsweek* 3 (9 June 1934): 3–4; "Agriculture: Unprecedented Heat Brings Death and Destruction to Half of the United States," *Newsweek* 4 (4 August 1934): 6–7; "Drought: Uncle Sam Looks at His Lean Larder and Acts to Hold Prices Down," *Newsweek* 4 (18 August 1934): 5–6; "Agriculture: 500,000,000 Tons of Dust Cover Kansas and Points East," *Newsweek* 5 (30 March 1935): 5–6; "Dust: More Storms Wreak Destruction in the Southwest," *Newsweek* 5 (20 April 1935): 11.

14. Russell B. Porter, "Drought Produces Lean Kine of Egypt," *New York Times,* 2 August 1934, 6.

15. Harlan Miller, "When Searing Drought Smites the Farm," *New York Times Magazine,* 27 May, 1934, 7, 22; Miller, "Dust Rides the Wind Out of the West," *New York Times Magazine,* 31 March 1935, 11, 14.

16. A. W. Malone, "Desert Ahead!" *New Outlook* 164 (August 1934): 14–17.

17. Ibid.

18. Morris Markey, "Nature the Farmer," *Saturday Evening Post* 207 (21 July 1934): 5–7,

81–83; Putnam Dana McMillan, "Marginal Land and Marginal Thinking," *Saturday Evening Post* 208 (1 June 1935): 27, 88–89.

19. Meridel Le Sueur, "Cows and Horses Are Hungry," *American Mercury* 33 (September 1934): 53–56; see also Linda Ray Pratt, "Woman Writer in the CP: The Case of Meridel Le Sueur," *Women's Studies* 14 (1988): 247–64.

20. "The Call of the Land," *Commonweal* 20 (25 May 1934): 85–86.

21. "Past Panics and Panacea," *Boise City News* (Oklahoma), 21 March 1935; "Tactless Texan," *Amarillo Globe* (Texas), 10 April 1935; "Garden of Eden Destroyed When Man Turned the Sod on the Prairie of Kansas," *Topeka Daily State Journal* (Kansas), 3 April 1935; "Dark Palm Sunday," *Meade Globe News* (Kansas), 18 April 1935; "Beaver County Enveloped in Dust," *Herald-Democrat* (Beaver, Oklahoma), 18 April 1935; see also Lookingbill, "A God-Forsaken Place," 273–86.

22. Charles Fitzhugh Talman, "Big and Little Dust Storms," *Nature Magazine* 25 (March 1935): 103–6.

23. Robert Geiger, "If It Rains . . ." *Washington Evening Star,* 15 April 1935, A-2.

24. Avis Carlson, "Dust," *New Republic* 82 (1 May 1935): 332–33; Carlson, "Dust Blowing," *Harper's Magazine* 171 (July 1935): 149–58.

25. Alfred Klausler, "It Can't Rain Here," *Nation* 143 (8 August 1936): 152; M. E. Poyer, "Fighting the Drought," *Nation* 143 (1 August 1936): 139; see also "The Shape of Things," *Nation* 143 (11 July 1936): 29; William Gropper, "The Dust Bowl," *Nation* 145 (21 August 1937): 194.

26. W. I. Drummond, "Dust Bowl," *Review of Reviews* 93 (June 1936): 37–40; "Drought," *New Republic* 87 (15 July 1936): 284.

27. "Drought: A Merciless Sun and a Scourge of Insects Destroy Crops, Cattle and Men," *Newsweek* 8 (18 July 1936): 7–11; "Drought: Rain of Relief Brings New Planning for Arid States," *Newsweek* 8 (25 July 1936): 22; "Drought: Worst in History of United States Leads to Relief Flight and Political Arguments," *Newsweek* 8 (15 August 1936): 17.

28. A. B. Macdonald, "It's No Longer the Dust Bowl," *Kansas City Star,* 7 June 1936.

29. Ernie Pyle, *Home Country* (New York: William Sloane Associates, 1947), 49–57; Pyle, "The Dust Bowl," in *Ernie's America: The Best of Ernie Pyle's 1930s Travel Dispatches,* ed. David Nichols (New York: Harper Collins, 1990), 113–26.

30. Pyle, *Home Country,* 49–57; Pyle, *Ernie's America,* 113–26.

31. Pyle, *Home Country,* 49–57; Pyle, *Ernie's America,* 113–26.

32. Archibald MacLeish, "Grasslands," *Fortune* 12 (November 1935): 58–67; see also Worster, *Dust Bowl,* 45–48, 63, 66.

33. MacLeish, "Grasslands," 67, 190.

34. Archibald MacLeish, *Land of the Free* (New York: Harcourt Brace, 1938), passim.

35. "Two Poems of Drought," *New Republic* 81 (5 December 1934): 99; Marion Ellet, "Kansas," *Kansas Magazine* (1936): 50; Kenneth Porter, "Anthology of Kansas Verse," *Kansas Magazine* (1937) 35–37; Bader, *Hayseeds, Moralizers, and Methodists:* 87–88.

36. Julia Lott, "Drought Survivors," *Kansas Magazine* (1936): 93.

37. Kenneth Porter, "Dust Cloud over Kansas," *Kansas Magazine* (1937): 64–65.

38. Elmyr Doran Warren, "The Dust Storm," in John L. McCarty, *Wind in the Cottonwoods* (Dalhart, Tex.: Dalhart, 1936), 211.

39. George Greenfield, "Unto Dust—A Great American Desert in the Making," *Reader's Digest* 30 (May 1937): 37–38.

40. Francis Flood, "The Dust Bowl Is Being Tamed," *Oklahoma Farmer-Stockman,* 1 July 1937, 3, 23.

41. John M. Collins, "A Dust Bowl Revives," *Christian Science Monitor,* 4 August 1937; Mark A. Dawber, "The Churches in the Dust Bowl," *Missionary Review of the World* 62 (September 1939): 394–97; see also John M. Collins, "Best Kansas Wheat Is in the Dust Bowl," *New York Times,* 19 February 1939, F3.

42. Ward West, "Hope Springs Green in the Dust Bowl," *New York Times Magazine,* 16 July 1939, 7, 21; see also Harold Ward, "Conquering the Dust Bowl," *Travel* 74 (February 1940): 24–25, 48.

43. Lisa Dorill, "Picturing the Dirty Thirties: Paintings and Prints of the Dust Bowl" (Ph.D. dissertation, University of Kansas, 1998); see also Matthew Baigell, *The American Scene: American Painting of the 1930s* (New York: Praeger, 1974); Barbara Melosh, *Engendering Culture: Manhood and Womanhood in New Deal Public Art and Theater* (Washington, D.C.: Smithsonian Institution Press, 1991); Jonathan Harris, *Federal Art and National Culture: The Politics of Identity in New Deal America* (Cambridge: Cambridge University Press, 1995).

44. "The U.S. Dust Bowl: Its Artist Is a Texan Portraying Man's Mistakes," *Life* 2 (21 June 1937): 60–65; DeLong, *Nature's Forms/Nature's Forces,* 1–27, 45, 130; Worster, *Dust Bowl,* 32–33.

45. DeLong, *Nature's Forms/Nature's Forces,* 21, 44, 104.

46. Ibid., 116.

47. Ibid., 7, 39, 120; see also Jane Tompkins, *West of Everything: The Inner Life of the Westerns* (New York: Oxford University Press, 1983).

48. Carolyn Merchant, "Reinventing Eden: Western Culture as a Recovery Narrative," in *Uncommon Ground,* ed. Cronon, 132–59.

Chapter 3

1. Richard Lowitt, *The New Deal and the West* (Bloomington: Indiana University Press, 1984), 8–63; see also Tim Lehman, *Public Values, Private Lands: Farmland Preservation Policy, 1933–1985* (Chapel Hill: University of North Carolina Press, 1995); Michael Schuyler, *Dread of Plenty: Agricultural Relief Activities of the Federal Government in the Middle West, 1933–1939* (Manhattan, Kans.: Sunflower University Press, 1989); Hurt, *Dust Bowl.*

2. Anthony Badger, *The New Deal: The Depression Years, 1933–1940* (New York: Hill and Wang, 1989), 147–89; see also Christopher Clarke-Hazlett, "The Road to Dependency:

Policy, Planning, and the Rationalization of American Agriculture, 1920–1945" (Ph.D. dissertation, University of Rochester, 1986); Harry C. McDean, "Federal Farm Policy and the Dust Bowl: The Half-Right Solution," *North Dakota History* 47 (Summer 1980): 21–31.

3. Wilburn Cartwright, "Drought Relief," 14 January 1931, in Wilburn Cartwright Collection, Carl Albert Center, University of Oklahoma, Norman, Oklahoma.

4. Harold Ickes, "The National Domain and the New Deal," *Saturday Evening Post* 206 (23 December 1933): 10–11, 55; see also Ickes, *The New Democracy* (New York: Norton, 1934).

5. R. V. Smrha, "Irrigation for Crop Insurance," *Biennial Report of Kansas State Board of Agriculture* 28 (1933): 138–41; James E. Sherow, *Watering the Valley: Development Along the High Plains Arkansas River, 1870–1950* (Lawrence: University Press of Kansas, 1990), 120–40.

6. N. E. Hansen, "Shall We Abandon or Shall We Develop Our Dry Western Uplands?" unpublished paper, 8 February 1934, in Elmer Thomas Collection, Carl Albert Center, University of Oklahoma, Norman, Oklahoma; see also Benjamin H. Hibbard, "The Drought and the AAA Program," *Nation* 139 (4 July 1934): 15–16.

7. "Do Something about It!" *Collier's* 94 (22 September 1934): 58; "Don't Bet on the Bad Lands," *Collier's* 98 (3 October 1936): 62.

8. "Dry Blizzards and Erosion," *Literary Digest* 117 (26 May 1934): 19; "Drought Leads to Provision for Lean Years," *Literary Digest* 117 (16 June 1934): 4.

9. Margaret Bourke-White, "Dust Changes America," *Nation* 140 (22 May 1935): 597–98.

10. Bernard W. Snow, "Flirting with Famine," *Farm Journal* 57 (December 1933): 5; Snow, "Prices and Failures," *Farm Journal* 58 (September 1934): 9, 23; Snow, "Crops and Weather," *Farm Journal* 60 (May 1936): 13; Snow, "Wheat and Water," *Farm Journal* 62 (April 1938): 18.

11. H. L. Freudenberger, "Black Blizzards," *Farm Journal* 62 (January 1938): 30–31; see also Clifford B. Anderson, "The Metamorphosis of American Agrarian Idealism in the 1920s and 1930s," *Agricultural History* 35 (October 1961): 182–88.

12. Leland W. Mann, "Packers Take Up Theology," *Christian Century* 51 (20 June 1934): 833–34; see also Lookingbill, "A God-Forsaken Place."

13. Buren Sparks, "Dust Storms and Providence," *Baptist Standard,* 9 May 1935.

14. Gerald B. Winrod, "Joseph of Egypt and Wallace of Iowa," *Revealer,* 15 August 1935; Winrod, "Disturbances in Nature," *Defender* 11 (August 1936): 21–22; see also Leo Ribuffo, *The Old Christian Right: The Protestant Far Right from the Great Depression to the Cold War* (Philadelphia: Temple University Press, 1983), 101–5, 119–24.

15. Winrod, "Joseph of Egypt and Wallace of Iowa," *Revealer,* 15 August 1935.

16. "Egypt Had No Chicago Board of Trade," *Capper's Weekly* (Topeka, Kansas), 9 June 1934; "To Put an End to Soil Robbing," *Capper's Weekly,* 28 March 1936.

17. T. A. McNeal, "New Crop Pest Visits Egypt," *Kansas Farmer,* 17 August 1935.

18. Alva Johnston, "Wheat, Drought, and the New Deal," *Saturday Evening Post* 207 (13 April 1935): 5–7, 78–83; Johnston, "The Hamburger Bonanza," *Saturday Evening Post* 207 (4 May 1935): 18–19, 99–104.

19. Joseph H. Fichter, "A Comparative View of Agrarianism," *Catholic World* 143 (September 1936): 654–59; see also J. M. Campbell, "In the Country," *Commonweal* 15 (3 February 1932): 378–80; Virgil Michel, "Agriculture and Reconstruction," *Commonweal* 29 (13 January 1939): 317–18.

20. Ernest A. Dewey, "Duster," *Commonweal* 27 (4 March 1938): 519; see also Edward S. Shapiro, "Catholic Agrarian Thought and the New Deal," *Catholic Historical Review* 65 (October 1979): 583–99.

21. Henry A. Wallace, *New Frontiers* (New York: Reynal and Hitchcock, 1934), 239–48, 269–71; see also Edward L. Schapsmeier and Frederick H. Schapsmeier, "Henry A. Wallace: Agrarian Idealist or Agricultural Realist?" *Agricultural History* 41 (April 1967): 127–37; Theodore Rosenof, "The Economic Ideas of Henry A. Wallace, 1933–1948," *Agricultural History* 41 (April 1967): 143–53.

22. Wallace, *New Frontiers,* 269–71.

23. Henry A. Wallace, "The Next Four Years in Agriculture," *New Republic* 89 (2 December 1936): 133–36; Wallace, "The Ever-Normal Granary," *Literary Digest* 124 (20 November 1937): 13–15; see also "Wallace on Future of Great Plains Area," *New York Times,* 16 December 1936, 8A.

24. Rexford Tugwell, "The Reason for Resettlement," unpublished paper, 1935, in Elmer Thomas Collection, Carl Albert Center, University of Oklahoma, Norman, Oklahoma; see also Tugwell, *The Battle for Democracy* (New York: Columbia University Press, 1935).

25. Rexford Tugwell, "Our New National Domain," *Scribner's Magazine* 99 (March 1936): 164–68; Tugwell, "Changing Acres," *Current History* 44 (September 1936): 57–63.

26. Resettlement Administration pamphlet, U.S. Government Printing Office, 1936, in Elmer Thomas Collection, Carl Albert Center, University of Oklahoma, Norman, Oklahoma.

27. Frieda Knobloch, *The Culture of Wilderness: Agriculture as Colonization in the American West* (Chapel Hill: University of North Carolina Press, 1996).

28. Pare Lorentz, *The Plow That Broke the Plains,* United States Resettlement Administration, Washington, D.C., 1936; "Documented Dust," *Time* 127 (25 May 1936): 47; Mark Van Doren, "Further Documents," *Nation* 142 (10 June 1936): 753–54; "Federal Movie Furor," *Business Week,* 11 July 1936, 14; "Dust Storm Film," *Literary Digest* 121 (16 May 1936): 22; see also Robert Snyder, *Pare Lorentz and the Documentary Film* (Norman: University of Oklahoma Press, 1968); Pare Lorentz, *FDR's Moviemaker: Memoirs and Scripts* (Reno: University of Nevada Press, 1992).

29. Dorothea Lange and Paul Taylor, *An American Exodus: A Record of Human Erosion* (New York: Reynal and Hitchcock, 1939); William H. Goetzmann and William N. Goetzmann, *The West of the Imagination* (New York: Norton, 1986), 388–94; see also William Stott, *Documentary Expression and Thirties America* (New York: Oxford University Press, 1973); James Curtis, *Mind's Eye, Mind's Truth: FSA Photography Reconsidered* (Philadelphia: Temple University Press, 1989).

30. Chester C. Davis, "Toward Planned Harvests," *Review of Reviews* 88 (December 1933): 19–21, 52; Davis, "If Drought Strikes Again," *Saturday Evening Post* 207 (27 April 1935): 23, 76–77, 79–80; Davis, "Rise of Grass," *Country Gentleman* 106 (January 1936): 18, 66, 68, 69.

31. Chester C. Davis, "Lost Acres," *American Magazine* 121 (February 1936): 63, 127–29; Davis, "Has the New Deal Helped the Farmer?" *Forum* 95 (February 1936): 76–79.

32. Report of the Great Plains Drought Area Committee, August 1936, in Elmer Thomas Collection, Carl Albert Center, University of Oklahoma, Norman, Oklahoma.

33. M. L. Wilson, "The Challenge to Agriculture," *Sooner State Conservation News,* March 1936, 2; Wilson, "Agricultural Conservation—An Aspect of Land Utilization," *Journal of Farm Economics* 19 (February 1937): 3–12.

34. Joseph L. Dailey, "Is the West Drying Up?" *Nation's Agriculture* 11 (September 1936): 2–3, 10.

35. P. H. Stephens, "Why the Dust Bowl?" *Journal of Farm Economics* 19 (August 1937): 750–57; see also Ewing Jones, "Dust Storms through the Years," *The Land Today and Tomorrow* 2 (April 1935): 1–4.

36. E. D. G. Roberts, "The Land Utilization Program in the Southern Great Plains," *Science* 88 (30 September 1938): 289–92; see also W. F. Peel, "The Soil Conservation Service Drought Program of 1936," *Soil Conservation* 2 (March 1937): 204–7.

37. L. C. Gray, "Our Land Policy Today," *Land Policy Review* 1 (May–June 1938): 3–8; Gray, "Federal Purchase and Administration of Submarginal Land in the Great Plains," *Journal of Farm Economics* 21 (February 1939): 123–31; see also Richard S. Kirkendall, "L. C. Gray and the Supply of Agricultural Land," *Agricultural History* 37 (October 1963): 205–16.

38. Roy Kimmel, "United Front to Reclaim the Dust Bowl," *New York Times Magazine,* 14 August 1938, 10–11, 20; Kimmel, "Planning for the Southern Great Plains," *Soil Conservation* 5 (November 1939): 120–22.

39. Herbert C. Hanson, "Ecology in Agriculture," *Ecology* 20 (April 1939): 111–17.

40. R. S. Kifer and H. L. Stewart, *Farming Hazards in the Drought Area,* Research Monograph 16, Works Progress Administration, Division of Social Research (Washington, D.C.: U.S. Government Printing Office, 1938), 3–28; see also F. D. Cronin and H. W. Beers, *Areas of Intense Drought Distress, 1930–1936,* Research Bulletin, Series 5, Works Progress Administration, Division of Social Research (Washington, D.C.: U.S. Government Printing Office, 1937), 3–28.

41. Bushrod W. Allin and Ellery A. Foster, "The Challenge of Conservation," in *Farmers in a Changing World,* Yearbook of Agriculture (Washington, D.C.: U.S. Government Printing Office, 1940), 416–28.

42. Smith, *Virgin Land.*

Chapter 4

1. "Storm Climax," *Liberal News* (Kansas), 15 April 1935; Paul Carlson, "Black Sunday: The South Plains Dust Blizzard of April 14, 1935," *West Texas Historical Association Yearbook* 67 (1991): 5–17.

2. Peter Farb, "Hugh Bennett: Messiah of the Soil," *American Forests* 66 (January 1960): 19, 40, 42; Garry L. Nall, "The Struggle to Save the Land: The Soil Conservation Effort in the Dust Bowl," in *The Depression in the Southwest,* ed. Donald D. Whisenhunt (Port-Washington, N.Y.: Kennikat Press, 1980), 26–41; "To Lay the Dust," *Extension Service Review* 9 (March 1938): 43; see also Lowitt, *The New Deal and the West,* 53–80.

3. Richard White, "Are You an Environmentalist or Do You Work for a Living: Work and Nature," in *Uncommon Ground,* ed. Cronon, 171–85.

4. F. E. Clements and Ralph Chaney, *Environment and Life in the Great Plains,* Carnegie Institution, Supplemental Publication 24 (Washington, D.C.: Carnegie Institution, 1937); Worster, *Nature's Economy,* 205–53; see also Ronald C. Tobey, *Saving the Prairies: The Life Cycle of the Founding School of American Plant Ecology, 1895–1955* (Berkeley: University of California Press, 1981).

5. Frederic E. Clements, "Climatic Cycles and Human Populations in the Great Plains," *Scientific Monthly* 47 (September 1938): 193–210.

6. Roger C. Smith, "Upsetting the Balance of Nature, with Special Reference to Kansas and the Great Plains," *Science* 75 (24 June 1932): 649–54; see also Hays, *Conservation and the Gospel of Efficiency.*

7. John Weaver and Evan Flory, "Stability of Climax Prairie and Some Environmental Changes Resulting from Breaking," *Ecology* 15 (October 1934): 333–47; see also John Weaver and F. W. Albertson, "Effects of the Great Drought on the Prairies of Iowa, Nebraska, and Kansas," *Ecology* 17 (October 1936): 567–639; Weaver and Albertson, "Deterioration of Midwestern Ranges," *Ecology* 21 (April 1940): 216–36.

8. E. A. Sherman, quoted in "Agriculture: Mother Nature Lays Down a Withering, Calamitous New Deal"; "The Recent Destructive Dust Cloud," *Science* 79 (25 May 1934): 473; E. A. Sherman, "Saving Our Soil," *Nation* 139 (12 April 1933): 401–3.

9. Clyde M. Brundy, "Trees for the Prairies," *American Forests* 39 (December 1933): 553–55, 574; see also William H. Droze, *Trees, Prairies, and People* (Denton, Tex.: Texas Women's University Press, 1977); Worster, *Dust Bowl,* 40, 220–23.

10. Ellsworth Huntington, "Marginal Land and the Shelter Belt," *Journal of Forestry* 32 (November 1934): 804–12.

11. Raphael Zon, "Shelterbelts—Futile Dream or Workable Plan," *Science* 81 (26 April 1935): 391–94; see also T. Russell Reitz, "A Traveler Sees the Shelterbelts," *Progress in Kansas* 7 (December 1940): 11–12.

12. "Drought Strikes Home," *Business Week,* 28 July 1934, 5–6; "Creeping Disaster," *Business Week,* 28 July 1934, 36; see also "Drought Results," *Business Week,* 9 June 1934, 7–8.

13. "Drought Strikes Home," *Business Week,* 28 July 1934, 5–6.

14. Wilson Compton, "Government versus Desert: The Fallacy of the Shelter Belt," *Forum* 93 (April 1935): 237–39.

15. "Western Kansas Can Have More Grass," *Kansas Farmer,* 13 April 1935.

16. J. N. Darling, "Desert Makers," *Country Gentleman* 105 (October 1935): 5–7, 81.

17. Stuart Chase, "Disaster Rides the Plains," *American Magazine* 124 (September

1937): 46–47, 66–70; Chase, *Rich Land, Poor Land* (New York: McGraw-Hill, 1936), 100–117.

18. Stuart Chase, "When the Crop Lands Go," *Harper's Magazine* 173 (August 1936): 225–33; see also Chase, "Behind the Drought," *Harper's Magazine* 173 (September 1936): 368–77.

19. Rexford Tugwell, quoted in James C. Malin, *History and Ecology: Studies of the Grassland,* ed. by Robert P. Swierenga (Lincoln: University of Nebraska Press, 1984), 45–46; see also R. Douglass Hurt, "National Grasslands: Origin and Development in the Dust Bowl," *Agricultural History* 59 (April 1985): 246–59; Michael E. Lewis, "National Grasslands in the Dust Bowl," *Geographical Review* 79 (April 1989): 161–71.

20. Tugwell, *Battle for Democracy,* 63–64, 123.

21. Ibid., 123, 158–59, 172, 238–39.

22. Morris L. Cooke, "Twenty Years of Grace," *Survey Graphic* 24 (June 1935): 277–82; Wilson, "Agricultural Conservation." See also Jean Christie, "New Deal Resources Planning: The Proposals of Morris L. Cooke," *Agricultural History* 53 (July 1979): 598–602.

23. Wallace, *New Frontiers,* 239–48; see also Schapsmeier and Schapsmeier, "Henry A. Wallace"; Rosenof, "Economic Ideas of Henry A. Wallace."

24. Henry A. Wallace, quoted in Russell Lord, *To Hold This Soil,* Miscellaneous Publication 321, United States Department of Agriculture (Washington, D.C.: U.S. Government Printing Office, 1938), 102–3.

25. Paul Sears, *Deserts on the March* (Norman: University of Oklahoma Press, 1935), passim; Worster, *Dust Bowl,* 199–209; see also Paul Sears, "The Black Blizzards," in *America in Crisis: Fourteen Crucial Episodes in American History,* ed. Daniel Aaron (New York: Knopf, 1952), 287–302.

26. Paul Sears, "Floods and Dust Storms," *Science* 83 (27 March 1936): 9; Sears, "Death from the Soil," *American Mercury* 42 (December 1937): 440–47.

27. Paul Sears, "O, Bury Me Not, Or The Bison Avenged," *New Republic* 90 (12 May 1937): 7–10.

28. Ibid.

29. Isaiah Bowman, "Our Expanding and Contracting Desert," *Geographical Review* 25 (January 1935): 43–61; Bowman, "The Land of Your Possession," *Science* 82 (27 September 1935): 285–93.

30. "Drought and Engineering," *Science* 84 (10 July 1936): 6; see also Sherow, *Watering the Valley,* 120–40.

31. William E. Warne, "Why Irrigation?" *Reclamation Era* 29 (April 1939): 74–76; see also R. Douglass Hurt, "Federal Land Reclamation in the Dust Bowl," *Great Plains Quarterly* 6 (September 1986): 94–106.

32. John C. Page, "Reclamation Fulfills Its Mission," *Reclamation Era* 28 (July 1938): 125–27; see also Page, "Reclamation Offers Solution for Migrant Farmer Problem in the West," *Reclamation Era* 30 (November 1940): 304–8; John Opie, *Ogallala: Water for a Dry Land* (Lincoln: University of Nebraska Press, 1993).

33. National Resources Committee, quoted in "Forestry in Soil Conservation," *Forestry News Digest,* February 1937, 22; see also National Resources Board, *A Report on National Planning and Public Works in Relation to Natural Resources and Including Land Use and Water Resources with Findings and Recommendations* (Washington, D.C.: U.S. Government Printing Office, 1934); Maxwell S. Stewart, *Saving Our Soil,* Public Affairs Pamphlet 14 (New York, 1940), 2.

34. Great Plains Committee, *The Future of the Great Plains,* U.S. Document 144, 75th Congress (Washington, D.C.: U.S. Government Printing Office, 1937), 1, 11, 14, 87.

35. Ibid., 1–6, 16; Gilbert F. White, "The Future of the Great Plains Revisited," *Great Plains Quarterly* 6 (Spring 1986): 84–93; Lowitt, *The New Deal and the West,* 45–46, 60–61.

36. M. M. Leighton, "Geology of Soil Drifting on the Great Plains," *Scientific Monthly* 47 (July 1938): 22–33.

37. "The Prairies Remember," *Science News Letter* 35 (15 April 1939): 239.

38. Graham V. Jacks and Robert O. Whyte, *The Rape of the Earth: A World Survey of Soil Erosion* (London: Faber and Faber, 1939), 170–73.

39. Raymond J. Pool, "White Man versus the Prairie," *Science* 91 (19 January 1940): 53–58.

40. H. H. Bennett, "A Major Effort at Erosion Control," *The Land Today and Tomorrow* 1 (October 1934): 1–4, 20–21; see also Farb, "Hugh Bennett," 19, 40, 42; Wellington Brink, *Big Hugh: The Father of Soil Conservation* (New York: Macmillan, 1951).

41. H. H. Bennett, "Highwayman of the Fields," *Farm Journal* 58 (November 1934): 5, 17; Bennett, "Facing the Erosion Problem," *Science* 81 (5 April 1935): 321–26; see also Bennett, "The Problem of Water and Soil Conservation," February 1935, in Elmer Thomas Collection, Carl Albert Center, University of Oklahoma, Norman, Oklahoma.

42. H. H. Bennett, "A Look at Some of the Western Projects," *Soil Conservation* 1 (November 1935): 1–8; Bennett, "The Vague, Roaming Dust Bowl," *New York Times Magazine,* 26 July 1936, 1, 2, 17.

43. H. H. Bennett, "Emergency and Permanent Control of Wind Erosion in the Great Plains," *Scientific Monthly* 47 (November 1938): 381–99; see also H. H. Finnell, "Control of Wind Erosion on the Southern Great Plains," *The Land Today and Tomorrow* 2 (March 1935): 4–6; Finnell, "Yardsticks and the Four-Card Draw," *Land Policy Review* 3 (October 1940); 19–23.

44. Hugh Hammond Bennett, *Soil Conservation* (New York: McGraw-Hill, 1939), 1–15, 727–31.

45. Ibid., 1–15.

46. Annette Kolodny, *The Lay of the Land: Metaphor as Experience and History in American Life and Letters* (Chapel Hill: University of North Carolina Press, 1975).

47. Jean François Lyotard, *The Postmodern Condition: A Report on Knowledge,* trans. Geoff Bennington and Brian Massumi (Minneapolis: University of Minnesota Press, 1979), 18–31.

Chapter 5

1. Franklin D. Roosevelt, "The Drought," *Vital Speeches* 2 (15 September 1936): 765–68; see also "Drought: Candidate Roosevelt on His Way to a Talk with Candidate Landon," *Newsweek* 8 (5 September 1936): 7.

2. James N. Gregory, *American Exodus: The Dust Bowl Migration and the Okie Culture in California* (New York: Oxford University Press, 1989); see also Roxanne Dunbar-Ortiz, "One or Two Things I Know about Us: Okies in American Culture," *Radical History Review* 59 (Spring 1994): 4–34; Charles J. Shindo, *Dust Bowl Migrants in the American Imagination* (Lawrence: University Press of Kansas, 1997); Benedict Anderson, *Imagined Communities* (London: Verso, 1983).

3. John L. McCarty, "Thou Shalt Not Bear False Witness," John L. McCarty Collection, Amarillo Public Library; Hurt, *Dust Bowl,* 53–60; Vance Johnson, *Heaven's Tableland: The Dust Bowl Story* (New York: Farrar, Straus, 1947), 190–99.

4. John L. McCarty, "A Tribute to Our Sandstorms," John L. McCarty Collection, Amarillo Public Library.

5. "The Tactless Texan," *Amarillo Globe,* 10 April 1935; Hurt, *Dust Bowl,* 54–57; *Amarillo Globe,* 27 March, 24 April 1935; David L. Nail, *One Short Sleep Past: A Profile of Amarillo in the Thirties* (Canyon, Tex.: Staked Plains Press, 1973), 21–27, 113–18.

6. J. F. Jarrell, "Erroneous Impressions of the Dust Bowl Corrected," *Earth* 32 (October 1935): 6–7; J. C. Mohler, "Kansas Comes through Bad Crop Season despite State's Defamers," *Earth* 31 (August 1934): 4; see also "Absurd Statements about Dust Storms in the Great Southwest," *Earth* 34 (April 1937): 12.

7. T. A. McNeal, "I Pay Tribute to Real Courage," *Kansas Farmer,* 11 April 1936.

8. George Riley Hall, "Our Big Problem in the Next 50 Years," *Daily Oklahoman,* 23 April 1939; see also W. Richard Fossy, "Talkin' Dust Bowl Blues: A Study of Oklahoma's Cultural Identity during the Great Depression," *Chronicles of Oklahoma* 55 (Spring 1977): 12–33.

9. The metaphor of the "stickers" may be traced to a collection of essays by Wallace Stegner. See Stegner, *Where the Bluebird Sings to the Lemonade Springs: Living and Writing in the American West* (New York: Penguin, 1992), xxii–xiii, 115–16; see also Paula Nelson, *The Prairie Winnows Out Its Own.*

10. Caroline A. Henderson, "Letters from the Dust Bowl," *Atlantic Monthly* 157 (May 1936): 540–51; see also Evelyn Harris and Caroline Henderson, "Letters of Two Women Farmers. I," *Atlantic Monthly* 152 (August 1933): 236–45; Harris and Henderson, "Letters of Two Women Farmers. II," *Atlantic Monthly* 152 (September 1933): 349–56; Virginia C. Purdy, "Dust to Eat: A Document from the Dust Bowl," *Chronicles of Oklahoma* 58 (Winter 1980–81): 440–54.

11. Henderson, "Letters from the Dust Bowl," 540–51; Caroline A. Henderson, "Spring in the Dust Bowl," *Atlantic Monthly* 159 (June 1937): 615–17; see also Gregory, *American Exodus,* 148.

12. Lawrence S. Morris, "The Economics of Eden," *Christian Century* 51 (4 July 1934):

891–93; Paul C. Ellis, "Next Spring," *Christian Century* 52 (20 February 1935): 239–40; Buren Sparks, "When Rain Came to the Desert," *Baptist Standard* (Texas), 31 January 1935; J. S. Ploughe, "Out of the Dust," *Christian Century* 52 (22 May 1935): 691–92.

13. "Wheat and Dust," *Time* 25 (22 April 1935): 66–68.

14. "Agriculture: Mother Nature Lays Down a Withering, Calamitous New Deal," 3–4; "Agriculture: Unprecedented Heat Brings Death and Destruction to Half of the United States"; "Drought: Uncle Sam Looks at His Lean Larder and Acts"; "Agriculture: 500,000,000 Tons of Dust Cover Kansas and Points East"; "Dust: More Storms Wreak Destruction in the Southwest"; "Drought: Worst in History of United States."

15. H. L. Mencken, "The Dole for Bogus Farmers," *American Mercury* 39 (December 1936): 400–408.

16. Ibid.

17. Ibid., 404, 407.

18. Sherwood Anderson, *Puzzled America* (New York: Charles Scribner's Sons, 1935), 203–17; see also Harvey Swados, *The American Writer and the Great Depression* (Indianapolis: Bobbs-Merrill, 1969).

19. Walter Davenport, "How Dry We Are," *Collier's* 87 (11 April 1931): 25, 43–44; Davenport, "Land Where Our Children Die," *Collier's* 100 (18 September 1937): 12–13, 73–77.

20. Davenport, "Land Where Our Children Die."

21. O. D. Duncan Papers, Special Collections and University Archives, Oklahoma State University, Stillwater, Oklahoma; Ralph Perkins, "Relief Work in a Dust Bowl Community," *Sociology and Social Research* 23 (July–August 1939): 539–45; Herbert Heaton, "Migration and Cheap Land: The End of Two Chapters," *Sociological Review* 26 (July 1934): 231–48; Harry C. McDean, "Social Scientists and Farm Poverty on the North American Plains, 1933–1940," *Great Plains Quarterly* 3 (Winter 1983): 17–29.

22. Josephine Strode, "Kansas Grit," *Survey* 72 (August 1936): 230–31.

23. Paul S. Taylor, "Again the Covered Wagon," *Survey Graphic* 24 (July 1935): 348–51, 368; see also Lange and Taylor, *American Exodus;* Shindo, *Dust Bowl Migrants,* 47–50.

24. Eric Thane, "Dark Retreat," *Frontier and Midland* 18 (Winter 1937–38): 73–76.

25. Morrow Mayo, "The Man with a Tractor," *Harper's Magazine* 177 (November 1938): 622–24.

26. "Boren Answers *The Grapes of Wrath*," *Daily Oklahoman,* 24 January 1940; Jerry Wilson, "Depression, Dust, and Defiance: Literature of the Dust Bowl Refugees," *North Dakota Quarterly* 56 (Winter 1988): 260–72; Marsha L. Weisiger, "The Reception of *The Grapes of Wrath* in Oklahoma: A Reappraisal," *Chronicles of Oklahoma* 70 (Winter 1992–93): 394–415; see also Louis Owens, *The Grapes of Wrath: Trouble in the Promised Land* (Boston: Twayne, 1989).

27. John Steinbeck, *The Grapes of Wrath* (1939; rpt. New York: Viking, 1986) 1–7; Michael G. Barry, "Degrees of Mediation and Their Political Value in Steinbeck's *Grapes of Wrath*," in *The Steinbeck Question: New Essays in Criticism,* ed. Don Noble (Troy, N.Y.: Whitston, 1993), 108–24; see also Susan Beegel, Susan Shillinglaw, and Wesley Tiffney Jr.,

eds., *Steinbeck and the Environment: Interdisciplinary Approaches* (Tuscaloosa: University of Alabama Press, 1997).

28. Steinbeck, *Grapes of Wrath*, 22–26; Owens, *Grapes of Wrath*, 21–95; Wilson, "Depression, Dust, and Defiance," 260–72; David N. Cassuto, "Turning Wine into Water: Water as Privileged Signifier in *The Grapes of Wrath*," in *Steinbeck and the Environment*, ed. Beegel, Shillinglaw, and Tiffney, 55–75.

29. Steinbeck, *Grapes of Wrath*, 35, 47.

30. Frederick Manfred, *The Golden Bowl*, introduction by John R. Milton (1944; rpt. Albuquerque: University of New Mexico Press, 1976), 3–10; Wilson, "Depression, Dust, and Defiance," 260–72.

31. Manfred, *Golden Bowl*, 11–39; see also Western Literature Association, *A Literary History of the American West* (Fort Worth: Texas Christian University Press, 1987), 792–805; Quantic, *Nature of the Place*, 83–86.

32. Manfred, *Golden Bowl*, 194–208, 209.

33. Ibid., 209–26.

34. Joe Klein, *Woody Guthrie: A Life* (New York: Knopf, 1980), 1–74; Malone, *Country Music, USA*, 32–135; Richard A. Pascal, "Walt Whitman and Woody Guthrie: American Prophet Singers and Their People," *Journal of American Studies* 24 (April 1990): 41–59; see also Brad Lookingbill, "Dusty Apocalypse and Socialist Salvation: A Study of Woody Guthrie's Dust Bowl Imagery," *Chronicles of Oklahoma* 72 (Winter 1994–95): 396–413.

35. Woody Guthrie, *Library of Congress Recordings* (Elektra Records, 1964), Side 1; Woody Guthrie, *Pastures of Plenty: A Self Portrait of Woody Guthrie*, ed. David Marsh and Harold Levanthol (New York: Harper Collins, 1990), 43–44.

36. Woody Guthrie, "Dust Storm Disaster," *Dust Bowl Ballads* (Folkways FH 5212, 1964): Side 1; Woody Guthrie, "Dusty Old Dust," *Dust Bowl Ballads* (Folkways FH 5212, 1964): Side 2.

37. Woody Guthrie, "Dust Can't Kill Me," *Dust Bowl Ballads* (Folkways FH 5212, 1964): Side 1; Woody Guthrie, "End of My Line," *The Woody Guthrie Songbook*, ed. Harold Levanthol and Marjorie Guthrie (New York: Grosset and Dunlap, 1976), 101.

38. Woody Guthrie, "I Ain't Got No Home," *Dust Bowl Ballads* (Folkways FH 5212, 1964): Side 1; Woody Guthrie, "Dust Bowl Refugee," *Dust Bowl Ballads* (Folkways FH 5212, 1964): Side 2; Woody Guthrie, "Talking Dust Bowl Blues," *Dust Bowl Ballads* (Folkways FH 5212, 1964): Side 1; Woody Guthrie, "Dust Bowl Blues," *Dust Bowl Ballads* (Folkways FH 5212, 1964): Side 2; Woody Guthrie, "Blowin' Down This Road," *Dust Bowl Ballads* (Folkways FH 5212, 1964): Side 2; Woody Guthrie, "Do Re Mi," *Dust Bowl Ballads* (Folkways FH 5212, 1964): Side 2.

39. Woody Guthrie, "Tom Joad," *Dust Bowl Ballads* (Folkways FH 5212, 1964): Side 2; H. R. Stoneback, "Rough People . . . Are the Best Singers: Woody Guthrie, John Steinbeck, and Folksong," in *Steinbeck Question*, 143–70.

40. Klein, *Woody Guthrie,* 143–44.

41. Lawrence Svobida, *An Empire of Dust* (Caldwell, Ida.: Caxton, 1940), 7–8; see also Riney-Kehrberg, *Rooted in Dust,* 112–13.

42. Svobida, *Empire of Dust,* 13–20, 29, 32, 172.

43. Ibid., 59, 70, 80–81.

44. Ibid., 95–96.

45. Ibid., 105, 123–24, 142, 166, 169, 185, 198–203.

46. Thomas A. Tripp, "Dust Bowl Tragedy," *Christian Century* 57 (24 January 1940): 108–10.

47. Don Eddy, "Up from the Dust," *American Magazine* 129 (April 1940): 54–55, 89–92.

48. Joseph Campbell, *The Hero with a Thousand Faces* (New York: Pantheon, 1949); see also Charles R. Hearn, *The American Dream in the Great Depression* (Westport, Conn.: Greenwood Press, 1977); Robert Sklar, *Movie-Made America* (New York: Random House, 1975).

49. John R. Wunder, Frances W. Kaye, and Vernon Carstensen, eds., *Americans View Their Dust Bowl Experience* (Niwot: University Press of Colorado, 1999), 113–19; Nail, *One Short Sleep Past,* 122–23.

50. William Leuchtenburg, *Franklin D. Roosevelt and the New Deal, 1932–1940* (New York: Harper & Row, 1963); Arthur M. Schlesinger Jr., *The Coming of the New Deal* (Boston: Houghton Mifflin, 1958); see also Alan Brinkley, *The End of Reform: New Deal Liberalism in Recession and War* (New York: Knopf, 1995); Steve Fraser and Gary Gerstle, eds., *The Rise and Fall of the New Deal Order, 1930–1980* (Princeton: Princeton University Press, 1989); Doris Kearns Goodwin, *No Ordinary Time* (New York: Simon and Schuster, 1994).

51. "The Tactless Texan," *Amarillo Globe,* 10 March 1933.

Chapter 6

1. T. Jackson Lears, *No Place of Grace: Antimodernism and the Transformation of American Culture* (1981; rpt. New York: Pantheon, 1983), xii; see also Warren I. Susman, *Culture as History: The Transformation of American Society in the Twentieth Century* (New York: Pantheon, 1984): 27–38; Klein, *Frontiers of Historical Imagination,* 58–91; Schama, *Landscape and Memory.* For an ironic view on the misinformation created by empirical methods, see Greil Marcus, *The Dustbin of History* (Cambridge, Mass.: Harvard University Press, 1995).

2. "Hail to the Pioneers," *Amarillo Sunday News-Globe* (Texas), 21 September 1930; Seth Holman, "Farmers of Plains Weather Hectic 1930 Economic Storm," *Amarillo Sunday News-Globe,* 28 December 1930, 5 January 1931.

3. F. D. Farrell, "The Story of Kansas, a Blooming Desert," *Earth* 28 (December 1931): 1–2.

4. "Editor Broadcasting," *Earth* 29 (December 1932): 10.

5. Webb, *Great Plains,* rpt. 140–225; see also William Cronon, "A Place for Stories: Nature, History, and Narrative," *Journal of American History* 78 (March 1992): 1155–56.

6. Webb, *Great Plains,* 184–202.

7. Ibid., 485–515; see also Martyn J. Bowden, "The Great American Desert in the American Mind," in *Geographies of the Mind,* ed. David Lowenthal and Martyn Bowden (New York: Oxford University Press, 1976), 119–47.

8. Isaiah Bowman, *The Pioneer Fringe* (New York: American Geographical Society, 1931), 111–42.

9. "Agriculture's Key Position," *Kansas Farmer* (Topeka), 23 January 1932; Arthur Capper, "Better Times on the Way Back," *Kansas Farmer,* 20 August 1933.

10. Hazel Barrington Selby, "Dirge for a Pioneer," *Frontier* 12 (May 1932): 309.

11. "Helping Themselves," *Clark County Clipper* (Kansas), 19 July 1934; see also Riney-Kehrberg, *Rooted in Dust,* 81, 169–70.

12. Garford Wilkinson, "Eastern Dust Damage Exaggerations Are Malicious Lies," *Amarillo Sunday News-Globe,* 5 April 1936; *Amarillo Daily News,* 17 December 1937.

13. William M. Wells, *The Desert's Hidden Wealth: The Life Story of a Man of the American People* (n.p. 1934), passim.

14. Ibid., 225–30.

15. Ibid., 13–14.

16. John A. Piquet, "Our Unconquered Frontier," *Scribner's Magazine* 96 (December 1934): 354–58.

17. Margaret Bourke-White, "The Drought," *Fortune* 10 (October 1934): 76–83.

18. E. Martindale, "The Great American Desert," *Warsaw Times* (Missouri), 4 April 1935.

19. F. D. Helm, "Reclamation as a Federal Investment," *Reclamation Era* 25 (March 1935): 63, 66; see also E. B. Debler, "Stabilization by Irrigation," *Reclamation Era* 30 (November 1940): 309–11; Hurt, "Federal Land Reclamation in the Dust Bowl."

20. N. E. Winters, "Declaration of Independence," *Sooner State Erosion News* 2 (July 1935): 1, in Elmer Thomas Collection, Carl Albert Center, University of Oklahoma, Norman, Oklahoma.

21. O. O. Waggener, *Western Agriculture and the Burlington* (Chicago: Agricultural Development Department of the Chicago, Burlington, and Quincy Railroad, 1938); see Val Kuska Collection, Nebraska State Historical Society, Lincoln, Nebraska.

22. Michel Foucault, "Nietzsche, Genealogy, History," in *The Postmodern History Reader,* ed. Keith Jenkins (London: Routledge, 1997), 124–26; see also Munslow, *Deconstructing History.*

23. John Ise, *Sod and Stubble* (New York: Wilson-Erickson, 1936), 2, 126, 258–59, 325.

24. Edith Kohl, *Land of the Burnt Thigh* (1938; rpt. St. Paul: Minnesota Historical Society, 1986), xxxiii–xxxiv.

25. Ibid., 228–35, 285, 296.

26. Bernard DeVoto, "The West: A Plundered Province," *Harper's Magazine* 169 (Au-

gust 1934): 355–64; Louis M. Hacker, "Plowing the Farmer Under," *Harper's Magazine* 169 (June 1934): 60–74; Louis B. Schmidt, "The Agricultural Revolution in the Prairies and Great Plains of the United States," *Agricultural History* 8 (October 1934): 169–95.

27. J. Evetts Haley, "Cow Business and Monkey Business," *Saturday Evening Post* 207 (8 December 1934): 26–29, 94–96; see also Howard Lamar, ed., "Haley, James Evetts, Sr." *The New Encyclopedia of the American West* (New Haven: Yale University Press, 1998), 465–66.

28. J. Evetts Haley, "Texas Control of Texas Soil," *West Texas Today,* July 1936, 14–16.

29. J. Evetts Haley, "Panhandle Hopeful of Future as Plans Made for Fight on Worst Dust Storm in History," *Dallas Morning News,* 17 April 1935, 1; Haley, "Texas Control of Texas Soil."

30. Rupert N. Richardson, "Some Historical Factors Contributing to the Problems of the Great Plains," *Southwestern Social Science Quarterly* 18 (June 1937): 1–14; see also Howard Lamar, ed., "Richardson, Rupert N." *New Encyclopedia of the American West,* 961–62.

31. William Allen White, *The Changing West* (New York: Macmillan, 1939), 5–6, 53–54, 71, 79, 89, 137; see also Shortridge, *Middle West,* 126–29.

32. White, *The Changing West,* 71, 79, 89, 137.

33. Alfred B. Sears, "The Desert Threat in the Southern Great Plains," *Agricultural History* 15 (January 1941): 1–11.

34. Ibid.

35. Frederick Lewis Allen, *Since Yesterday: The Nineteen Thirties in America* (New York: Harper Brothers, 1940), 196–214.

36. Ibid.

37. Kunigunde Duncan, "Reclaiming the Dust Bowl," *Nation* 149 (9 September 1939): 269–71.

38. Ibid., 271.

39. Bliss Isely, "Unwhipped Dust Bowl Heroes Won't Budge," *Nation's Business* 29 (November 1941): 27–28, 86–87.

Epilogue

1. "Letters," W. S. Campbell Collection, Box 34, Folders 14 and 15, Western History Collections, University of Oklahoma, Norman, Oklahoma; see also Gary Anderson, *Sitting Bull and the Paradox of Lakota Nationhood* (New York: Harper Collins, 1996), 175.

2. J. S. Russell, "We Know How to Prevent Dust Bowls," *Journal of Soil and Water Conservation* 10 (July 1955): 171–75; see R. Douglass Hurt, "Return of the Dust Bowl: The Filthy Fifties," *Journal of the West* 18 (October 1979): 85–93.

3. Deborah Epstein Popper and Frank J. Popper, "The Great Plains: From Dust to Dust," *Planning* 53 (December 1987): 12–18; Riney-Kehrberg, *Rooted in Dust,* 175–81; see also John R. Borchert, "The Dust Bowl in the 1970s," *Annals of the Association of American*

Geographers 61 (March 1971): 1–22; Richard Manning, *Grassland: The History, Biology, Politics, and Promise of the American Prairie* (New York: Penguin, 1995).

4. 10,000 Maniacs, "Dust Bowl," *Blind Man's Zoo,* Elektra 60815, 1989; William K. Stevens, "Great Plains or Great Desert? A Sea of Dunes Lies in Wait," *New York Times,* 28 May 1996, B5; Nancy Harbert, "Bone Dry," *Time* 147 (10 June 1996), 5–11; Hugh Sidey, "Echoes of the Great Dust Bowl," *Time* 147 (10 June 1996), 5–11; Mark Alan Hughes, "Welfare Dust Bowl," *Washington Post,* 25 September 1996, A23; "Surviving the Dust Bowl," *The American Experience,* PBS Home Video, A3276, 1998.

5. Yi-fu Tuan, *Landscapes of Fear* (New York: Pantheon, 1979); see also Manning, *Grassland,* 281–82; Klein, *Frontiers of Historical Imagination,* 297–99.

6. William E. Riebsame, "The Dust Bowl: Historical Image, Psychological Anchor, and Ecological Taboo," *Great Plains Quarterly* 6 (Spring 1986): 127–36; Cronon, "A Place for Stories"; Demeritt, "Nature of Metaphors"; Charles Shindo, "The Dust Bowl Myth," *Wilson Quarterly* 24 (Autumn 2000); 25–30.

Selected Bibliography

PRIMARY SOURCES

Manuscript Collections

Amarillo Public Library. Amarillo, Texas.
    John L. McCarty Collection.

Carl Albert Center. University of Oklahoma. Norman, Oklahoma.
    Elmer Thomas Collection.
    Wilburn Cartwright Collection.
    William H. Murray Collection.

Kansas State Historical Society. Topeka, Kansas.
    Arthur Capper Papers.

Nebraska State Historical Society. Lincoln, Nebraska.
    Val Kuska Collection.

No Man's Land Historical Museum. Goodwell, Oklahoma.
    Miscellaneous Poems and Scrapbooks.

Oklahoma Historical Society. Oklahoma City, Oklahoma.
    Foreman Collection.

Special Collections and University Archives. Oklahoma State University. Stillwater,
    Oklahoma.
    O. D. Duncan Papers.
    H. H. Finnell Papers.

Southwest Collection. Texas Tech University. Lubbock, Texas.
    Dust Bowl Clippings.

Western History Collection. University of Oklahoma. Norman, Oklahoma.
    W. S. Campbell Collection.

Government Publications

Bell, Earl H. *Culture of a Contemporary Rural Community: Sublette, Kansas.* Rural Life Stud-
    ies: 2. Bureau of Agricultural Economics, United States Department of Agriculture.
    Washington, D.C.: U.S. Government Printing Office, 1942.

Chilcott, E. F. *Preventing Soil Blowing.* Farmer's Bulletin 1771. United States Department of
    Agriculture. Washington, D.C.: U.S. Government Printing Office, 1937.

Cole, J. S., and G. W. Morgan. *Implements and Methods of Tillage to Control Soil Blowing on
    the Northern Great Plains.* Farmer's Bulletin 1797. United States Department of Agri-
    culture. Washington, D.C.: U.S. Government Printing Office, 1938.

Cronin, F. D., and H. W. Beers. *Areas of Intense Drought Distress, 1930–1936.* Research Bul-
    letin. Series 5. National Division of Social Research. Works Progress Administration.
    Washington, D.C.: U.S. Government Printing Office, 1937.

Edwards, A. D. *Influence of Drought and Depression on a Rural Community: A Case Study in
    Haskell County Kansas.* Social Research Report 7. Farm Security Administration and
    Bureau of Agricultural Economics. United States Department of Agriculture. Wash-
    ington, D.C.: U.S. Government Printing Office, 1939.

Great Plains Committee (Harlan H. Barrows; H. H. Bennett; Morris L. Cooke, Chairman;
    L. C. Gray; F. C. Harrington; Richard C. Moore; John C. Page; Harlow S. Person). *The
    Future of the Great Plains.* Washington, D.C.: U.S. Government Printing Office, 1937.

Johnstone, Paul F. *Farmers in a Changing World.* Yearbook of Agriculture. United States De-
    partment of Agriculture. Washington, D.C.: U.S. Goverment Printing Office, 1940.

Kifer, R. S., and H. L. Stewart. *Farming Hazards in the Drought Area.* Research Monograph
    16. National Division of Social Research. Works Progress Administration. Washington,
    D.C.: U.S. Government Printing Office, 1938.

Link, Irene. *Relief and Rehabilitation in the Drought Area.* Research Bulletin Series 5, No. 3.
    National Division of Social Research. Works Progress Administration. Washington,
    D.C.: U.S. Government Printing Office, 1937.

Lord, Russell. *To Hold This Soil.* Miscellaneous Publication 321. United States Department
    of Agriculture. Washington, D.C.: U.S. Government Printing Office, 1938.

National Resources Board. *A Report on National Planning and Public Works in Relation to
    Natural Resources and Including Land Use and Water Resources with Findings and Rec-
    ommendations.* Washington, D.C.: U.S. Government Printing Office, 1934.

Rule, Glenn K. *Crops Against the Wind.* Farmer's Bulletin 1833. United States Department
    of Agriculture. Washington, D.C.: U.S. Government Printing Office, 1939.

Taeuber, Conrad, and Carl C. Taylor. *The People of the Drought States.* Research Bulletin Se-
    ries 5, No. 2. National Division of Social Research. Works Progress Administration.
    Washington, D.C.: U.S. Government Printing Office, 1937.

U.S. Bureau of the Census. *Census of Religious Bodies: 1936.* Washington, D.C.: U.S. Gov-
    ernment Printing Office, 1941.

U.S. Department of Commerce. *Thirteenth Census of the United States: 1910.* Washington, D.C.: U.S. Government Printing Office, 1913.

U.S. Department of Commerce. *Fourteenth Census of the United States: 1920.* Washington, D.C.: U.S. Government Printing Office, 1923.

U.S. Department of Commerce. *Fifteenth Census of the United States: 1930.* Washington, D.C.: U.S. Government Printing Office, 1933.

U.S. Department of Commerce. *Sixteenth Census of the United States: 1940.* Washington, D.C.: U.S. Government Printing Office, 1941.

Whitfield, Charles. J., and J. A. Perrin. *Sand-Dune Reclamation in the Southern Great Plains.* Farmer's Bulletin 1825. United States Department of Agriculture. Washington, D.C.: U.S. Government Printing Office, 1939.

Pamphlets

American National Cattlemen's Association. *If and When It Rains: The Stockman's View of the Range Question.* Denver: n.p., 1938.

Clements, Frederic, and Ralph Chaney. *Environment and Life in the Great Plains.* Supplemental Publication 24. Carnegie Institution. Washington, D.C.: Carnegie Institution, 1937.

Public Affairs Committee. *Farm Policies Under the New Deal.* Public Affairs Pamphlet 16. New York: Public Affairs Committee, 1938.

Sanderson, Dwight. *Research Memorandum on Rural Life in the Great Depression.* New York: Social Science Research Council, 1937.

Stewart, Maxwell S. *Saving Our Soil.* Public Affairs Pamphlet 14. New York: Public Affairs Committee, 1940.

Vance, Rupert B. *Farmers Without Land.* Public Affairs Pamphlet 12. New York: Public Affairs Committee, 1937.

Waggener, O. O. *Western Agriculture and the Burlington.* Chicago: Agricultural Development Department of the Chicago, Burlington, and Quincy Railroad Company, 1938.

Monographs

Allen, Frederick Lewis. *Since Yesterday: The Nineteen Thirties in America.* New York: Harper Brothers, 1940.

Baker, O. E., Ralph Bordosi, and M. L. Wilson. *Agriculture in Modern Life.* New York: Harper, 1939.

Bennett, Hugh Hammond. *Soil Conservation.* New York: McGraw-Hill, 1939.

Bowman, Isaiah. *The Pioneer Fringe.* New York: American Geographical Society, 1931.

Brunner, Edmund, and Irving Lorge. *Rural Trends in Depression Years.* New York: Columbia University Press, 1937.

Chase, Stuart. *Rich Land, Poor Land.* New York: McGraw-Hill, 1936.

Ickes, Harold L. *The New Democracy.* New York: Norton, 1934.

Ise, John. *Sod and Stubble.* New York: Wilson-Erickson, 1936.

Jacks, Graham V., and Robert O. Whyte. *Rape of the Earth: A World Survey of Soil Erosion.* London: Faber and Faber, 1939.

Kohl, Edith. *Land of the Burnt Thigh.* 1938; reprint, St. Paul: Minnesota Historical Society, 1986.

Kolb, J. H., and Edmund S. Brunner. *Rural Social Trends.* New York: McGraw-Hill, 1933.

Landon, Alfred M. *America at the Crossroads.* New York: Dodge, 1936.

McWilliams, Cary. *Ill Fares the Land.* Boston: Little, Brown, 1942.

Minton, Bruce, and John Stuart. *The Fat Years and the Lean.* New York: Modern Age Books, 1940.

Mitchell, Lucy Sprang, et al. *My Country 'tis of Thee: The Use and Abuse of Natural Resources.* New York: Macmillan, 1940.

Sears, Paul. *Deserts on the March.* Norman: University of Oklahoma Press, 1935.

Tugwell, Rexford. *The Battle for Democracy.* New York: Columbia University Press, 1935.

Turner, Frederick Jackson. *The Frontier in American History.* 1920; reprint, New York: Holt, Rinehart and Winston, 1960.

Van Hise, Charles Richard. *The Conservation of Natural Resources in the United States.* New York: Macmillan, 1910.

Wallace, Henry A. *New Frontiers.* New York: Reynal and Hitchcock, 1934.

White, William Allen. *The Changing West.* New York: Macmillan, 1939.

Webb, Walter P. *Divided We Stand: The Crisis of a Frontierless Democracy.* New York: Farrar and Rinehart, 1937.

———.*The Great Plains.* 1931; reprint, Lincoln: University of Nebraska Press, 1981.

Wells, William M. *The Desert's Hidden Wealth: The Life Story of a Man of the American People.* N.p., 1934.

Literature and Memoirs

Anderson, Sherwood. *Puzzled America.* New York: Charles Scribner's Sons, 1935.

Burton, Richard. *The City of the Saints and Across the Rocky Mountains to California.* Reprinted as *The Look of the West, 1860: Across the Plains to California.* Lincoln: University of Nebraska Press, n.d.; originally published 1862.

Garland, Hamlin. *Jason Edwards: An Average Man.* Boston: Arena, 1892.

Guthrie, Woody. *Bound for Glory.* New York: E. P. Dutton, 1943.

———. *Pastures of Plenty: A Self Portrait of Woody Guthrie.* Edited by David Marsh and Harold Levanthol. New York: Harper Collins, 1990.

———. *The Woody Guthrie Songbook.* Edited by Harold Levanthol and Marjorie Guthrie. New York: Grosset and Dunlap, 1976.

Hudson, Lois. *The Bones of Plenty.* Boston: Atlantic Monthly Press, 1962.

———. *Reapers of the Dust.* Boston: Little, Brown, 1964.

Lorentz, Pare. *FDR's Moviemaker: Memoirs and Scripts.* Reno: University of Nevada Press, 1992.

Low, Ann Marie. *Dust Bowl Diary.* Lincoln: University of Nebraska Press, 1984.

MacLeish, Archibald. *Land of the Free.* New York: Harcourt Brace, 1938.

Manfred, Fredrick. *The Golden Bowl.* Introduction by John R. Milton. 1944; reprint, Albuquerque: University of New Mexico Press, 1976.

McCarty, John L., ed. *Wind in the Cottonwoods.* Dalhart, Tex.: Dalhart, 1936.

Parkman, Francis. *The Oregon Trail.* 1849; reprint New York: Signet, 1950.

Pyle, Ernie. *Ernie's America: The Best of Ernie Pyle's 1930s Travel Dispatches.* Edited by David Nichols, New York: Harper Collins, 1990.

———. *Home Country.* New York: William Sloane Associates, 1947.

Steinbeck, John. *The Grapes of Wrath.* 1939; reprint, New York: Viking, 1986.

Svobida, Lawrence. *An Empire of Dust.* Caldwell, Ida.: Caxton, 1940.

Vestal, Stanley. *Short Grass Country.* New York: Duell, Sloan, and Pearce, 1941.

Audio/Visual Texts

Guthrie, Woody. *Dust Bowl Ballads.* Victor Records, two discs (P-28,P-27), 1940; RCA Victor (LPV 502), n.d.; Folkways (FH 5212), 1964.

———. *Library of Congress Recordings.* Elektra Records, 1965.

Lange, Dorothea, and Paul Taylor. *An American Exodus: A Record of Human Erosion.* New York: Reynal and Hitchcock, 1939.

Lorentz, Pare. *The Plow That Broke the Plains: A U.S. Documentary Film.* United States Resettlement Administration. Washington, D.C., 1936.

"Surviving the Dust Bowl." *The American Experience.* PBS Home Video. A3276, 1998.

10,000 Maniacs. *Blind Man's Zoo.* Elektra 60815, 1989.

Articles

"Absurd Statements about Dust Storms in the Great Southwest." *Earth* 34 (April 1937): 12.

Adams, Hancock. "Better Days for Farmers." *National Republic* 19 (August 1931): 5–6, 45.

"Agriculture: Mother Nature Lays Down a Withering, Calamitous New Deal." *Newsweek* 3 (9 June 1934): 3–4.

"Agriculture: 500,000,000 Tons of Dust Cover Kansas and Points East." *Newsweek* 5 (30 March 1935): 5–6.

"Agriculture: Unprecedented Heat Brings Death and Destruction to Half of the United States." *Newsweek* 4 (4 August 1935): 6–7.

Allin, Bushrod W. "Migration Required for Best Land Use." *Journal of Farm Economics* 18 (August 1936): 493–99.

"Areas of Drought Pray for Rain." *Literary Digest* 121 (20 June 1936): 32.

"Arid Farming and Ecology." *Scientific American* 159 (November 1938): 233.

"At the Observation Post." *Literary Digest* 118 (11 August 1934): 9.

"Attack on Drought." *Literary Digest* 122 (25 July 1936): 4.

"Autumn Drought." *Newsweek* 14 (6 November 1939): 57.

Bach, Julian S. "Corn, Hogs, and Drought." *New Republic* 81 (5 December 1934): 98–99.

Bainer, H. M. "Panhandle and South Plains of Texas." *Earth* 33 (August 1936): 6–7.

Bennett, H. H. "Emergency and Permanent Control of Wind Erosion in the Great Plains." *Scientific Monthly* 47 (November 1938): 381–99.

———. "Facing the Erosion Problem." *Science* 81 (5 April 1935): 321–26.

———. "Highwayman of the Fields." *Farm Journal* 58 (November 1934): 5, 17.

———. "A Look at Some of the Western Projects." *Soil Conservation* 1 (November 1935): 1–8.

———. "A Major Effort at Erosion Control." *The Land Today and Tomorrow* 1 (October 1934): 1–4, 20–21.

———. "The Vague, Roaming Dust Bowl." *New York Times Magazine*, 26 July 1936, 1, 2, 17.

"Best Part of the Earth." *Earth* 29 (December 1932): 10.

Blackmer, Francesca M. "The West, Water, and the Grazing Laws." *Survey Graphic* 26 (July 1937): 387.

Bourke-White, Margaret. "The Drought." *Fortune* 10 (October 1934): 76–83.

———. "Dust Changes America." *Nation* 140 (22 May 1935): 597–98.

Bowman, Isaiah. "Land of Your Possession." *Science* 82 (27 September 1935): 285–93.

———. "Our Expanding and Contracting Desert." *Geographical Review* 25 (January 1935): 43–61.

Boyle, James. "The AAA: An Epitaph." *Atlantic Monthly* 157 (February 1936): 217–25.

Brown, Earl, et al. "Dust Storms and Their Possible Effect on Health with Special Reference to the Dust Storms of Kansas in 1935." *Public Health Reports* 50 (4 October 1935): 1369–83.

Bruere, M. B. "Lifting the Drought." *Survey Graphic* 23 (November 1934): 544–47.

Brundy, Clyde M. "Trees for the Prairies." *American Forests* 39 (December 1933): 553–55, 574.

Burrill, Meredith F. "Geography and the Relief Problem in Texas and Oklahoma." *Southwestern Social Science Quarterly* 17 (December 1936): 294–302.

Call, L. E. "Conditions in Western Kansas." *The Land Today and Tomorrow* 2 (April 1935): 8–11.

———. "The Plains Farmer and the Changing World." *Biennial Report of Kansas State Board of Agriculture* 37 (1939–40): 13–24.

"The Call of the Land." *Commonweal* 20 (25 May 1934): 85–86.

Campbell, J. M. "In the Country." *Commonweal* 15 (3 February 1932): 378–80.

Carlson, Avis. "Dust." *New Republic* 82 (1 May 1935): 32–33.

———. "Dust Blowing." *Harper's Magazine* 171 (July 1935): 149–58.

Carroll, Raymond G. "Shelterbelt." *Saturday Evening Post* 208 (5 October 1935): 23, 81–85.

Caulfield, John H. "The Dust Storm Serves Notice." *Farm and Ranch* 53 (15 September 1934): 2, 3, 9.

Chase, Stuart. "Behind the Drought." *Harper's Magazine* 173 (September 1936): 368–77.

———. "Disaster Rides the Plains." *American Magazine* 124 (September 1937): 46–47, 66–70.

———. "When the Crop Lands Go." *Harper's Magazine* 173 (August 1936): 225–33.

Choun, F. H. "Duststorms in the Southwestern Plains Area." *Monthly Weather Review* 64 (June 1936): 198–99.

Clayton, C. F. "Program of the Federal Government for the Purchase and Use of Submarginal Land." *Journal of Farm Economics* 17 (February 1935): 55–63.

Cleave, Van. "Some of the Biological Effects of Drought." *Scientific Monthly* 33 (October 1931): 301–6.

Clements, Frederic. "Climatic Cycles and Human Populations in the Great Plains." *Scientific Monthly* 47 (September 1938): 193–210.

Collins, John M. "Best Kansas Wheat Is in the Dust Bowl." *New York Times*, 19 February 1939, Section 3, 1–2.

————. "A Dust Bowl Revives." *Christian Science Monitor* (Weekly Magazine), 4 August 1937, 1–2.

Compton, Wilson. "The Government versus Desert: The Fallacy of the Shelter Belt." *Forum* 93 (April 1935): 237–39.

Cooke, Morris L. "Twenty Years of Grace." *Survey Graphic* 24 (June 1935): 277–82.

Cox, William T. "Do Droughts Explain the Prairies?" *American Forests* 42 (December 1936): 556–57.

"Creeping Disaster." *Business Week*, 28 July 1934, 36.

Dailey, Joseph L. "Is the West Drying Up?" *Nation's Agriculture* 11 (September 1936): 2–3, 10.

Darling, J. N. "Desert Makers." *Country Gentleman* 105 (October 1935): 5–7, 81.

"Data on the Drought." *Science* 80 (24 August 1934): 179.

Davenport, Walter. "How Dry We Are." *Collier's* 87 (11 April 1931): 25, 43–44.

————. "Land Where Our Children Die." *Collier's* 100 (18 September 1937): 12–13, 73–77.

Davis, Chester. "Farmers Still Want the AAA." *Forum* 95 (February 1936): 76–79.

————. "If Drought Strikes Again." *Saturday Evening Post* 207 (27 April 1935): 23, 76–80.

————. "Lost Acres." *American Magazine* 121 (February 1936): 63, 127–29.

————. "Rise of Grass." *Country Gentleman* 106 (January 1936): 18, 66, 68, 69.

————. "Toward Planned Harvests." *Review of Reviews* 88 (December 1933): 19–21, 52.

Dawber, Mark A. "The Churches in the Dust Bowl." *Missionary Review of the World* 62 (September 1939): 394–97.

Debler, E. B. "Stabilization by Irrigation." *Reclamation Era* 30 (November 1940): 309–12.

"Deep-Well Irrigation in Dust Bowl." *Business Week*, 11 September 1937, 40–42.

De Kruif, Paul. "If We Get Rain." *Ladies' Home Journal* 51 (September 1934): 8–9, 78, 80.

De Voto, Bernard. "The West: A Plundered Province." *Harper's Magazine* 169 (August 1934): 355–64.

Dewey, Ernest A. "Duster." *Commonweal* 27 (4 March 1938): 519.

Dickinson, L. L. "Crop Control Brings Serfdom." *Forum* 95 (February 1936): 79–82.

Dobkins, D. A., and Virgil S. Beck. "Stabilizing the Dust Bowl." *Soil Conservation* 3 (December 1937): 157–58, 167.

"Documented Dust." *Time* 27 (25 May 1936): 47–48.

"Does Prayer Change the Weather?" *Christian Century* 47 (10 September 1930): 1084–86.

"Don't Bet on the Bad Lands." *Collier's* 98 (3 October 1936): 62.

"Do Something about It!" *Collier's* 94 (22 September 1934): 58.

Drake, Raymond. "Wind Erosion and Its Control." *Agricultural Engineering* 18 (May 1937): 197–98, 200.

"Drought." *New Republic* 66 (21 February 1931): 37–41.

"Drought." *New Republic* 87 (15 July 1936): 284.

"Drought." *Science* 84 (10 July 1936): 6.

"Drought." *Science* 91 (23 February 1940): 9.

"Drought: A Merciless Sun and a Scourge of Insects Destroy Crops, Cattle and Men." *Newsweek* 8 (18 July 1936): 7–11.

"Drought: Candidate Roosevelt on His Way to a Talk with Candidate Landon." *Newsweek* 8 (5 September 1936): 7–8.

"Drought: Dry Spell and Grasshoppers Inspire Grain-Belt Prayers for Rain and Federal Aid." *Newsweek* 8 (4 July 1936): 10.

"Drought: Experts Act to Ration Cattle for Nation's Larder." *Newsweek* 4 (25 August 1934): 10.

"Drought: In Lieu of Rainfall Relief Money Begins to Flow." *Newsweek* 8 (11 July 1936): 13.

"Drought: Rain of Relief Brings New Planning for Arid States." *Newsweek* 8 (25 July 1936): 22.

"Drought: Uncle Sam Looks at His Lean Larder and Acts to Hold Prices Down." *Newsweek* 4 (18 August 1934): 5–6.

"Drought: Unprecedented Heat." *Newsweek* 4 (4 August 1934): 6–7.

"Drought: Worst in History of United States Leads to Relief Flight and Political Arguments." *Newsweek* 8 (15 August 1936): 17.

"Drought Aftermath." *Business Week*, 15 September 1934, 14.

"Drought Again Scorches the West." *Scholastic* 29 (19 September 1936): 14.

"Drought Ahead." *Business Week*, 9 March 1935, 5–6.

"Drought and Autumn Rains." *Science* 81 (11 January 1935): 39.

"Drought and Engineering." *Science* 84 (10 July 1936): 6.

"Drought and Its Effects on Agricultural Crops." *Scientific Monthly* 39 (September 1934): 288.

"Drought Area Covers Entire Middle West." *Oklahoma Farmer-Stockman*, 15 July 1936, 6.

"Drought Centers." *Science* 74 (August 1931): 11.

"Drought Cuts Grain Crops to Thirty Year Low." *Literary Digest* 118 (18 August 1934): 5, 38.

"Drought Damage." *Literary Digest* 107 (18 October 1930): 53.

"Drought Damage Still in Doubt." *Business Week*, 10 September 1930, 13–14.

"Drought Effects Deepen." *Business Week*, 11 August 1934, 5–6.

"Drought Hangs On." *Newsweek* 15 (4 March 1940): 51–52.

"Drought Is the Moon's Fault." *Literary Digest* 106 (6 September 1930): 16.

"Drought Isn't Over; Farms, Utilities, Cities Worry." *Business Week* (11 February 1931): 20–21.

"Drought Leads to Provision for Lean Years." *Literary Digest* 117 (16 June 1934): 4.

"Drought Parches Farm Income." *Business Week*, 11 July 1936, 13.

"Drought Relief." *Survey* 65 (15 March 1931): 13–14.

"Drought Relief—A Worm's-Eye View." *New Republic* 64 (1 October 1930): 175–76.

"Drought Relief Machinery May Have Permanent Job." *Business Week*, 10 September 1930, 15.

"Drought Results." *Business Week*, 9 June 1934, 7–8.

"Drought Spreads." *Business Week*, 25 July 1936, 23–24.

"Drought Strikes Home." *Business Week*, 28 July 1934, 5–6.

"Drought Strikes the Plains Again." *Business Week*, 18 November 1939, 16, 18.

"Droughts Don't Last Forever." *Scientific American* 156 (February 1937): 135.

Drucker, Peter. "The Industrial Revolution Hits the Farmer." *Harper's Magazine* 179 (November 1939): 592–93.

Drummond, W. I. "Dust Bowl." *Review of Reviews* 93 (June 1936): 37–40.

"Dry Blizzards and Erosion." *Literary Digest* 117 (26 May 1934): 19.

Duley, F. L. "Wind Erosion in the Great Plains." *The Land Today and Tomorrow* 2 (April 1935): 5–8.

Duncan, Kunigunde. "Reclaiming the Dust Bowl." *Nation* 149 (9 September 1939): 269–71.

"Dust: More Storms Wreak Destruction in the Southwest." *Newsweek* 5 (20 April 1935): 11.

"Dust and Politics." *Business Week*, 20 April 1935, 15–16.

"Dust and the Nation's Breadbasket." *Literary Digest* 119 (30 April 1935): 10.

"Dust Bowl Area." *Science* 84 (31 July 1936): 113–14.

"Dust Bowl into Grazing Land." *Literary Digest* 121 (7 March 1936): 9.

"Dust Bowls of the Past." *Science* 86 (8 October 1937): 8.

"Dust Crop." *Business Week*, 30 March 1935, 12.

"Dust Hurls a Challenge." *Popular Mechanics* 66 (August 1936): 161–63.

"Dust Storm Collection." *Kansas Authors Bulletin Yearbook* 10 (1934): 50–53.

"Dust Storm Film." *Literary Digest* 121 (16 May 1936): 22.

"Dust Storm Forecasts." *Literary Digest* 120 (13 July 1935): 19.

"Dust Storms' Aftermath." *Literary Digest* 120 (2 November 1935): 15.

"Dust Storms and Their Possible Effects on Health." *American City* 52 (March 1937): 19.

Eddy, Don. "Up from the Dust." *American Magazine* 129 (April 1940): 54–55, 89–92.

"Effects of Drought on Prairie Trees." *Science* 81 (8 March 1935): 7.

"Effects of the Drought." *Science* 72 (15 August 1930): 10.

Ellis, Paul C. "Next Spring." *Christian Century* 52 (20 February 1935): 239–40.

"Farmers: Dragon's Teeth." *Time* 25 (13 May 1935): 15–18.

"Farmers: Worse Than 1934." *Time* 28 (13 July 1936): 13–14.

"Farming Crisis." *Literary Digest* 122 (11 July 1936): 6–7.

Farrell, F. D. "The Story of Kansas, a Blooming Desert." *Earth* 28 (December 1931): 1–2.

"Federal Movie Furor." *Business Week*, 11 July 1936, 14.

Fichter, Joseph H. "A Comparative View of Agrarianism." *Catholic World* 143 (September 1936): 654–59.

Finnell, H. H. "Control of Wind Erosion on the Southern Great Plains." *The Land Today and Tomorrow* 2 (March 1935): 4–6.

———. "High Plains Wheat." *Farm Journal* 54 (September 1930): 7–8, 51.

———. "Yardsticks and the Four-Card Draw." *Land Policy Review* 3 (October 1940): 19–23.

Fletcher, John Gould. "Two Poems of Drought." *New Republic* 81 (5 December 1934): 99.

Flood, Francis. "The Dust Bowl Is Being Tamed." *Oklahoma Farmer-Stockman*, 1 July 1937, 3, 23.

Freudenberger, H. L. "Black Blizzards." *Farm Journal* 62 (January 1938): 30.

Fuller, Norman G. "Walter Plagge—One Who Stayed in the Dust Bowl." *Land Policy Review* 3 (October 1940): 37–39.

Garrett, Garet. "The AAA in Its Own Dust Bowl." *Saturday Evening Post* 213 (2 March 1940): 12–13, 60–63.

Gates, Floyd P. "Duststorm Words." *American Speech* 13 (February 1938): 71–72.

Geiger, Robert. "If It Rains . . ." *Washington Evening Star*, 15 April 1935, A-2.

"God, Send Us Rain." *Outlook* 155 (20 August 1930): 612.

Godwin, Harriet. "Manna in the Cactus." *Scholastic* 25 (19 January 1935): 7.

"Good and Evil Effects of the Drought." *Literary Digest* 106 (23 August 1930): 5–6.

Gray, Lewis C. "Federal Purchase and Administration of Submarginal Land in the Great Plains." *Journal of Farm Economics* 21 (February 1939): 123–31.

———. "Our Land Policy." *Land Policy Review* 1 (May–June 1938): 3–8.

"Great Drought." *Nation* 131 (20 August 1930): 195.

"Great Drought of 1930." *Literary Digest* 106 (16 August 1930): 5–6.

Greenfield, George. "Unto Dust—A Great American Desert in the Making." *Reader's Digest* 30 (May 1937): 37–38.

Gregg, Willis R. "Meteorological Aspects of the 1936 Drought." *Scientific Monthly* 43 (August 1936): 190.

Gropper, William. "The Dust Bowl." *Nation* 145 (21 August 1937): 194.

Hacker, Louis M. "Plowing the Farmer Under." *Harper's Magazine* 169 (June 1934): 60–74.

Haecker, A. L. "Prepare for Drouth." *Farm and Ranch* 53 (1 May 1934): 21.

Haley, J. Evetts. "Cow Business and Monkey Business." *Saturday Evening Post* 207 (8 December 1934): 26–29, 94–96.

———. "Panhandle Hopeful of Future as Plans Made for Fight on Worst Dust Storm in History." *Dallas Morning News*, 17 April 1935, 1.

———. "Texas Control of Texas Soil." *West Texas Today*, July 1936, 14–16.

Hanson, Herbert C. "Ecology in Agriculture." *Ecology* 20 (April 1939): 111–17.

Harbert, Nancy. "Bone Dry." *Time* 147 (10 June 1996): 5–11.

Harger, Charles Moreau. "Brighter Skies Out West." *American Monthly Review of Reviews* 70 (October 1924): 420–23.

———. "The Next Commonwealth: Oklahoma." *Outlook* 67 (December 1904): 273–81.

———. "The Passing of the Promised Land." *Atlantic Monthly* 104 (October 1909): 461–66.

———. "The West's New Vision." *Atlantic Monthly* 120 (July 1917): 121–28.

Harris, Evelyn, and Caroline Henderson. "Letters of Two Women Farmers." *Atlantic Monthly* 152 (August–September 1933): 236–45, 349–56.

"Harvests Draw to a Close in Santa Fe Southwest." *Earth* 33 (November 1936): 1–2.

"He Is Here to Stay—The New American: Farmer Everlasting." *Farm Journal* 60 (December 1936): 18.

Heaton, Herbert. "Migration and Cheap Land: The End of Two Chapters." *Sociological Review* 26 (July 1934): 231–48.

Helm, F. D. "Reclamation as a Federal Investment." *Reclamation Era* 25 (March 1935): 63, 66.

Henderson, Caroline A. "Letters from the Dust Bowl." *Atlantic Monthly* 157 (May 1936): 540–51.

———. "Spring in the Dust Bowl." *Atlantic Monthly* 159 (June 1937): 615–17.

Henson, Edwin R. "Borrowed Time in the Dust Bowl." *Land Policy Review* 3 (October 1940): 3–7.

Hibbard, Benjamin Horace. "The Drought and the AAA Program." *Nation* 139 (4 July 1934): 15–16.

Hibbs, Ben. "Dust Bowl." *Country Gentleman* 106 (March 1936): 5, 6, 83–87.

———. "The Dust Bowl Can Be Saved." *Saturday Evening Post* 210 (18 December 1937): 36–37, 77–78, 80–82.

———. "Governor Landon Answers." *Country Gentleman* 105 (January 1935): 12, 13, 54.

———. "Reaping the Wind." *Country Gentleman* 104 (May 1934): 15, 45, 48.

Hinde, R. R. "Dust Bowl Experience with Strip Cropping." *Soil Conservation* 4 (October 1938): 103–5, 107–8.

Hoffman, Charles S. "Drought and Depression Migration." *Monthly Labor Review* 46 (January 1938): 27–35.

"How Things Look in Washington." *Oklahoma Farmer-Stockman*, 15 August 1938, 4.

"How Will the Drought Affect Health?" *Literary Digest* 118 (18 August 1934): 15.

Howe, Gene. "In the Panhandle of Texas." *Earth* 28 (July 1931): 12.

Hughes, Mark Alan. "Welfare Dust Bowl." *Washington Post*, 25 September 1996, A23.

Huntington, Ellsworth. "Marginal Land and the Shelter Belt." *Journal of Forestry* 32 (November 1934): 804–12.

Huse, Harry G. "Two Against the Sky." *Frontier* 13 (November 1932): 25–33.

Ickes, Harold. "The National Domain and the New Deal." *Saturday Evening Post* 206 (23 December 1933): 10–11, 55.

Isley, Bliss. "The Case History of Wheat." *Atlantic Monthly* 165 (May 1940): 632–38.

———. "Unwhipped Dust Bowl Heroes Won't Budge." *Nation's Business* 29 (November 1941): 26–28, 86–87.

Janow, Seymour, and Davis McEntire. "The Migrants: Migration to California." *Land Policy Review* 3 (July–August 1940): 24–36.

Jarrell, J. F. "Erroneous Impressions of the Dust Bowl Corrected." *Earth* 32 (October 1935): 6–7.

Johnston, Alva. "The Hamburger Bonanza." *Saturday Evening Post* 207 (4 May 1935): 18–19, 99–104.

———. "Wheat, Drought, and the New Deal." *Saturday Evening Post* 207 (13 April 1935): 5–7, 78–83.

Jones, Ewing. "Dust Storms through the Years." *The Land Today and Tomorrow* 2 (April 1935): 1–4.

———. "A Rookie Looks at Soil Erosion." *The Land Today and Tomorrow* 1 (November 1934): 8–11.

Kellog, Royal S. "The Shelterbelt Scheme." *Journal of Forestry* 32 (December 1934): 974–77.

Kellogg, Paul U. "Drought and the Red Cross." *Survey* 65 (15 February 1931): 645.

Kenney, F. R. "Water for the West." *Land Policy Review* 1 (September–October 1938): 1–5.

Kifer, R. S., and H. L. Stewart. "Farming Hazards in the Drought Area." *Rural Sociology* 4 (1939): 359–60.

Kimmel, Roy. "Planning for the Southern Great Plains." *Soil Conservation* 5 (November 1939): 120–22.

———. "United Front to Reclaim the Dust Bowl." *New York Times Magazine*, 14 August 1938, 10–11, 20.

Kincer, J. B. "Drought of 1934." *Scientific Monthly* 39 (July 1934): 95–96.

———. "Effect of the 1936 Drought on Crops." *Scientific Monthly* 43 (August 1936): 191.

Klausler, Alfred. "It Can't Rain Here." *Nation* 143 (8 August 1936): 152.

Kresensky, Raymond. "Drought." *New Republic* 79 (8 August 1934): 340.

Lane, Neil. "The Dust Farmer Goes West." *Land Policy Review* 1 (May–June 1938): 21–25.

Lang, Martha Nell. "Prayer for West Texas." *The Land Today and Tomorrow* 2 (April 1935): 10.

Law, Albert H. "The Dust Bowl Comes Back." *Farm and Ranch* 55 (15 February 1936): 1, 10.

———. "Returning Protection to the Land." *Farm and Ranch* 54 (15 January 1935): 1, 4, 16.

Leighton, M. M. "Geology of Soil Drifting on the Great Plains." *Scientific Monthly* 47 (July 1938): 22–33.

Le Sueur, Meridel. "Cows and Horses Are Hungry." *American Mercury* 33 (September 1934): 53–56.

Lord, Russell. "Back to the Farm?" *Forum* 89 (February 1933): 97–103.

Lott, Julia. "Drought Survivors." *Kansas Magazine*, 1936, 93.

MacLeish, Archibald. "Grasslands." *Fortune* 12 (November 1935): 58–67, 185–90, 198–203.

MacMillan, Robert. "Farm Families in the Dust Bowl." *Land Policy Review* 1 (September–October 1938): 14–17.

Malin, James C. "The Adaption of the Agricultural System to Sub-Humid Environment." *Agricultural History* 10 (July 1936): 118–41.

———. "The Turnover of Farm Population in Kansas." *Kansas Historical Quarterly* 4 (1935): 339–72.

Malone, A. W. "Desert Ahead!" *New Outlook* 164 (August 1934): 14–17.

Mann, Leland W. "Packers Take Up Theology." *Christian Century* 51 (20 June 1934): 883–84.

Markey, Morris. "Nature the Farmer." *Saturday Evening Post* 207 (21 July 1934): 5–7, 81–83.

Martin, Robert J. "Duststorms of 1938 in the United States." *Monthly Weather Review* 67 (January 1939): 12–15.

———. "Duststorms of January–April 1937 in the United States." *Monthly Weather Review* 65 (April 1937): 151–52.

———. "Duststorms of May 1936 in the United States." *Monthly Weather Review* 64 (May 1936): 176.

———. "Duststorms of May–December 1937 in the United States." *Monthly Weather Review* 66 (January 1938): 9–12.

Martindale, E. "The Great American Desert." *Warsaw Times* (Missouri), 4 April 1935.

Mattice, W. A. "Dust Storms." *Monthly Weather Review* 63 (March 1935): 113–15.

———. "Dust Storms, November 1933 to May 1934." *Monthly Weather Review* 63 (February 1935): 53–55.

Mayo, Morrow. "The Man with the Tractor." *Harper's Magazine* 177 (November 1938): 622–24.

McGinnis, B. W. "Utilization of Crop Residues Against Wind Erosion." *The Land Today and Tomorrow* 2 (April 1935): 12–14.

McMillan, Putnam Dana. "Marginal Land and Marginal Thinking." *Saturday Evening Post* 208 (1 June 1935): 27, 88–89.

Mead, Frank S. "God's Green Acres." *Farm Journal* 59 (November 1935): 19, 53.

Mencken, H. L. "The Dole for Bogus Farmers." *American Mercury* 39 (December 1936): 400–408.

Merkel, H. "Who's Afraid of the Drought?" *Better Homes and Gardens* 17 (June 1939): 16–17.

Merrill, Arthur Truman. "The Pioneer." *Frontier* 10 (January 1930): 96.

Meyerhoff, H. A. "Floods and Dust Storms." *Science* 83 (26 June 1936): 622.

Michel, Virgil. "Agriculture and Reconstruction." *Commonweal* 29 (13 January 1939): 317–18.

"Mid-West Brought to Knees by Searing Heat." *Literary Digest* 118 (4 August 1934): 4.

Miller, Harlan. "When Searing Drought Smites the Farm." *New York Times Magazine*, 27 May 1934, 7, 22.

———. "Dust Rides the Wind Out of the West." *New York Times Magazine*, 31 March 1935, 11, 14.

Miller, K. K. "Dust Unto Dust." *Kansas Magazine*, 1936, 61–62.

Mitchell, I. H. "Nation Benefitted by Irrigation." *Reclamation Era* 25 (February 1935): 27–28, 36.

Mohler, J. C. "Kansas Comes through Bad Crop Season despite State's Defamers." *Earth* 31 (August 1934): 4.

"More Than Dust Blows Away." *Science News Letter* 32 (31 July 1937): 73.

Morris, Lawrence S. "The Economics of Eden." *Christian Century* 51 (4 July 1934): 891–93.

Morris, Ralph C. "The Notion of a Great American Desert East of the Rockies." *Mississippi Valley Historical Review* 13 (September 1926): 190–200.

Mullen, C. W. "Driving in the Rain." *Oklahoma Farmer-Stockman*, 1 October 1936, 3.

———. "Farmers Will Boost Wheat Acreage." *Oklahoma Farmer-Stockman*, 1 November 1936, 3, 14.

———. "High Plains Will Bloom Again." *Oklahoma Farmer-Stockman*, 1 April 1935, 3, 18.

"Nature and Source of Dust Storms." *Literary Digest* 116 (16 December 1933): 20.

Newport, Fred C., and Robert R. Hinde. "Farming Level Terraces in the Dust Bowl." *Soil Conservation* 4 (November 1938): 115–18.

"1934 Dry?" *Literary Digest* 118 (1 September 1934): 17.

Norris, Ada Buell. "Black Blizzard." *Kansas Magazine*, 1941, 103–4.

Norris, George W. "Trees vs. Drought and Dust." *Washington Sunday Star*, 25 June 1939, C-3.

Odum, Howard P. "New Frontiers of American Life." *Southwest Review* 18 (July 1933): 418–29.

"Our Dependent Cities." *Farm Journal* 55 (February 1931): 10.

"Our Great Drought Still." *Literary Digest* 108 (21 March 1931): 23.

Owen, Russell. "Where Drought Sears Land and People." *New York Times Magazine*, 15 February 1931, 7.

Page, John C. "Reclamation Fulfills Its Mission." *Reclamation Era* 28 (July 1938): 125–27.

———. "Reclamation Offers Solution for Migrant Farmer Problem in the West." *Reclamation Era* 30 (November 1940): 304–8.

"Parched Plains." *Literary Digest* 122 (29 August 1936): 7–8.

Peel, W. F. "The Soil Conservation Service Drought Program of 1936." *Soil Conservation* 2 (March 1937): 204–7.

Perkins, Ralph. "Relief Work in a Dust Bowl Community." *Sociology and Social Research* 23 (July–August 1939): 539–45.

Peterson, Elmer. "The Dust Bowl Sends Flowers." *Kansas Magazine*, 1937, 68–69.

Piquet, John A. "Our Unconquered Frontier." *Scribner's Magazine* 96 (December 1934): 354–58.

"Plants That Defy Drought in a Desert." *Science* 80 (20 July 1934): 8.

Ploughe, J. S. "Out of the Dust." *Christian Century* 52 (22 May 1935): 691–92.

Pool, Raymond J. "White Man versus the Prairie." *Science* 91 (19 January 1940): 53–58.

Porter, Kenneth. "Dust Cloud over Kansas." *Kansas Magazine*, 1937, 64–65.

———. "Anthology of Kansas Verse." *Kansas Magazine*, 1937, 35–37.

Porter, Russell B. "Drought Produces Lean Kine of Egypt." *New York Times*, 2 August 1934, 6.

Poyer, M. E. "Fighting the Drought." *Nation* 143 (1 August 1936): 139.

"Principle and Precedent." *National Republic* 18 (March 1931): 12.

"Profitable Disaster." *Collier's* 86 (20 September 1930): 74.

"Program for Parched Land." *Nation* 143 (25 July 1936): 89.

Ravenel, Mazyck P. "Drought and Health." *American Journal of Public Health* 21 (November 1931): 1198–1202.

"The Recent Destructive Dust Cloud." *Science* 79 (25 May 1934): 473.

"Recurring Drought." *Literary Digest* 122 (4 July 1936): 6–7.

"Red Cross Ill-Advised." *Outlook* 157 (11 February 1931): 205–7.

Reitz, T. Russell. "A Traveler Sees the Shelterbelts." *Progress in Kansas* 7 (December 1940): 11–12.

"Relief: Needs of Drought Victims Continue to Mount." *Newsweek* 8 (29 August 1936): 15.

Richardson, Rupert N. "Some Historical Factors Contributing to the Problems of the Great Plains." *Southwestern Social Science Quarterly* 18 (June 1937): 1–14.

"Right Side Up." *Saturday Evening Post* 211 (27 May 1939): 22.

Roberts, E. D. G. "Land Utilization Program in the Southern Great Plains." *Science* 88 (30 September 1938): 289–92.

Robinson, M. L. "The Response of Kansas Farmers to the Wheat Adjustment Program." *Journal of Farm Economics* 19 (February 1937): 359–62.

Roosevelt, Franklin D. "The Drought." *Vital Speeches* 2 (15 September 1936): 765–68.

"Roosevelt and the Drought." *Nation* 143 (18 July 1936): 61–62.

"Row over Feeding Our Hungry Farmers." *Literary Digest* 108 (31 January 1931): 8–9.

Rowell, Edward J. "Drought Refugee and Labor Migration to California in 1936." *Monthly Labor Review* 43 (December 1936): 1355–63.

Rugg, H. "Sustained Yield Principle: America Rebuilds." *Scholastic* 36 (26 February 1940): 11–13.

"Santa Fe Earth." *Earth* 34 (November 1937): 6.

"Scattering of Light in Dust Storms." *Science* 81 (5 April 1935): 8.

Schafer, A. L. "When Hunger Followed Drought." *Survey* 65 (1 March 1931): 581–83, 627.

Schmidt, Louis B. "The Agricultural Revolution in the Prairies and Great Plains of the United States." *Agricultural History* 8 (October 1934): 169–96.

"Science Arms Farmers Against Four Foes." *Literary Digest* 120 (6 July 1935): 16–17.

Seagreaves, Charles. "Why Pay Rent?" *Earth* 31 (September 1934): 12.

Sears, Alfred B. "The Desert Threat in the Southern Great Plains." *Agricultural History* 15 (January 1941): 1–11.

Sears, Paul B. "Death from the Soil." *American Mercury* 42 (December 1937): 440–47.

———. "Floods and Dust Storms." *Science* 83 (27 March 1936): 9.

———. "The Great American Shelterbelt." *Ecology* 17 (October 1936): 683–84.

———. "O, Bury Me Not; Or, The Bison Avenged." *New Republic* 90 (12 May 1937): 7–10.

"Second Year of Drought." *New Republic* 66 (1 April 1931): 169–70.

Seibert, Victor C. "A New Menace to the Middle West: The Dust Storms." *Aerend* 8 (Fall 1937): 209–26.

Selby, H. E. "How Many Acres Do We Require?" *Land Policy Review* 3 (September 1940): 8–11.

Selby, Hazel B. "Dirge for a Pioneer." *Frontier* 12 (May 1932): 309.

"Self Help Drought-Relief Program." *Literary Digest* 106 (30 August 1930): 9.

"The Shape of Things." *Nation* 143 (11 July 1936): 29.

Sherman, E. A. "Saving Our Soil." *Nation* 139 (12 April 1933): 401–3.

Sidey, Hugh. "Echoes of the Great Dust Bowl." *Time* 147 (10 June 1996): 5–11.

Smrha, R. V. "Irrigation for Crop Insurance." *Biennial Report of Kansas State Board of Agriculture* 28 (1933): 138–41.

Smith, J. R. "Drought—Act of God and Freedom." *Survey Graphic* 23 (September 1934): 412–15.

Smith, Roger C. "Upsetting the Balance of Nature, with Special Reference to Kansas and the Great Plains." *Science* 75 (24 June 1932): 649–54.

Snow, Bernard W. "As I Said in January—." *Farm Journal* 59 (June 1935): 9.

———. "Crops and Weather." *Farm Journal* 60 (May 1936): 13.

———. "Flirting with Famine." *Farm Journal* 57 (December 1933): 5.

———. "A 1935 Wheat Shortage." *Farm Journal* 59 (January 1935): 7.

———. "Prices and Failures." *Farm Journal* 58 (September 1934): 9, 23.

———. "Wheat and Water." *Farm Journal* 62 (April 1938): 18.

Soule, M. H. "Microorganism Carried by the Dust Storm." *Science* 80 (6 July 1934): 14–15.

Spearman, Frank H. "The Great American Desert." *Harper's Monthly Magazine* 77 (July 1888): 232–45.

Starch, E. A. "Type of Farming Modification Needed in the Great Plains." *Journal of Farm Economics* 21 (February 1939): 114–20.

Stephens, P. H. "Why the Dust Bowl?" *Journal of Farm Economics* 19 (August 1937): 750–57.

Stevens, William K. "Great Plains or Great Desert? A Sea of Dunes Lies in Wait." *New York Times*, 28 May 1996, B5.

Stoeckeler, J. H. "Shelterbelt Planting Reduces Wind Erosion Damages in Western Oklahoma." *Journal of the American Society of Agronomy* 30 (November 1938): 923–31.

Strode, Josephine. "Kansas Grit." *Survey* 72 (August 1936): 230–31.

"Study of the Effect of Drought on Trees." *Science* 84 (7 August 1936): 136.

Talman, Charles F. "Big and Little Dust Storm." *Nature Magazine* 25 (March 1935): 103–6.

Taylor, Paul S. "Again the Covered Wagon." *Survey Graphic* 24 (July 1935): 348–51.

Taylor, Paul S., and Edward J. Rowell. "Refugee Labor Migration to California, 1937." *Monthly Labor Review* 47 (August 1938): 240–50.

Thane, Eric. "Dark Retreat." *Frontier and Midland* 18 (Winter 1937–38): 73–76.

"There's Still a Drought." *Business Week*, 17 November 1934, 12.

"This Drought Is the Worst." *Business Week*, 8 August 1936, 11–12.

Thone, Frank. "Prairies Remember." *Science News Letter* 35 (15 April 1939): 239.

Throckmorton, R. I. "Aftermath of the Drouth." *Country Gentleman* 105 (January 1935): 9, 53.

———. "Yardstick for Wheatgrowers." *Country Gentleman* 106 (March 1936): 19, 109, 115.

Tisdale, E. S. "1930–31 Drought." *American Journal of Public Health* 21 (November 1931): 1203–18.

"To Lay the Dust." *Extension Service Review* 9 (March 1938): 43.

"Too Much Weather." *Nation* 139 (8 August 1934): 145–46.

"Transforming the Panhandle of Texas." *Earth* 3 (April 1906): 12.

Tripp, Thomas A. "Dust Bowl Tragedy." *Christian Century* 57 (24 January 1940): 108–10.

Troxell, Willard W., and W. Paul O'Day. "The Migrants: Migration to the Pacific Northwest." *Land Policy Review* 3 (January–February 1940): 32–43.

Tugwell, Rexford. "Changing Acres." *Current History* 44 (September 1936): 57–63.

———. "Our New National Domain." *Scribner's Magazine* 99 (March 1936): 164–68.

———. "The Place of Government in a National Land Program." *Journal of Farm Economics* 16 (January 1934): 55–69.

"The U.S. Dust Bowl: Its Artist Is a Texan Portraying Man's Mistakes." *Life* 2 (2 June 1937): 60–65.

"U.S. Wages War on Devastating Drought." *Scholastic* 25 (22 September 1934): 17, 22.

Van Doren, Mark. "Further Documents." *Nation* 142 (10 June 1936): 753.

Van Royen, William. "Prehistoric Droughts in the Central Great Plains." *Geographical Review* 27 (October 1937): 637–50.

Van Wagenen, Jared. "A Farmer Counts His Blessings." *Atlantic Monthly* 150 (July 1932): 33–39.

Wallace, Henry A. "The Ever-Normal Granary." *Literary Digest* 124 (20 November 1937): 13–15.

———. "The Next Four Years in Agriculture." *New Republic* 89 (2 December 1936): 133–36.

———. "Relief for the Farmer." *Forum* 89 (March 1933): 158–60.

———. "The Value of Scientific Research to Agriculture." *Science* 77 (19 May 1933): 475–80.

"Wallace on Future of Great Plains Area." *New York Times*, 16 December 1936, 8A.

Ward, Harold. "Conquering the Dust Bowl." *Travel* 74 (February 1940): 24–25, 48.

Warne, William E. "Why Irrigation?" *Reclamation Era* 29 (April 1939): 74–76.

"Washington Notes." *New Republic* 80 (15 August 1934): 17–18.

Watson, E. H. "Note on the Dust Storm." *Science* 79 (6 April 1934): 320.

Watson, W. R. "Economic Units for the Dust Bowl." *Soil Conservation* 4 (September 1938): 80–88.

Weaver, John, and F. W. Albertson. "Deterioration of Midwestern Ranges." *Ecology* 21 (April 1940): 216–36.

———. "Effects of the Great Drought on the Prairies of Iowa, Nebraska, and Kansas." *Ecology* 17 (October 1936): 567–639.

Weaver, John, and Evan Flory. "Stability of Climax Prairie and Some Environmental Changes Resulting from Breaking." *Ecology* 15 (October 1934): 333–47.

Wehrwein, George. "Wind Erosion Legislation in Texas and Kansas." *Journal of Land and Public Utility Economics* 12 (August 1936): 312–13.

"West in Black Crisis of Drought." *Literary Digest* 122 (18 July 1936): 3–5.

West, Ward. "Hope Springs Green in the Dust Bowl." *New York Times Magazine*, 16 July 1939, 7, 21.

"What Can Science Do about the Drought?" *Popular Mechanics* 64 (August 1935): 206–7.

"What the Drought Means." *Business Week*, 23 June 1934, 9–10.

"Wheat and Dust." *Time* 25 (22 April 1935): 66–68.

Whitfield, Charles. J. "Sand Dunes in the Great Plains." *Soil Conservation* 2 (March 1937): 208–9.

———. "Wind Erosion Endangering Colorado Vegetation." *The Land Today and Tomorrow* 1 (December 1934): 27–28.

"Will Prayer Bring Rain?" *Literary Digest* 106 (27 September 1930): 18–19.

"Will the Drought Return This Summer?" *Literary Digest* 119 (6 April 1935): 16.

Wilson, Charles M. "Saga of Drought." *Commonweal* 20 (14 September 1934): 464–65.

———. "The Surviving Frontier." *Current History* 34 (May 1931): 189–92.

Wilson, M. L. "Agricultural Conservation—An Aspect of Land Utilization." *Journal of Farm Economics* 19 (February 1937): 3–12.

———. "Economic Democracy in Soil Conservation." *Agricultural Situation* 21 (September 1937): 9–10.

———. "A Land Use Program for the Federal Government." *Journal of Farm Economics* 15 (April 1933): 216–27.

Wimberly, Ware W. "Parable of the Drouth." *Christian Century* 53 (5 August 1936): 1061–62.

Winrod, Gerald B. "A Biblical Analysis of the Nation's Plight." *Defender* 11 (January 1937): 3–6.

———. "A Bust in the Brain Trust." *Defender* 8 (April 1934): 6–9.

———. "Disturbances in Nature." *Defender* 11 (August 1936): 21–22.

———. "Revival of Ruin." *Defender* 5 (January 1931): 1.

Winters, S. R. "New Plants to Check Drought and Dust." *Literary Digest* 119 (13 April 1935): 19.

Woodman, H. V. "Pasture Development in Texas." *The Land Today and Tomorrow* 2 (March 1935): 7–11.

"WPA, RA, and Drought." *Survey* 72 (September 1936): 272.

Zon, Raphael. "Shelterbelts—Futile Dream or Workable Plan." *Science* 81 (26 April 1935): 390–94.

Newspapers

Amarillo Daily News (Texas). 1930–40.

Amarillo Globe (Texas). 1935.

Baptist Messenger (Oklahoma City, Oklahoma). 1930–40.

Baptist Standard (Dallas, Texas). 1930–40.

Beaver Herald-Democrat (Oklahoma). 1934–39.

Boise City News (Oklahoma). 1934–39.

Capper's Weekly (Topeka, Kansas). 1930–40.

Catholic Advance (Wichita, Kansas). 1930–40.

Church Advocate and Good Way. (Ft. Scott, Kansas). 1930–40.

Clark County Clipper (Ashland, Kansas). 1934.

Custer County Chief (Broken Bow, Nebraska). 1930–40.

Daily Oklahoman (Oklahoma City, Oklahoma). 1930–40.

Dalhart Texan (Texas). 1933–40.

Dodge City Daily Globe (Kansas). 1934–39.

Elkhart Tri-State News (Kansas). 1939.

Hastings Daily Tribune (Nebraska). 1936–39.

Hutchinson News (Kansas). 1930–40.

Kansas City Star (Kansas). 1934–39.

Kansas Farmer. (Topeka, Kansas). 1930–40.

Liberal News (Kansas). 1934–35.

Lincoln Evening Journal (Nebraska). 1930–40.

Meade County Press (Kansas). 1934–39.

Meade Globe News (Kansas). 1934–39.

Morton County Farmer (Kansas). 1935.

Nebraska Farmer (Lincoln, Nebraska). 1930–40.

Nebraska Signal (Geneva, Nebraska). 1936.

Omaha World Herald (Nebraska). 1930–40.

Revealer (Wichita, Kansas). 1934–36.

Sooner State Conservation News. (Oklahoma). 1935–37.

Southwest Daily Times (Liberal, Kansas). 1935–39.

Sublette Monitor (Kansas). 1930–40.

Topeka Daily State Journal (Kansas). 1934–39.

SECONDARY SOURCES

Books

Abrams, David. *The Spell of the Sensuous: Perception and Language in a More-Than-Human World.* New York: Random House, 1996.

Anderson, Gary C. *Sitting Bull and the Paradox of Lakota Nationhood.* New York: Harper-Collins, 1996.

Armitage, Katie. *Making Do and Doing Without: Kansas in the Great Depression.* Lawrence: University of Kansas, Division of Continuing Education, 1983.

Athearn, Robert G. *The Mythic West in Twentieth Century America.* Lawrence: University Press of Kansas, 1986.

Bader, Robert Smith. *Hayseeds, Moralizers, and Methodists: The Twentieth Century Image of Kansas.* Lawrence: University Press of Kansas, 1988.

Badger, Anthony. *The New Deal: The Depression Years, 1933–1940.* New York: Hill and Wang, 1989.

Baigell, Matthew. *The American Scene: American Painting of the 1930s.* New York: Praeger, 1974.

Baker, Robert S. *Brave New World: History, Science, and Dystopia.* New York: Twayne, 1989.

Barkun, Michael. *Disaster and the Millennium.* New Haven: Yale University Press, 1974.

Beegel, Susan, Susan Shillinglaw, and Wesley Tiffney Jr., eds. *Steinbeck and the Environment: Interdisciplinary Approaches.* Tuscaloosa: University of Alabama Press, 1997.

Bennett, John. *The Ecological Transition: Cultural Anthropology and Human Adaption.* New York: Pergamon, 1966.

Bercovitch, Sacvan. *The American Jeremiad.* Madison: University of Wisconsin Press, 1978.

Blodgett, Jan. *Land of Bright Promise: Advertising the Texas Panhandle and South Plains, 1870–1917.* Austin: University of Texas Press, 1988.

Blouet, Brian W., and Lawson, Merlin P., eds. *Images of the Plains.* Lincoln: University of Nebraska Press, 1975.

Blouet, Brian W., and Frederick C. Luebke, eds. *The Great Plains: Environment and Culture.* Lincoln: University of Nebraska Press, 1979.

Bogue, Allan. *Frederick Jackson Turner.* Norman: University of Oklahoma Press, 1998.

Bonnifield, Paul. *The Dust Bowl: Men, Dirt, and Depression.* Albuquerque: University of New Mexico Press, 1979.

Booker, M. Keith. *Dystopian Literature: A Theory and Research Guide.* Westport, Conn.: Greenwood, 1994.

Boyer, Paul. *When Time Shall Be No More: Prophecy Belief in Modern American Culture.* Cambridge, Mass.: Harvard University Press, 1992.

Brink, Wellington. *Big Hugh: The Father of Soil Conservation.* New York: Macmillan, 1951.

Brinkley, Alan. *The End of Reform: The New Deal Liberalism in Recession and War.* New York: Knopf, 1995.

Bryant, Keith. *Alfalfa Bill.* Norman: University of Oklahoma Press, 1968.

Burbank, Garin. *When Farmers Voted Red: The Gospel of Socialism in the Oklahoma Countryside, 1910–1924.* Westport, Conn.: Greenwood Press, 1976.

Campbell, Joseph. *The Hero with a Thousand Faces.* New York: Pantheon, 1949.

Conrad, David. *The Forgotton Farmers: The Story of Sharecroppers in the New Deal.* Urbana: University of Illinois Press, 1965.

Cronon, William, ed. *Uncommon Ground: Rethinking the Human Place in Nature.* New York: Norton, 1996.

Curtis, James. *Mind's Eye, Mind's Truth: FSA Photography Reconsidered.* Philadelphia: Temple University Press, 1989.

Dale, E. E. *Frontier Ways: Sketches of Life in the Old West.* Austin: University of Texas Press, 1959.

DeLong, Lea Rosson. *Nature's Forms/Nature's Forces: The Art of Alexandre Hogue.* Norman: University of Oklahoma Press, 1984.

Dorman, Robert L. *Revolt of the Provinces: The Regionalist Movement in America, 1920–1945.* Chapel Hill: University of North Carolina Press, 1993.

Droze, Wilmon H. *Trees, Prairies, and People.* Denton, Tex.: Texas Women's University, 1977.

Eden, Robert. *The New Deal and Its Legacy: Critique and Its Reappraisal.* New York: Greenwood Press, 1989.

Ekirch, Arthur A. Jr. *Man and Nature in America*. New York: Columbia University Press, 1963.

Eliade, Mircea. *The Myth of the Eternal Return: Or, Cosmos and History*. Translated by Willard R. Trask. Princeton: Princeton University Press, 1991.

Emmons, David. *Garden in the Grassland: Boomer Literature of the Central Great Plains*. Lincoln: University of Nebraska Press, 1971.

Faulkner, Virginia, and Frederick Luebke. *Vision and Refuge: Essays on the Literature of the Great Plains*. Lincoln: University of Nebraska Press, 1982.

Fite, Gilbert. *Conquering the Great American Desert*. Lincoln: Nebraska Historical Society, 1975.

Fraser, Steve, and Gary Gerstle, eds. *The Rise and Fall of the New Deal Order, 1930–1980*. Princeton: Princeton University Press, 1989.

French, Warren, ed. *A Companion to* The Grapes of Wrath. New York: Viking, 1963.

Ganzel, Bill. *Dust Bowl Descent*. Lincoln: University of Nebraska Press, 1984.

Gare, Arran E. *Postmodernism and the Environmental Crisis*. London: Routledge, 1995.

Gilman, Carolyn, and Mary Jane Schneider. *The Way to Independence: Memories of a Hidatsa Indian Family, 1840–1920*. St. Paul: Minnesota Historical Society Press, 1987.

Glantz, Michel H., ed. *Drought Follows the Plow: Cultivating Marginal Areas*. London: Cambridge University Press, 1994.

Goetzmann, William H., and William N. Goetzmann. *The West of the Imagination*. New York: Norton, 1986.

Gray, James H. *Men Against the Desert*. Saskatoon: Western Producer Prairie Book, 1967.

Green, Donald E. *Land of the Underground Rain*. Austin: University of Texas Press, 1973.

————, ed. *Rural Oklahoma*. Oklahoma City: Oklahoma Historical Society, 1977.

Gregory, James N. *American Exodus: The Dust Bowl Migration and Okie Culture in California*. New York: Oxford University Press, 1989.

Haley, James L. *The Buffalo War*. Austin: State House Press, 1998.

Hamilton, David. *From New Day to New Deal: American Farm Policy from Hoover to Roosevelt*. Chapel Hill: University of North Carolina Press, 1991.

Handy, Robert T. *The American Religious Depression, 1925–1935*. Philadelphia: Fortress Press, 1968.

Hardin, Charles M. *The Politics of Agriculture: Soil Conservation and the Struggle for Power in Rural America*. Glencoe, Ill.: Free Press, 1952.

Hargreaves, Mary W. M. *Dry Farming in the Northern Great Plains, 1900–1925*. Cambridge, Mass.: Harvard University Press, 1957.

Harris, Jonathan. *Federal Art and National Culture: The Politics of Identity in New Deal America*. Cambridge: Cambridge University Press, 1995.

Hays, Samuel P. *Conservation and the Gospel of Efficiency: The Progressive Conservation Movement, 1890–1920*. Cambridge, Mass.: Harvard University Press, 1959.

Hearn, Charles R. *The American Dream in the Great Depression*. Westport, Conn.: Greenwood Press, 1977.

Hendrickson, Kenneth E., ed. *Hard Times in Oklahoma: The Depression Years.* Oklahoma City: Oklahoma Historical Society, 1983.

Hewes, Leslie. *The Suitcase Farming Frontier.* Lincoln: University of Nebraska Press, 1973.

Hofstadter, Richard. *The Age of Reform.* New York: Vintage, 1955.

Hollon, W. Eugene. *The Great American Desert, Then and Now.* New York: Oxford University Press, 1966.

Hoy, Jim, and Tom Isern. *Plains Folk: A Commonplace of the Great Plains.* Norman: University of Oklahoma Press, 1987.

Hudson, John C. *Plains Country Towns.* Minneapolis: University of Minnesota Press, 1985.

Hull, William H. *The Dirty Thirties.* Edina, Minn.: Stanton Publishing Services, 1989.

Hurt, R. Douglass. *The Dust Bowl: An Agricultural and Social History.* Chicago: Nelson-Hall, 1981.

Huth, Hans. *Nature and the American: Three Centuries of Changing Attitudes.* Lincoln: University of Nebraska Press, 1957.

Irwin, Lee. *The Dream Seekers: The Native American Visionary Traditions of the Great Plains.* Norman: University of Oklahoma Press, 1994.

Jenkins, Keith, ed. *The Postmodern History Reader.* London: Routledge, 1997.

Johnson, Vance. *Heaven's Tableland: The Dust Bowl Story.* New York: Farrar, Straus, 1947.

Karl, Barry. *The Uneasy State: The United States from 1915 to 1945.* Chicago: University of Chicago Press, 1983.

Kirkendall, Richard S. *Social Scientists and Farm Politics in the Age of Roosevelt.* Columbia: University of Missouri Press, 1966.

Klein, Joe. *Woody Guthrie: A Life.* New York: Knopf, 1980.

Klein, Kerwin Lee. *Frontiers of Historical Imagination: Narrating the European Conquest of Native America, 1890–1990.* Berkeley: University of California Press, 1997.

Knobloch, Frieda. *The Culture of Wilderness: Agriculture as Colonization in the American West.* Chapel Hill: University of North Carolina Press, 1996.

Kolodny, Annette. *The Lay of the Land: Metaphor as Experience and History in American Life and Letters.* Chapel Hill: University of North Carolina Press, 1975.

Kraenzel, Carl F. *The Great Plains in Transition.* Norman: University of Oklahoma Press, 1955.

Kromm, David E., and Stephen F. White, eds. *Groundwater Exploitation in the High Plains.* Lawrence: University Press of Kansas, 1992.

Kyvig, David E., and Mary-Ann Blasio. *New Day/New Deal: A Bibliography of the Great American Depression.* Westport, Conn.: Greenwood Press, 1988.

Lamar, Howard, ed. *The New Encyclopedia of the American West.* New Haven: Yale University Press, 1998.

Lawson, Merlin P. *The Climate of the Great American Desert.* Lincoln: University of Nebraska Press, 1974.

Lears, T. Jackson. *No Place of Grace: Antimodernism and the Transformation of American Culture.* 1981. Reprint. New York: Pantheon, 1983.

Lehman, Tim. *Public Values, Private Lands: Farmland Preservation Policy, 1933–1985.* Chapel Hill: University of North Carolina Press, 1995.

Leuchtenburg, William. *Franklin D. Roosevelt and the New Deal, 1932–1940.* New York: Harper & Row, 1963.

Limerick, Patricia. *Desert Passages: Encounters with the American Deserts.* Albuquerque: University of New Mexico Press, 1985.

———. *Legacy of Conquest: The Unbroken Past of the American West.* New York: Norton, 1987.

Linderman, Frank. *Plenty Coups, Chief of the Crows.* Lincoln: University of Nebraska Press, 1962.

Lowitt, Richard. *The New Deal and the West.* Bloomington: Indiana University Press, 1984.

Lowitt, Richard, and Maurine Beasley, eds. *One Third of a Nation: Lorena Hickock Reports on the Great Depression.* Urbana: University of Illinois Press, 1981.

Lyotard, Jean François. *The Postmodern Condition: A Report on Knowledge.* Translated by Geoff Bennington and Brian Massumi. Minneapolis: University of Minnesota Press, 1979.

Malin, James C. *The Grassland of North America: A Prolegomena to Its History with Addenda.* Lawrence, Kans.: Privately published, 1947.

———. *History and Ecology: Studies of the Grassland.* Edited by Robert P. Swierenga. Lincoln: University of Nebraska Press, 1984.

Malone, Bill. *Country Music, USA.* Austin: University of Texas Press, 1985.

Mangione, Jerry. *The Dream and the Deal: The Federal Writers Project, 1935–1943.* Boston: Little, Brown, 1972.

Manning, Richard. *Grassland: The History, Biology, Politics, and Promise of the American Prairie.* New York: Penguin, 1995.

Marcus, Greil. *The Dustbin of History.* Cambridge, Mass.: Harvard University Press, 1995.

Marx, Leo. *The Machine in the Garden: Technology and the Pastoral Ideal in America.* New York: Oxford University Press, 1964.

Mathews, Jane De Hart. *The Federal Theatre, 1935–1939: Plays, Relief, and Politics.* Princeton: Princeton University Press, 1967.

McCoy, Donald R. *Landon of Kansas.* Lincoln: University of Nebraska, 1966.

McDaniel, Marylou, ed. *God, Grass, and Grit: History of the Sherman County Trade Area.* Hereford, Tex.: Pioneer Book Publishers, 1971.

McKinzie, Richard D. *The New Deal for Artists.* Princeton: Princeton University Press, 1973.

Melosh, Barbara. *Engendering Culture: Manhood and Womanhood in New Deal Public Art and Theater.* Washington, D.C.: Smithsonian Institution Press, 1991.

Miller, Robert M. *American Protestantism and Social Issues, 1919–1939.* Chapel Hill: University of North Carolina Press, 1958.

Miner, Craig. *West of Wichita: Settling the High Plains of Kansas, 1865–1890.* Lawrence: University Press of Kansas, 1986.

Morris, John Miller. *El Llano Estacado: Exploration and Imagination on the High Plains of Texas and New Mexico.* Austin: Texas State Historical Association, 1997.

Munslow, Alun. *Deconstructing History.* London: Routledge, 1997.

Nail, David L. *One Short Sleep Past: A Profile of Amarillo in the Thirties.* Canyon, Tex.: Staked Plains Press, 1973.

Nash, Gerald. *Creating the West: Historical Interpretations, 1890–1990.* Albuquerque: University of New Mexico Press, 1991.

Nash, Roderick. *Wilderness and the American Mind.* 3d ed. New Haven: Yale University Press, 1982.

Nelson, Paula. *The Prairie Winnows Out Its Own: The West River Country of South Dakota in the Years of Depression and Dust.* Iowa City: University of Iowa Press, 1996.

Nietzsche, Frederick. *The Portable Nietzsche.* Edited and translated by Walter Kaufmann. New York: Viking Press, 1954.

Noble, Don, ed. *The Steinbeck Question: New Essays in Criticism.* Troy, New York: Whitston, 1993.

Nobles, Gregory H. *American Frontiers: Cultural Encounters and Continental Conquest.* New York: Hill and Wang, 1997.

Opie, John. *Nature's Nation: An Environmental History of the United States.* New York: Harcourt Brace, 1998.

———. *Ogallala: Water for a Dry Land.* Lincoln: University of Nebraska Press, 1993.

Owens, Louis. *The Grapes of Wrath: Trouble in the Promised Land.* Boston: Twayne, 1989.

———. *John Steinbeck's Re-Vision of America.* Athens: University of Georgia Press, 1985.

Pautenaude, Lionel. *Texans, Politics, and the New Deal.* New York: Garland, 1983.

Pells, Richard H. *Radical Visions and American Dreams: Culture and Social Thought in the Depression Years.* New York: Harper Torchbooks, 1974.

Quantic, Diane Dufva. *The Nature of the Place: A Study of Great Plains Fiction.* Lincoln: University of Nebraska Press, 1995.

Ribuffo, Leo. *The Old Christian Right: The Protestant Far Right from the Great Depression to the Cold War.* Philadelphia: Temple University Press, 1983.

Riney-Kehrberg, Pamela. *Rooted in Dust: Surviving Drought and Depression in Southwestern Kansas.* Lawrence: University Press of Kansas, 1994.

Rister, Carl C. *No Man's Land.* Norman: University of Oklahoma Press, 1948.

Saarinen, Thomas F. *The Perception of Drought Hazard on the Great Plains.* Department of Geography Research Paper No. 106. Chicago: University of Chicago Press, 1966.

Saloutos, Theodore. *The American Farmer and the New Deal.* Ames: Iowa State University Press, 1982.

Schama, Simon. *Landscape and Memory.* New York: Knopf, 1995.

Schlebecker, John T. *Cattle Raising on the Plains, 1900–1961.* Lincoln: University of Nebraska Press, 1963.

Schlesinger, Arthur M. Jr. *The Coming of the New Deal.* Boston: Houghton Mifflin, 1958.

Schruben, Francis. *Kansas in Turmoil, 1930–1936.* Columbia: University of Missouri Press, 1969.

Schultz, Constance, ed. *Bust to Boom: Documentary Photographs of Kansas, 1936–1949.* Lawrence: University Press of Kansas, 1996.

Schuyler, Michael. *Dread of Plenty: Agricultural Relief Activities of the Federal Government in the Middle West, 1933–1939.* Manhattan, Kans.: Sunflower University Press, 1989.

Sherow, James E. *Watering the Valley: Development Along the High Plains Arkansas River, 1870–1950.* Lawrence: University Press of Kansas, 1990.

Shindo, Charles J. *Dust Bowl Migrants in the American Imagination.* Lawrence: University Press of Kansas, 1997.

Short, John R. *Imagined Country: Society, Culture, and Environment.* London: Routledge, 1991.

Shortridge, James. *The Middle West: Its Meaning in American Culture.* Lawrence: University Press of Kansas, 1989.

Simonson, Harold P. *Beyond the Frontier: Writers, Western Regionalism, and a Sense of Place.* Fort Worth: Texas Christian University Press, 1989.

Sisk, David. *Transformations of Language in Modern Dystopias.* Westport, Conn.: Greenwood, 1997.

Sklar, Robert. *Movie-Made America.* New York: Random House, 1975.

Slotkin, Richard. *Fatal Environment: The Myth of the Frontier in the Age of Industrialization, 1800–1890.* New York: Atheneum, 1985.

Smith, Henry Nash. *Virgin Land: The American West as Symbol and Myth.* New York: Vintage, 1950.

Snyder, Robert. *Pare Lorentz and the Documentary Film.* Norman: University of Oklahoma Press, 1968.

Spence, Clark C. *The Rainmakers: Pluviculture to World War II.* Lincoln: University of Nebraska Press, 1980.

Stegner, Wallace. *Where the Bluebird Sings to the Lemonade Springs: Living and Writing in the American West.* New York: Penguin, 1992.

Stein, Walter J. *California and the Dust Bowl Migration.* Westport, Conn.: Greenwood Press, 1973.

Stewart, Rick. *Lone Star Regionalism: The Dallas Nine and Their Circle.* Austin: Texas Monthly Press, 1985.

Stott, William. *Documentary Expression and Thirties America.* New York: Oxford University Press, 1973.

Susman, Warren I. *Culture as History: The Transformation of American Society in the Twentieth Century.* New York: Pantheon, 1984.

Swados, Harvey. *The American Writer and the Great Depression.* Indianapolis: Bobbs-Merrill, 1969.

Szasz, Ferenc Morton. *The Protestant Clergy in the Great Plains and Mountain West, 1865–1915.* Albuquerque: University of New Mexico Press, 1988.

Tannehill, Ivan. *Drought: Its Causes and Effects.* Princeton: Princeton University Press, 1947.

Taylor, Bob Pepperman. *Our Limits Transgressed: Environmental Political Thought in America.* Lawrence: University Press of Kansas, 1992.

Terkel, Studs. *Hard Times.* New York: Pantheon, 1970.

Thomas, David S. G. and Nicholas J. Middleton. *Desertification: Exploding the Myth.* New York: Chichester, 1994.

Thomas, William, ed. *Man's Role in Changing the Face of the Earth.* Chicago: University of Chicago Press, 1956.

Thompson, John. *Closing the Frontier: Radical Response in Oklahoma, 1889–1923.* Norman: University of Oklahoma Press, 1986.

Tobey, Ronald C. *Saving the Prairies: The Life Cycle of the Founding School of American Plant Ecology, 1895–1955.* Berkeley: University of California Press, 1981.

Tuan, Yi-Fu. *Landscapes of Fear.* New York: Pantheon, 1979.

Turner, Frederick W. *Beyond Geography: The Western Spirit Against the Wilderness.* New York: Viking, 1980.

Tuveson, Ernest. *Redeemer Nation: The Idea of America's Millennial Role.* Chicago: University of Chicago Press, 1968.

Utley, Robert. *The Lance and the Shield: The Life and Times of Sitting Bull.* New York: Henry Holt, 1993.

Ward, Geoffrey C. *The West: An Illustrated History.* Boston: Little, Brown, 1996.

Watkins, T. H. *The Great Depression: America in the 1930s.* Boston: Little, Brown, 1993.

West, Elliot. *The Contested Plains: Indians, Goldseekers, and the Rush to Colorado.* Lawrence: University Press of Kansas, 1998.

———. *The Way to the West: Essays on the Central Plains.* Albuquerque: University of New Mexico Press, 1995.

Western Literature Association. *A Literary History of the American West.* Fort Worth: Texas Christian University Press, 1987.

Whisenhunt, Donald D. *The Environment and the American Experience.* Port Washington, N.Y.: Kennikat Press, 1974.

———, ed. *The Depression in the Southwest.* Port Washington, N.Y.: Kennikat Press, 1980.

White, Hayden. *The Content of the Form: Narrative Discourse and Historical Representation.* Baltimore: Johns Hopkins University Press, 1987.

White, Richard. *It's Your Misfortune and None of My Own: A New History of the American West.* Norman: University of Oklahoma Press, 1991.

Williams, George. *Wilderness and Paradise in Christian Thought.* New York: Harper and Brothers, 1962.

Worster, Donald. *Dust Bowl: The Southern Plains in the 1930s.* New York: Oxford University Press, 1979.

———. *Nature's Economy: A History of Ecological Ideas.* New York: Cambridge University Press, 1994.

———. *Under Western Skies: Nature and History and the American West.* New York: Oxford University Press, 1992.

———. *Wealth of Nature: Environmental History and the Ecological Imagination.* New York: Oxford University Press, 1993.

Wright, James, and Sarah Rosenberg, eds. *The Great Plains Experience.* Lincoln: University of Mid-America, 1978.

Wrobel, David. *The End of American Exceptionalism: Frontier Anxiety from the Old West to the New Deal.* Lawrence: University Press of Kansas, 1993.

Wunder, John R., Frances W. Kaye, and Vernon Carstensen, eds. *Americans View Their Dust Bowl Experience.* Niwot: University Press of Colorado, 1999.

Wyatt, William K. *Westward in Eden: The Public Lands and the Conservation Movement.* Berkeley: University of California Press, 1982.

Zamora, Lois P., ed. *The Apocalyptic Vision in America: Interdisciplinary Essays on Myth and Culture.* Bowling Green, Ohio: Bowling Green University Press, 1982.

Articles

Allen, John L. "The Garden-Desert Continuum: Competing Views of the Great Plains in the Nineteenth Century." *Great Plains Quarterly* 5 (Fall 1985): 207–20.

———. "Horizons of the Sublime: The Invention of the Romantic West." *Journal of Historical Geography* 18 (January 1992): 27–40.

Anderson, Clifford B. "The Metamorphosis of American Agrarian Idealism in the 1920s and 1930s." *Agricultural History* 35 (October 1961): 182–88.

Baird, W. David. "Agriculture in the Oklahoma Panhandle, 1898–1942." *Chronicles of Oklahoma* 72 (Summer 1994): 116–37.

Baker, William. "A History of Cimarron County." *Chronicles of Oklahoma* 31 (Autumn 1953): 255–67.

Baltensperger, B. H. "Plains Boomers and the Creation of the Great American Desert Myth." *Journal of Historical Geography* 18 (January 1992): 59–73.

Beddow, James B. "Depression and the New Deal: Letters from the Plains." *Kansas Historical Quarterly* 43 (Summer 1977): 140–53.

Berkhofer, Robert F. "Space, Time, Culture, and the American Frontier," *Agricultural History* 38 (January 1964): 21–30.

Bogue, Allan G. "The Heirs of James C. Malin: A Grassland Historiography." *Great Plains Quarterly* 1 (Spring 1981): 105–31.

Borchert, John R. "The Dust Bowl in the 1970s." *Annals of the Association of American Geographers* 61 (March 1971): 1–22.

Bourke-White, Margaret. "Dust Plague Upon the Land." *Life* 36 (3 May 1954): 34–38, 41.

Bowden, Martyn J. "The Invention of American Tradition." *Journal of Historical Geography* 18 (January 1992): 3–26.

———. "The Great American Desert in the American Mind." In *Geographies of the Mind,* ed. D. Lowenthal and M. Bowden, 119–47. New York: Oxford University Press, 1976.

Burmeister, Charles. "Six Decades of Rugged Individualism: The American National Cattleman's Association." *Agricultural History* 30 (October 1956): 143–50.

Carlson, Paul H. "Black Sunday: The South Plains Dust Blizzard of April 14, 1935." *West Texas Historical Association Yearbook* 67 (1991): 5–17.

Christie, Jean. "New Deal Resources Planning: The Proposals of Morris L. Cooke." *Agricultural History* 53 (July 1979): 598–602.

Coffey, Marilyn. "The Dust Storms of the 1930s." *Natural History* 87 (February 1978): 73–82.

Conrat, Richard, and Maisie Conrat. "The Great Migrations into the Agricultural Lands of the West." *American West* 14 (March–April 1977): 22–33.

Cronon, William. "Modes of Prophecy and Production: Placing Nature in History." *Journal of American History* 76 (March 1990): 1122–31.

———. "A Place for Stories: Nature, History, and Narrative." *Journal of American History* 78 (March 1992): 1347–76.

Demeritt, David. "The Nature of Metaphors in Cultural Geography and Environmental History." *Progress in Human Geography* 18 (June 1994): 163–85.

Dodds, Gordon B. "Conservation and Reclamation in the Trans-Mississippi West: A Critical Bibliography." *Arizona and the West* 13 (Summer 1971): 143–71.

Doerr, Arthur H. "Dry Conditions in Oklahoma in the 1930s and 1950s as Delimited by the Original Thornthwaite Climatic Classification." *Great Plains Journal* 2 (Spring 1963): 67–77.

Dunbar-Ortiz, Roxanne. "One or Two Things I Know about Us: Okies in American Culture." *Radical History Review* 59 (Spring 1994): 4–34.

Farb, Peter. "Hugh Bennett: Messiah of the Soil." *American Forests* 66 (January 1960): 19, 40, 42.

Fearon, Peter. "From Self-Help to Federal Aid: Unemployment and Relief in Kansas, 1929–1932." *Kansas History* 13 (Summer 1990): 107–22.

Finnell, H. H. "The Plowup of the Western Grasslands and the Resultant Effect upon Great Plains Agriculture." *Southwestern Social Science Quarterly* 32 (September 1951): 94–100.

Fite, Gilbert. "Farmer Opinion and the Agricultural Adjustment Act, 1933." *Mississippi Valley Historical Review* 48 (March 1962): 656–73.

Flores, Dan. "Bison Ecology and Bison Diplomacy: The Southern Plains from 1800 to 1850," *Journal of American History* 78 (September 1991): 465–85.

Forsythe, John L. "Clifford Hope of Kansas: Practical Congressman and Agrarian Idealist." *Agricultural History* 51 (April 1977): 406–20.

Fossy, W. Richard. "Talkin' Dust Bowl Blues: A Study of Oklahoma's Cultural Identity During the Great Depression." *Chronicles of Oklahoma* 55 (Spring 1977): 12–33.

Garwood, Darrell D. "Gerald Burton Winrod and the Politics of Kansas During the Depression." *Heritage of the Great Plains* 17 (Winter 1984): 27–34.

Glaab, Charles N. "Visions of Metropolis: William Gilpin and Theories of City Growth in the American West." *Wisconsin Magazine of History* 45 (1961): 21–31.

Gordon, Ira J. "The Kansas Wheat Culture." *Transactions, Kansas Academy of Science* 35 (1952): 56–60.

Green, Donald E. "The Idea of an Inexhaustible Supply of Ground Water on the Texas High Plains: The Obstacle of a Myth to Water Conservation." *Proceedings of the Oklahoma Academy of Science* 50 (1970): 151–54.

Grider, Silvia, "Black Easter: April 14, 1935." In *Diamond Bessie and the Shepherds*, ed. Wilson M. Hudson, 261–71. Austin, Tex.: Encino Press, 1972.

Guttenberg, Albert Z. "The Land Utilization Movement of the 1920s." *Agricultural History* 50 (July 1976): 477–90.

Hargreaves, Mary W. M. "Land-Use Planning in Response to Drought: The Experience of the Thirties." *Agricultural History* 50 (October 1976): 561–82.

Haslam, Gerald. "What about the Okies?" *American History Illustrated* 12 (April 1977): 28–29.

Herman, Alan. "Dust, Depression, and Demagogues: Political Radicals of the Great Plains, 1930–1936." *Journal of the West* 16 (January 1977): 57–62.

Hope, Clifford. "Kansas in the 1930s." *Kansas Historical Quarterly* 36 (Spring 1970): 2–13.

———. "Strident Voices in Kansas Between the Wars." *Kansas History* 2 (Spring 1979): 54–64.

Howarth, William. "Beyond the Dust Bowl." *National Geographic* 166 (September 1984): 322–49.

Hurt, R. Douglass. "The Dust Bowl." *American West* 14 (July–August 1977): 22–27, 56–57.

———. "Federal Land Reclamation in the Dust Bowl." *Great Plains Quarterly* 6 (Spring 1986): 94–106.

———. "Irrigation on the Kansas Plains Since 1930." *Red River Valley Historical Review* 4 (Summer 1979): 64–72.

———. "Letters from the Dust Bowl." *Panhandle-Plains Historical Review* 52 (1979): 1–13.

———. "National Grasslands: Origin and Development in the Dust Bowl." *Agricultural History* 59 (April 1985): 246–59.

———. "Return of the Dust Bowl: The Filthy Fifties." *Journal of the West* 18 (October 1979): 85–93.

Hyde, Anne F. "Cultural Filters: The Significance of Perception in the History of the American West." *Western Historical Quarterly* 24 (August 1993): 351–74.

Isley, C. C. "Will the Dust Bowl Return?" *Northwest Miller*, 20 November 1945, 18, 35, 38–39.

Judd, B. Ira. "The Dust Came at Noon." *Cattleman* 60 (May 1974): 64, 66, 74.

Kirkendall, Richard S. "L. C. Gray and the Supply of Agricultural Land." *Agricultural History* 37 (October 1963): 205–16.

Kollmorgen, Walter M. "The Woodsman's Assaults on the Domain of the Cattleman." *Annals of the Association of American Geographers* 59 (June 1969): 215–39.

Kracht, James B. "Perception of the Great Plains in Nineteenth Century Folk Songs." *Journal of Geography* 88 (November–December 1989): 206–12.

Lamar, Howard. "Comparing Depressions: The Great Plains and the Canadian Prairie Experience, 1929–1941." In *The Twentieth Century West: Historical Interpretations*, ed. Michael P. Malone and Richard W. Etulain, 175–206. Lincoln; University of Nebraska Press, 1989.

Lambert, C. Roger. "The Drought Cattle Purchase, 1934–1935: Problems and Complaints." *Agricultural History* 45 (April 1971): 85–93.

———. "Drought Relief for Cattlemen: The Emergency Purchase Program of 1934–35." *Panhandle-Plains Historical Review* 45 (1972): 21–35.

————. "Slaughter of the Innocents: The Public Protests AAA Killing of Little Pigs." *Midwest Quarterly* 14 (April 1973): 247–54.

————. "Texas Cattlemen and the AAA, 1933–1935." *Arizona and the West* 14 (Summer 1972): 137–54.

————. "Want and Plenty: The Federal Surplus Relief Corporation and the AAA." *Agricultural History* 46 (July 1972): 390–400.

Lewis, Michael. "National Grasslands in the Dust Bowl." *Geographical Review* 79 (April 1989): 161–71.

Lockeretz, William. "Lessons of the Dust Bowl." *American Scientist* 66 (September–October 1978): 560–69.

Logsdon, Guy. "The Dust Bowl and the Migrant." *American Scene* 12 (1971).

Lookingbill, Brad. "Dusty Apocalypse and Socialist Salvation: A Study of Woody Guthrie's Dust Bowl Imagery." *Chronicles of Oklahoma* 72 (Winter 1994–95): 396–413.

————. "A God-Forsaken Place: Folk Eschatology and the Dust Bowl." *Great Plains Quarterly* 14 (Fall 1994): 273–86.

————. "The Living and the Dead Land: The Great Plains Environment and the Literature of Depression America." *Heritage of the Great Plains* 29 (Fall–Winter 1996): 38–48.

Lowitt, Richard. "Regionalism at the University of Oklahoma." *Chronicles of Oklahoma* 73 (Summer 1995): 150–71.

————. "Shelterbelts in Nebraska." *Nebraska History* 57 (Fall 1976): 405–22.

Luebke, Frederick C. "Regionalism and the Great Plains: Problems of Concept and Method." *Western Historical Quarterly* 15 (January 1984): 17–38.

Malin, James C. "Dust Storms." *Kansas Historical Quarterly* 14 (May–November 1946): 129–44, 265–96, 391–413.

May, Irvin M., Jr. "Cotton and Cattle: The FSRC and Emergency Work Relief." *Agricultural History* 46 (July 1972): 401–13.

————. "Marvin Jones: Agrarian and Politician." *Agricultural History* 51 (April 1977): 421–40.

————. "Southwestern Agricultural Experiment Stations During the New Deal." *Journal of the West* 18 (October 1979): 75–84.

McDean, Harry C. "Dust Bowl Historiography." *Great Plains Quarterly* 6 (Spring 1986): 117–26.

————. "Federal Farm Policy and the Dust Bowl: The Half-Right Solution." *North Dakota History* 47 (Summer 1980): 21–31.

————. "The Okie Migration as a Socio-Economic Necessity in Oklahoma." *Red River Valley Historical Review* 3 (Winter 1978): 77–91.

————. "Social Scientists and Farm Poverty on the North American Plains, 1933–1940." *Great Plains Quarterly* 3 (Winter 1983): 17–29.

McGinty, Brian. "The Dawn Came, But No Day: The Dust Bowl." *American History Illustrated* 11 (November 1976): 8–18.

Mehls, Steven F. "Garden in the Grassland Revisited: Railroad Promotional Efforts and the

Settlement of the Texas Plains." *West Texas Historical Association Year Book* 55 (1984): 47–66.

Merchant, Carolyn. "Gender and Environmental History." *Journal of American History* 76 (March 1990): 1117–21.

Miller, Terin. "Panhandle's Black Sunday Remembered." *Amarillo News-Globe.* 14 April 1985.

Nall, Garry. "Dust Bowl Days: Panhandle Farming in the 1930s." *Panhandle-Plains Historical Review* 48 (1975): 50–51.

———. "The Farmer's Frontier in the Texas Panhandle." *Panhandle-Plains Historical Review* 45 (1972): 1–20.

———. "Panhandle Farming in the 'Golden Era' of American Agriculture." *Panhandle-Plains Historical Review* 46 (1973): 68–93.

———. "Specialization and Expansion: Panhandle Farming in the 1920s." *Panhandle-Plains Historical Review* 47 (1974): 1–20.

Neel, Susan Rhoades. "A Place of Extremes: Nature, History, and the American West." *Western Historical Quarterly* 25 (Winter 1994): 489–506.

Neugebauer, Janet M. "The Diary of William G. Deloach: A West Texas Farmer." *West Texas Historical Association Yearbook* 59 (1983): 108–21.

Parfit, Michael. "The Dust Bowl." *Smithsonian* 20 (June 1989): 44–56.

Pascal, Richard A. "Walt Whitman and Woody Guthrie: American Prophet Singers and Their People." *Journal of American Studies* 24 (April 1990): 41–59.

Peterson, Tarla Rai. "The Will to Conservation: A Burkean Analysis of Dust Bowl Rhetoric and American Farming Motives." *Southern Speech Communication Journal* 52 (Fall 1986): 1–21.

Popper, Deborah Epstein, and Frank J. Popper. "The Great Plains: From Dust to Dust." *Planning* 53 (December 1987): 12–18.

Potter, Barrett G. "The 'Dirty Thirties' Shelterbelt Project." *American Forests* 82 (January 1976): 36–39.

Pratt, Linda Ray. "Woman Writer in the CP: The Case of Meridel Le Sueur." *Women's Studies* 14 (1988): 247–64.

Purdy, Virginia C., ed. "Dust to Eat: A Document from the Dust Bowl." *Chronicles of Oklahoma* 58 (Winter 1980–81): 440–54.

Riebsame, William E. "The Dust Bowl: Historical Image, Psychological Anchor, and Ecological Taboo." *Great Plains Quarterly* 6 (Spring 1986): 127–36.

———. "The United States Great Plains." In *The Earth as Transformed by Human Action: Global and Regional Changes in the Biosphere over the Past 300 Years*, ed. B. L. Turner II et al., 561–75. Cambridge: Cambridge University Press, 1990.

Riefenberg, Anne. "Black Sunday: The Day the Dust Bowl Got Its Name." *Dallas Morning News*, 14 April 1985, 1A, 28A, 29A.

Riney-Kehrberg, Pamela. "From the Horse's Mouth: Dust Bowl Farmers and Their Solutions to the Problem of Aridity." *Agricultural History* 66 (Spring 1992): 137–50.

————. "Hard Times—Hungry Years: Failure of the Poor Relief in Southwestern Kansas." *Kansas History* 15 (Autumn 1992): 154–67.

————. "In God We Trusted, in Kansas We Busted . . . Again." *Agricultural History* 63 (Spring 1989): 137–50.

Roberts, Roy. "Population Changes in the Great Plains." *Rural Sociology* 7 (March 1942): 40–48.

Rosenof, Theodore. "The Economic Ideas of Henry A. Wallace, 1933–1948." *Agricultural History* 41 (April 1967): 143–53.

Russell, J. S. "We Know How to Prevent Dust Bowls." *Journal of Soil and Water Conservation* 10 (July 1955): 171–75.

Saloutos, Theodore. "The New Deal and Farm Policy in the Great Plains." *Agricultural History* 43 (July 1969): 345–55.

Schapsmeier, Edward L., and Frederick H. Shapsmeier. "Agriculture in the West." *Journal of the West* 18 (October 1979): 3–8.

————. "Henry A. Wallace: Agrarian Idealist or Agricultural Realist?" *Agricultural History* 41 (April 1967): 127–37.

Sears, Paul. "The Black Blizzards." In *America in Crisis: Fourteen Crucial Episodes in American History*, ed. Daniel Aaron, 287–302. New York: Knopf, 1952.

Shapiro, Edward S. "Catholic Agrarian Thought and the New Deal." *Catholic Historical Review* 65 (October 1979): 583–99.

Shaver, James H. "Drought, Dust, and the Good Times." *Kansas Quarterly* 12 (Spring 1980): 17–22.

Shindo, Charles J. "The Dust Bowl Myth." *Wilson Quarterly* 24 (Autumn 2000): 25–30.

Smith, Henry Nash. "Rain Follows the Plow." *Huntington Library Quarterly* 10 (February 1947): 169–93.

Steiner, Michael C. "Regionalism and the Great Depression." *Geographical Review* 73 (October 1983): 430–46.

Stout, Joe A., Jr. "Cattlemen, Conservationists, and the Taylor Grazing Act." *New Mexico Historical Review* 45 (October 1970): 311–22.

Swain, Donald C. "The Bureau of Reclamation and the New Deal, 1933–1940." *Pacific Northwest Quarterly* 61 (July 1970): 137–46.

Thompson, Gerald. "New Western History: A Critical Analysis." In *Old West/New West*, ed. Gene Gressley, 51–71. Norman: University of Oklahoma Press, 1997.

Vindex, Charles. "Survival on the High Plains." *Montana: The Magazine of Western History* 28 (October 1978): 2–11.

Waltner, John. "Gerald B. Winrod: Deluded Defender of the Faith." *Mennonite Life* 34 (January 1969): 30–33.

Weisiger, Marsha L. "The Reception of *The Grapes of Wrath* in Oklahoma: A Reappraisal." *Chronicles of Oklahoma* 70 (Winter 1992–93): 394–415.

Wessel, Thomas R. "Roosevelt and the Great Plains Shelterbelt." *Great Plains Journal* 8 (Spring 1969): 57–74.

Whisenhunt, Donald W. "The Texas Attitude toward Relief, 1929–1933." *Panhandle-Plains Historical Review* 46 (1973): 94–109.

White, Gilbert F. "The Future of the Great Plains Revisited." *Great Plains Quarterly* 6 (Spring 1986): 84–93.

White, Lynn. "The Historical Roots of Our Ecological Crisis." *Science* 155 (10 March 1967): 1203–7.

White, Richard. "American Environmental History: The Development of a New Historical Field." *Pacific Historical Review* 54 (August 1985): 297–335.

———. "Environmental History, Ecology, and Meaning." *Journal of American History* 76 (March 1990): 1111–16.

Williams, Raymond. "Ideas of Nature." In *Problems in Materialism and Culture*, 67–85. London: NLB, 1980.

Wilson, Jerry. "Depression, Dust, and Defiance: Literature of the Dust Bowl Refugees." *North Dakota Quarterly* 56 (Winter 1988): 260–72.

Worster, Donald. "The Dirty Thirties: A Study in Agricultural Capitalism." *Great Plains Quarterly* 6 (Spring 1986): 107–16.

———. "Grass to Dust: Ecology and the Great Plains in the 1930s." *Environmental Review* 3 (1977): 2–13.

———. "Transformations of the Earth: Toward an Agroecological Perspective in History." *Journal of American History* 76 (March 1990): 1087–1106.

Zabel, Orville H. "To Reclaim the Wilderness: The Immigrants' Image of Territorial Nebraska." *Nebraska History* 46 (December 1965): 315–24.

Theses

Adams, Ruby Winona. "Social Behavior in a Drought Stricken Texas Panhandle Community." M.A. thesis, University of Texas, 1939.

Aslup, Francis M. "A History of the Panhandle of Texas." M.A. thesis, University of Southern California, 1943.

Babcock, John Gilbert Chittenden. "The Role of Public Discourse in the Soil Conservation Movement, 1865–1935." Ph.D. dissertation, University of Michigan, 1985.

Beberet, William G. "The Evolution of a New Deal Agricultural Program: Soil Conservation Districts and Comprehensive Land and Water Development in Nebraska." Ph.D. dissertation, University of Nebraska, 1970.

Birdwell, Bobby Thomas. "The Relationship Between Farmers' Soil Conservation Ethics and Soil Erosion." Ph.D. dissertation, Oklahoma State University, 1982.

Button, Jean Stoddard. "Social and Political Attitudes of a Kansas Town." M.A. thesis, University of Kansas, 1946.

Clarke-Hazlett, Christopher. "The Road to Dependency: Policy, Planning, and the Rationalization of American Agriculture, 1920–1945." Ph.D. dissertation, University of Rochester, 1986.

Cooper, Norman W. "Oklahoma in the Great Depression, 1930–1940: The Problem of Emergency Relief." M.A. thesis, University of Oklahoma, 1973.

Day, Barbara T. "The Oil and Gas Industry and Texas Policies, 1930–1935." Ph.D. dissertation, Rice University, 1973.

Dorill, Lisa. "Picturing the Dirty Thirties: Paintings and Prints of the Dust Bowl." Ph.D. dissertation, University of Kansas, 1998.

Floyd, Fred. "A History of the Dust Bowl." Ph.D. dissertation, University of Oklahoma, 1950.

Gilbert, Judith A. "Migrations of the Oklahoma Farm Population, 1930–1940." M. A. thesis, University of Oklahoma, 1965.

Hamaker, Gene. "Irrigation Pioneers: A History of the Tri-County Project to 1935." Ph.D. dissertation, University of Nebraska, 1958.

Johnson, William R. "Farm Policy in Transition: 1932, Year of Crisis." Ph.D. dissertation, University of Oklahoma, 1963.

Lang, James B. "The Shelterbelt Project in the Southern Great Plains—1934–1970—A Geographic Appraisal." M.A. thesis, University of Oklahoma, 1970.

McMillan, Robert Turner. "The Interrelation of Migration and Socio-economic Status of Open-Country Families in Oklahoma." Ph.D. dissertation, Louisiana State University, 1943.

Rasinger, Hurshal. "Social and Economic Study of Texas County." M.A. thesis, University of Oklahoma, 1937.

Sindell, Gail Ann. "Gerald B. Winrod and the Defender: A Case Study of the Radical Right." Ph.D. dissertation, Case Western Reserve University, 1973.

Smith, Wilda M. "Reaction of Kansas Farmers to the New Deal Farm Programs." Ph.D. dissertation, University of Illinois, 1961.

Ware, James Wesley. "Black Blizzard: The Dust Bowl of the 1930s." Ph.D. dissertation, Oklahoma State University, 1977.

Wickens, J. F. "Colorado in the Great Depression." Ph.D. dissertation, University of Denver, 1964.

Index